General Sports English
体育通识英语 2

主　编：刘振忠　荣　晶

分册主编：潘　浪　关景军　杜思民　田国立

分册副主编：倪　萍　朱　静　金兴玉　吕红梅

编　者（按姓氏音序排列）：

艾　群　蔡其伦　陈洪特　陈玉玲　高　斌　杭花平　焦悦梅
兰　洁　李　晖　李　茜　李晓玲　李英涛　刘汝丰　刘影倩
罗　欣　孟　娴　任　峰　任　哲　施珊珊　孙　斌　汤棣华
王　芳　王海娟　吴日升　谢超波　徐美云　薛　梅　闫　蕾
于宝英　张　宏　张立萍　张盈利　赵　平　钟圆成　朱　荔

U0361883

清华大学出版社
北京

内 容 简 介

《体育通识英语》系列教材按体育运动项目和体育基础知识两大板块编写,共三册。本书为第二册,主题内容涵盖水上运动、冰上运动、雪上运动、重竞技及其他项目、户外与休闲文体活动,共23课,每课包括听说、阅读、练习、规则与概念、拓展阅读五个板块。教材视角多元,涵盖与体育项目和赛事相关的各个领域;活动设计贴近专业实践,切合体育专业学生学习需求。教材以语言学习、专业学习与通识教育三者融合为编写理念,具有广泛性、通识性、实用性的特点。

本书可作为体育类专业大学英语拓展课程教材,也可适用于体育外事专业、英语专业(体育英语方向)的基础阶段体育英语教学。

图书在版编目(CIP)数据

体育通识英语. 2 / 刘振忠,荣晶主编;潘浪等分册主编. —北京:清华大学出版社,2016(2021.3重印)

ISBN 978-7-302-43051-3

Ⅰ. ①体⋯ Ⅱ. ①刘⋯ ②荣⋯ ③潘⋯ Ⅲ. ①体育–英语–高等学校–教材

Ⅳ. ①H31

中国版本图书馆CIP数据核字(2016)第034860号

责任编辑:曹诗悦
封面设计:平 原
责任校对:王凤芝
责任印制:杨 艳

出版发行:清华大学出版社
      网 址:http://www.tup.com.cn,http://www.wqbook.com
      地 址:北京清华大学学研大厦A座 邮 编:100084
      社 总 机:010-62770175 邮 购:010-62786544
      投稿与读者服务:010-62776969,c-service@tup.tsinghua.edu.cn
      质量反馈:010-62772015,zhiliang@tup.tsinghua.edu.cn
印 装 者:涿州市京南印刷厂
经 销:全国新华书店
开 本:185mm×260mm 印 张:16.75 字 数:273千字
版 次:2016年3月第1版 印 次:2021年3月第6次印刷
定 价:68.00元

产品编号:068355-04

《体育通识英语》编委会

顾　问：

张绰庵（河北体育学院）　田　慧（北京体育大学）

主　任：

刘振忠（河北体育学院）　孙　斌（河北体育学院）

委　员（按姓氏拼音排序）：

艾险峰（武汉体育学院）

白毅鸿（首都体育学院）

陈洪特（四川师范大学）

陈丽江（上海体育学院）

陈玉玲（广州体育学院）

杜思民（郑州大学体育学院）

冯　政（广州体育学院）

关景军（吉林体育学院）

金兴玉（哈尔滨体育学院）

李　晖（上海体育学院）

李正栓（河北师范大学）

刘海娜（天津体育学院）

陆晓玲（西安体育学院）

宁翠叶（山东体育学院）

潘　浪（南京体育学院）

邵丽君（河北科技师范学院）

魏晓红（邯郸学院）

吴日升（河北中医学院）

杨　梅（武汉体育学院）

赵林静（沧州师范学院）

赵　敏（沈阳体育学院）

郑　辉（北京体育大学）

周　栋（河北体育学院）

朱　静（江门职业技术学院）

前言

一、教材编写背景

英语作为全球目前使用最广泛的语言，在世界舞台上扮演着重要角色。进入 21 世纪以来，随着体育竞赛、体育科技与文化交流活动的日趋国际化，体育英语日渐呈现出其特有的地位与作用。为适应体育全球化的发展趋势，我们迫切需要加强体育英语教育，让更多的人掌握一些体育通识英语知识，这是摆在我们面前的重要教育任务。

培养学生的英语应用能力，使之能够在今后的工作和社会交往中有效使用英语进行口头和书面语言交流，同时具备一定的专业学术英语能力，这是目前我国高校大学英语教育的改革趋势与必然要求。体育院校作为体育人才培养的重要阵地，长期以来遵循以基础英语教育为主的教学模式，缺乏渗透体育元素的专业英语教育熏陶。转变教学观念，优化教学内容，构建融合型的英语教学体系势在必行。在确保提高学生英语水平的基础上，融入一些体育英语知识，将对提高英语教育教学质量、培养高素质应用型体育人才起到积极的促进作用。

基于体育领域的人才需求以及体育院校大学英语教学需要，遵循语言学习规律，结合体育专业学生特点、认知风格和学习策略，本书编写组历经三年多的策划、调研、编写与试用修改，现正式出版《体育通识英语》。

二、教材编写依据

教材以体育专业学生为教学对象，考虑到体育院校学生的英语基础、认知水平、学习策略和教学需要，依据"因材施教、学以致用"的教学理念，确定了"易学、易懂、易用"的编写思路。在选篇收集过程中，编者从国内外体育类书报杂志与网站的众多文章中精心筛选出了鲜活生动、富有体育元素、满足学生专业兴趣诉求的素材。选文题材广泛，涵盖与体育相关的各个领域，包括体育运动的起源与发展、体育项目现状、竞赛方式与相关规则、体育组织与机构、运动场地与设备、体育运动常识、人体科学知识、体育产业与管理、明星成长与培养等方面的知识与信息，让学习者提高英语交流能力与学术水平，同时感受体育魅力。

教材以即将颁布的《大学英语教学指南》中的基础目标与提高目标为指导，以提高学生体育英语能力为目标，借助丰富多样的素材、灵活实用的教学资源，让学生了解体育英语的语言特点，掌握体育项目技战术和体育赛事的专业术语及相关表达。在此基础上，使学生能听懂有关体育项目的一般对话，能够在对外体育文化活动与国际赛事上使用英语进行一般的交流，能够在国内外体育机构从事一般性的口译工作；使学生能读懂一般性题材的体育资料，承担基本的体育信息与资料的翻译工作；使学生能完成一般性写作，承担体育赛事的新闻采访、编稿与简要解说工作；使学生能够顺利通过裁判员等级英语考试，并能够在体育产业相关领域从事翻译、服务、组织和管理工作。

教材采取以语言学习、专业学习与通识教育三者并重的教育理念。以英语语言知识传授为导引，设有听说与阅读板块，配有写作、翻译练习，全面提高学生英语语言能力；以语言技能训练为基础，每单元设有与主题相关的情景对话和交互性任务，切合专业学习特点；以学习体育英语知识带动英语学习，任务活动包括口头、书面与亲身实践等形式，满足课堂内外的语言实践。

综上，本教材将语言学习、专业学习和通识教育有机结合，使学生在提升语言能力的同时拓展专业视野，提升人文素养，以适应未来职业发展需要。

三、教材特色

《体育通识英语》系列教程是一套理念新颖、视野开拓、内容丰富的以专业内容为依托的新型教材，具有广泛性、通识性、易懂性、实用性等特点。编者结合体育专业英语教学与学习的需求以及体育专业特性，对每一个话题进行了仔细讨论、推敲，在知识体系、主题内容、练习活动、授课讲解、结构设计、适用范围等方面呈现出以下特色。

知识体系： 从体育专业英语教学实际出发，教材将体育文化、体育历史、体育科技、赛事规则、场馆器材、运动科学、体育产业等知识与语言材料相结合，各单元设计了听说、情景对话、讨论、阅读、词汇、写作和拓展练习等活动，并配有详细的参考译文，构成完整的知识体系。知识分布点面结合，难度适中，贴近实际，让学习者所学的知识和技能在实际工作、学习、生活中能够得到应用。

主题内容： 教材内容丰富多彩，综合了体育学科下各专业的特点。素材视角多元，贴近专业教学需要，切合学生知识需求。材料涉及体育文化、赛事组织、体育机构、体育项目发展、专业术语、竞赛规则和体育明星等，覆盖体育教育、运动训练、社会体育、运动人体科学、民族传统武术、体育艺术等体育本科专业以及运动人体科学、运动康复、体育管理、体育新闻等体育相关专业。

练习活动： 教材将英语学习与体育知识相结合，练习多样，突出实践性。对话贴近实际，选取课堂、训练、赛场、治疗、旅途等场景，使学生亲身参与，创新思考，学以致用。此外，练习内容还包括体育解说词编写、赛事服务实践报告、体育信息与资料整理、赛事采访提纲撰写等写作训练，有效检测学生的知识运用能力。

授课讲解： 根据课程计划安排、学生英语水平和专业特点，教师可灵活选取不同单元作为教学材料，采取多样的教学方法，激发学生体育英语学习的兴趣。教师可运用现代多媒体手段，趣味、系统地传授体育英语知识，发挥教材特色，实现因材施教、寓教于乐，以培养学生英语应用能力、自主学习能力和体育文化素养。根据实际需要，教师可以选择三册同时进行教学，也可分册进行，其中有些内容可作为学生课外阅读材料。

结构设计： 教材框架、体例、结构设计新颖，具有一定的独特性。设计充分考虑到体育项目所涵盖的知识面，每一单元涉及的知识点既相辅相成，又相对独立，符合体育专业学生的知识需求、学习习惯与审美情趣。教材内容与艺术设计的有机结合，创设了轻松的学习环境，更能激发学生的学习兴趣。

适用范围： 教材适用于英语专业（体育英语方向）、体育外事专业基础阶段的体育英语教学，可作为体育类专业以及体育院校的新闻、管理、心理、体育人文等学科的大学英语教材，以拓宽学生知识面，培养学生语言能力、学习能力与思维能力；也可作为大学英语课程的拓展训练材料以及体育类专业英语选修课程教材，以开阔学生视野，培养学生跨文化体育英语交流能力；同时也可作为具有一定英语水平的教练员、运动员、体育工作者和体育爱好者的参考读物。

四、教材结构

《体育通识英语》按体育运动项目和体育基础知识两大板块编写，共三册。第一、二册主题为各类体育运动项目，涉及奥运比赛项目与非奥运项目共 50 个。第一册分为田径运动、体操、球类运动、武术及其他传统体育、舞蹈，五章，共 29 课；第二册分为水上运动、冰上运动、雪上运动、重竞技及其他项目、户外与休闲文体活动，五章，共 23 课；第三册主题为体育基础知识，分为体育基本形态、体育组织与管理、运动场地与设备、运动生物科学基础、体育产业与管理，五章，共 23 课。

每课的基本结构为：

第一部分：听说（Listening and Speaking）。根据单元主题设计一段情景对话，配有录音 *。此外，还配有相关的词汇和短语列表、交互性口语活动。

第二部分：阅读（Reading）。包括两篇短文，内容为与单元主题相关的体育运动项目、体育知识、体育赛事或组织机构的介绍。每篇文章后均配有相关的词汇和短语列表、体育专业词汇表，以及相应的思考题，引导学生加深对赛事项目的了解。

第三部分：练习（Exercises）。任务形式灵活，突出实践性，形式包括观赛讨论、赛事策划、资料翻译等口笔头活动，帮助学生巩固本单元所学内容。

第四部分：规则与概念（Rules and Concepts）/ 概念与常识（Definitions and General Knowledge）。简要介绍各项比赛的竞技规则或体育运动中涉及的相关概念，供学习者了解和参考。

第五部分：拓展阅读（Further Reading）。介绍与单元主题相关的体育名人、历史事件等，帮助学习者完善知识结构，提高学习兴趣。

五、编写团队

《体育通识英语》教程由河北体育学院张绰庵策划、刘振忠组织编写，由全国 22 所院校的教师共同参与完成。编写小组由英语教师和具有国内外大赛裁判、体育教学训练经历且理论功底深厚的体育教师组成，确保了英文编写和中文参考译文两方面的准确性、语言地道性和任务的真实性，保证了教材质量。

---

* 与本教程配套的音频，可从清华大学出版社的资源库里免费下载。请学习者访问 ftp://ftp.tup.tsinghua.edu.cn/，进入"外语分社"目录下，选择所需的音频文件。

　　《体育通识英语》教程在策划和编写过程中还得到了国内兄弟院校老师的指导和帮助，教材中凝聚了他们的经验和智慧。国内英语专家以及外籍教师Carl Malcolm Ramsey（英）、Brin Kerr（美）、Jason Robert Cormier（加拿大）、Coleman Javier Dixon（美）对教材的英文部分进行了详细、认真地审阅，并提出了许多建设性建议。在此一并表示衷心感谢！

　　《体育通识英语》系列教程涉及体育项目多、内容覆盖面广、编写难度较大，由于编写时间紧迫，加之编者水平有限，书中不当之处在所难免，敬请各位专家、学者和读者批评指正，以便再版更正。

《体育通识英语》编写组

2016 年 1 月

Contents

Contents

Chapter 1

Aquatics

Lesson 1 Swimming

Part One Listening and Speaking

Activity 1

🎧 Listen to the following conversation, and then work in pairs to act it out.

(Peter got a leg cramp while swimming. He started to cry out to the lifeguard for help.)

A: Lifeguard, can you give me a hand?

B: What's wrong, buddy?

A: I have a cramp in my legs.

B: Please don't move. Let me help you. Lean your upper body on mine and heel pedal your feet. Are you feeling better?

A: Much better.

B: Let's get you to the shore now. You will be all right after a rest.

A: Thank you very much!

Words and Expressions

cramp /kræmp/ *n.* 痉挛，抽筋

lifeguard /'laɪfgɑːd/ *n.* 救生员

lean /liːn/ *v.* 倚靠；屈身

heel /hɪl/ *n.* 脚后跟 *v.* 倾侧

pedal /'pedl/ *v.* 蹬，踩踏板 *n.* 踏板

get to the shore 上岸

Activity 2

👥 Work in pairs and answer the following questions.

> **Question 1:** If someone feels dizzy and nauseated when swimming, what should he do?
>
> **Question 2:** If water gets into someone's ears when swimming, how should he deal with it?

Part Two　Reading

Passage 1

Directions: Read the passage about swimming and discuss the following questions with your partner.

Swimming

Swimming is consistently among top public recreational activities. In some countries, swimming lessons are compulsory of the educational curriculum. The origin of swimming is quite early. Based on historical records, the ancients, who lived in coastal areas, learned to swim gradually by observing and imitating animals' swimming, such as fish and frogs.

Modern swimming began in the 19th century in England. The first indoor swimming pool was built in Liverpool George Wharf in 1828. Britain held the earliest swimming competition in 1837. Not until the year 1869 was swimming officially established as a specialized sport, and then it was introduced to British colonies. Swimming continued to spread across the globe, and in 1896 it was made an official competition in the first modern Olympic Games in Athens, Greece.

Swimming is classified into three categories: practical swimming, competitive swimming and synchronized swimming. Practical swimming has a quite useful value in military, production, and life service, and it mainly includes sidestroke, diving, counter-breaststroke, treading water, rescue, swimming in battle gear, etc. Competitive swimming has specific technical requirements, and it is a swimming event that complies with competition rules. In competitive swimming, four major styles have been established. They are: freestyle (front crawl), breaststroke, backstroke (back crawl), and butterfly. Events in competition may have only one of these styles except in the case of the individual medley, or IM, which consists of all four. Synchronized swimming, also known as "art swimming", is a type of competitive sport that combines dancing, gymnastics and swimming. Synchronized swimming competitions consist of solos, duets and team events. Because of its graceful movement and cooperation with music, it is also referred to as the "water ballet".

Words and Expressions

consistently /kən'sɪstəntlɪ/ adv. 一致地，一贯地

public /'pʌblɪk/ adj. 公共的；公众的，大众的

recreational /ˌrekrɪ'eɪʃənl/ adj. 娱乐的，消遣的

compulsory /kəm'pʌlsərɪ/ adj. 必须的；强制的；必修的

curriculum /kə'rɪkjələm/ n. 课程；课程大纲

observe /əb'zɜːv/ v. 观察；奉行，遵守

imitate /'ɪmɪteɪt/ v. 模仿

establish /ɪ'stæblɪʃ/ v. 确立；创立，建立

specialized /'speʃəlaɪzd/ adj. 专门的

colony /'kɒlənɪ/ n. 殖民地

spread /spred/ v. 传播，流传

classify /'klæsɪfaɪ/ v. 分类

category /'kætəgərɪ/ n. 类别，范畴

synchronized /'sɪŋkrənaɪzd/ adj. 同步的

rescue /'reskjuː/ n. & v. 救护

event /ɪ'vent/ n. 比赛项目；事件

comply /kəm'plaɪ/ v. 遵从，依从，顺从

individual /ˌɪndɪ'vɪdʒuəl/ adj. 个体的；单独的；个人的

consist of 由……组成，构成

graceful /'greɪsfl/ adj. 优雅的，优美的

water ballet 水上芭蕾

Sports Terms

swimming pool 游泳池

practical swimming 实用游泳

competitive swimming 竞技游泳

synchronized swimming 花样游泳

sidestroke /'saɪdstrəuk/ n. 侧泳

diving /'daɪvɪŋ/ n. 潜泳

counter-breaststroke /'kaʊntə(r)-'breststrəuk/ n. 反蛙泳

tread water 踩水

swimming in battle gear 武装泅渡

freestyle /'friːstaɪl/ n. (front crawl) 自由泳（爬泳）

Sports Terms

breaststroke /ˈbres(t)strəʊk/ *n.* 蛙泳

backstroke /ˈbækˌstrəʊk/ *n.*

(back crawl) 仰泳（背泳）

butterfly /ˈbʌtəflaɪ/ *n.* 蝶泳

individual medley 个人混合游泳

art swimming 艺术游泳

solo /ˈsəʊləʊ/ *n.* 单人（游泳）

duet /djuˈet/ *n.* 双人（游泳）

Questions:

    1. How did the ancients learn to swim?

    2. Where did modern swimming originate from?

    3. Can you tell the categorization of competitive swimming?

Passage 2

Directions: Read the passage about the International Swimming Federation and discuss the following questions with your partner.

International Swimming Federation

International Swimming Federation (FINA) is the international federation recognized by the International Olympic Committee (IOC) for administering international competitions in aquatic sports. It was set up in London in 1908 and its headquarters is located in Lausanne, Switzerland. Julio Maglione is the current president of FINA. English and French are its formal languages, and English is the working language.

The FINA oversees the following aquatic events: swimming, diving, synchronized swimming, water polo and open water swimming. The FINA is responsible for hosting competitions, including the Olympics swimming competitions, World Championships (since 1973) and World Cups (since 1979). It is also responsible for the Short-Course World Swimming Championships (since 1993), Diving Grand Prix (since 1994), the addition of synchronized diving to the Diving World Cups (since 1994), and the addition of junior women's water polo to the Water Polo World Tournaments (since 1995). China had been a member of the FINA before the foundation of the PRC, quitting in 1958 and regaining its membership in July 1980.

Words and Expressions

federation /ˌfedə'reɪʃn/ *n.* 联邦，联盟

recognize /'rekəgnaɪz/ *v.* 承认，认可；认出，辨出

aquatic /ə'kwɒtɪk/ *adj.* 水上的

set up 创立，建立

headquarters /ˌhed'kwɔːtəz/ *n.* 总部

formal language 正式用语

working language 工作用语

oversee /ˌəʊvə'siː/ *v.* 监督，监管

responsible /rɪ'spɒnsəbl/ *adj.* 负责任的

host /həʊst/ *v.* 主办，举办 *n.* 东道主

championship /'tʃæmpɪənʃɪp/ *n.* 锦标赛；冠军

tournament /'tʊənəmənt/ *n.* 锦标赛；联赛

foundation /faʊn'deɪʃn/ *n.* 建立，成立；基础；根基

regain /rɪ'geɪn/ *v.* 恢复，重新获得

membership /'membəʃɪp/ *n.* 会员资格

Sports Terms

International Swimming Federation (FINA) 国际游泳联合会

International Olympic Committee (IOC) 国际奥委会

diving /'daɪvɪŋ/ *n.* 跳水

water polo 水球

Open Water Swimming 公开水域游泳

World Championships 世界锦标赛

World Cups 世界杯赛

Short-Course World Swimming Championships 世界短池游泳锦标赛

Diving Grand Prix 跳水大奖赛

Diving World Cups 跳水世界杯

Water Polo World Tournaments 世界水球锦标赛

Questions:

1. Where is the FINA's headquarters? Who is the current president?

2. What aquatic events are governed by the FINA?

3. Can you list the main competitions organized by the FINA?

Part Three Exercises

Directions: Do the following exercises.

1. Your friends are practicing swimming today, and you explain to them how to recover after swimming.

2. Who is your favorite swimmer? Tell a story of a swimmer that you like and write an essay with no less than 150 words.

Part Four Rules and Concepts

1. An international standard swimming pool is 50 meters long, at least 21 meters wide and at least 1.8 meters deep. Each pool has eight lanes and each lane is 2.5 meters wide. The course rope is connected with a single buoy of 5–10 centimeters in diameter.

2. Athletes must stand on the starting platforms and assume a starting position (except for the backstroke). The starting platform is 50–75 centimeters above water and covers an area of 50 cm × 50 cm.

3. In a swimming competition, any swimmers starting before the signal has been given shall be disqualified.

4. Some events start with a jump from the starting platform, such as freestyle, breaststroke, butterfly and individual medley, but backstroke sets out in the water.

5. In freestyle and backstroke competition, swimmers can only touch the wall with one hand when arriving at the end. But in the breaststroke and butterfly competition, swimmers must use both hands to touch the wall at the same time. Swimming competitions of more than 50 meters must retrace on the way.

6. Freestyle and backstroke allow swimmers to use any part of their body to touch the wall when they turn around. This allows swimmers to push the wall with their feet after turning around underwater.

7. In the individual medley, when swimmers convert from backstroke to breaststroke, they must keep the backstroke position until reaching the wall.

8. Swimming time and place are determined automatically by an electronic system.

When swimmers set out, a pressure plate in the starting platform will record the data.

9. On both sides of the wall in each lane, there is a touch pad. If swimmers touch the wall, it will be recorded. Because the touch pad and starting platform are interconnected, the officials can determine whether swimmers participating in the relay competition enter the water after their teammate touches the wall.

10. In the relay competition, if any swimmer leaves the starting platform within 0.03 seconds before his teammate touches the wall, his team will automatically be disqualified.

Part Five Further Reading

Michael Fred Phelps

Michael Fred Phelps was born on June 30, 1985, in Baltimore, Maryland. He is a retired American swimming athlete who currently holds the world records in the 200-meter butterfly, the 200-meter individual medley, and the 400-meter medley. He is the Olympic champion, a rare swimming talent. At the 2004 Athens Olympic Games Phelps won six gold swimming medals. In winning eight gold medals at the 2008 Beijing Games, Phelps surpassed legendary athlete Mark Spitz's record-setting seven gold medals won at the 1972 Munich Olympics. This led him to become the athlete who won the most gold medals in the same Olympic Games. After the 2012 London Games, Phelps has claimed the highest number of gold medals (18) and the most total medals (22) in Olympic history. He announced his official retirement in August 2012.

Lesson 2 Diving

Part One Listening and Speaking

Activity 1

🎧 Listen to the following conversation, and then work in pairs to act it out.

(Peter and John are diving teammates. Before the competition, they are doing adaptive training together and are pointing out each other's deficiencies.)

A: The match will be around the corner. What will we practice today?

B: According to the requirements we need to do some adaptive training.

A: OK.

B: Your rhythm is good. But your pace is too fast, which may affect your jumping performance.

A: Indeed, all my jump attempts have not gone smoothly.

B: My opinion is that, you should make your last step smaller, which will help you to exert more strength for the jump.

A: I see. Thank you very much.

B: Then let's practice it a few more times, until we perfect it.

A: All right.

Words and Expressions

adaptive /əˈdæptɪv/ *adj.* 适应的；适合的	performance /pəˈfɔːməns/ *n.* 表现；表演
deficiency /dɪˈfɪʃnsɪ/ *n.* 不足，缺点	
around the corner 即将到来	attempt /əˈtempt/ *n.* 努力；尝试
rhythm /ˈrɪð(ə)m/ *n.* 节奏	exert strength 发力
pace /peɪs/ *n.* 步幅	perfect /pəˈfekt/ *v.* 完善，使完美

Activity 2

👥 Work in pairs and make conversations according to the given situations.

Situation 1: When an athlete can't finish movements in the diving training, the instructor suggests he use ground training aid.

Situation 2: An athlete strained his thigh in the training process. The doctor gave him first aid and advised him to have a few days off before training again.

Part Two Reading

Passage 1

Directions: Read the passage about diving and discuss the following questions with your partner.

Diving

Diving is a sporting event that came into being as a result of man's struggle with nature and the development of swimming skills. The picture of a group of boys diving head down is drawn on a ceramic vase displayed in a British museum in London. It is by far the earliest picture ever found of diving.

A kind of diving emerged in China during the Song dynasty period. It was called the aquatic swing, by which the performers threw their bodies into mid-air with the help of swings and plunged into the water after finishing several actions. As its actions are very breathtaking and graceful, it resembles modern acrobatic diving.

With its roots dating back to the 20th century, modern diving was performed by Swedish athletes at the second Olympic Games in 1900 and became an Olympic event in 1904. Competitive diving consists of platform diving and springboard diving. Platform diving is performed on the inelastic platform. The distance between the platform and water varies from 5 to 7.5 to 10 meters. The Olympics, World Championships, and World Cups employ the 10-meter ones exclusively. Springboard diving is performed on the elastic board of which one end is fixed and the other is elastic. The springboard could be either 1 or 3 meters above the water.

Diving falls into five groups according to the direction and structure of jumping actions, namely, forward dive, back dive, inward dive, reverse dive, and twist dive. Each group incorporates a required dive and an optional dive. Each action has different degrees of difficulty. The bearing of the body in the air can be classified into four kinds, namely, straight, bend, tuck, somersault and flip turn. In a dive, if the action is easy, the degree of difficulty will be lowered accordingly, and vice versa. Judges will give scores according to the approach, take-off, action in the air, and entry.

Words and Expressions

as a result of 作为……的结果

struggle /'strʌɡl/ *n.* 斗争

draw /drɔː/ *v.* 描绘

display /dɪ'spleɪ/ *v.* 展示，陈列

emerge /ɪ'mɜːdʒ/ *v.* 出现，显露

dynasty /'daɪnəstɪ/ *n.* 朝代

swing /swɪŋ/ *n.* 秋千

plunge /plʌndʒ/ *v.* 冲入，落入

breathtaking /'breθteɪkɪŋ/ *adj.* 惊险的；壮观的；惊人的，令人激动的

resemble /rɪ'zembl/ *v.* 相似，相像，类似

date back to 回溯到，追溯到

athlete /'æθliːt/ *n.* 运动员

inelastic /ɪnə'læstɪk/ *adj.* 无弹性的，无弹力的

vary /'veərɪ/ *v.* （依……而）变化，不同

exclusively /ɪk'skluːsɪvlɪ/ *adv.* 专门地，独有地

elastic /ɪ'læstɪk/ *adj.* 弹性的，弹力的

incorporate /ɪn'kɔːpəreɪt/ *v.* 包括，包含；合并

optional /'ɒpʃənl/ *adj.* 可选择的

Sports Terms

platform diving 跳台跳水	**straight** /streɪt/ *n.* 直体
springboard diving 跳板跳水	**bend** /bend/ *n.* 屈体
10-meter platform 10 米跳台	**tuck** /tʌk/ *n.* 抱膝
forward dive 向前跳水	**somersault** /ˈsʌməsɒlt/ *n.* 翻腾
back dive 向后跳水	**flip turn** 转体
inward dive 向内跳水	**approach** /əˈprəʊtʃ/ *n.* 助跑；接近；
reverse dive 反身跳水	进场
twist dive 转体跳水	**take-off** /ˈteɪk-ɔf/ *n.* 起跳；起飞
degree of difficulty 难度系数	**entry** /ˈentrɪ/ *n.* 入水；入口；进入

Questions:

 1. How was diving brought out in ancient China?

 2. What does competitive diving consist of?

 3. How is the diver's performance judged?

Passage 2

Directions: Read the passage about the Chinese Swimming Association and discuss the following questions with your partner.

Chinese Swimming Association

The Chinese Swimming Association (CSA) is the national federation which oversees aquatic sports in China. Founded in 1956 with Li Menghua as its first chairman, it is headquartered in Beijing. The CSA is recognized by the Chinese Olympic Committee (COC), and is China's only legal representative in swimming's world and regional governing bodies—the International Swimming Federation (FINA) and the Asia Swimming Federation (ASF). It organizes and conducts competitions in swimming, diving, synchronized swimming, water polo, and open water swimming. It has under its control the specific committees of coaching, scientific research, judging, children training instruction, long-distance swimming, senile swimming, winter swimming and life saving. The CSA hosts a number of aquatic events including the National Swimming Championships, National Synchronized Swimming Championships, National Diving Championships, National Water Polo Championships and National Junior Water Polo Games.

Words and Expressions

association /əˌsəʊʃɪ'eɪʃn/ *n.* 联合；联盟

found /faʊnd/ *v.* 成立，建立

legal /'liːgl/ *adj.* 合法的

representative /ˌreprɪ'zentətɪv/ *n.* 代表

adj. 有代表性的；代表的

conduct /kən'dʌkt/ *v.* 领导；指挥；操纵

life saving 救生

Sports Terms

Chinese Swimming Association (CSA) 中国游泳协会

Chinese Olympic Committee (COC) 中国奥委会

Questions:

1. What disciplines are overseen by the CSA?

2. What aquatic events are hosted by the CSA?

Part Three Exercises

Directions: Do the following exercises.

1. Suppose you are going to interview a very famous diving athlete. Draft an outline for the interview.

2. Watch a video clip of a diving match and discuss the posture, actions, and the scoring for diving.

Part Four Rules and Concepts

1. Dives include the following types: forward, back, inward, reverse, armstand, and twisting, and with the body positions of straight, bend, tuck, and free.

2. In judging a dive, the approach, take-off, elevation, execution, and entry must be

analyzed and evaluated, and an overall score is given.

3. The two criteria to be evaluated on entry are the angle, which should be near vertical with toes pointed, and the amount of splash, which should be as little as possible.

4. When a dive starts, the diver's body should be straight, head erect, heels together and arms straight to the sides.

5. Before the hurdle, the approach should be comprised of no less than three steps.

6. In back take-offs, the diver is not allowed to lift his feet from the board before actual take-off.

7. Each group of diving actions has its own number which indicates the group the action belongs to and how many circles the diver is to flip.

8. The number of actions in the first four groups consists of three digits. The first digit indicates the action group, the second indicates flying actions (0 means no flying actions) and the third reveals the circles of somersaults (1 stands for half a circle, 2 stands for a whole circle and 3 stands for one and a half circles). For instance, "201" represents the second group and backward 1/2 somersault. "305" represents the third group and backward 2.5 somersaults.

9. The fifth group is marked by 4-digit numbers. The first digit stands for group number, the second the direction of somersault, the third the number of circles of somersault and the fourth the number of twist circles which are counted as the previous four groups. For example, the number "5136": 5 stands for group 5; 1 means the direction of the somersault is the same as the first group; 3 stands for 1.5 somersaults and 6 means 3 twists. Another example is "5337": 5 stands for group 5; 3 means the somersault twist will be finished in a reverse direction, just as the third group; 3 stands for 1.5 somersaults; 7 stands for 3.5 twists.

10. The sixth group, the arm-stand actions, also employs 3-digit numbers. The first number stands for group, the second the direction of diving, and the third the number of somersault circles. For example, the number "614": 6 stands for group 6; 1 means the direction of the somersault is the same as the first group; 4 means 2 circles of somersaults. Another example is "632", which means the arm-stand diving action will be finished in a reversed direction with one somersault.

Part Five Further Reading

Queen of Diving

Born in Baoding, Hebei province in 1981, Guo Jingjing is a renowned Chinese diving athlete. As she set an almost unbeatable record of four Olympic gold medals, and five consecutive victories in both the individual and synchronized 3-meter springboard at the World Championships, she is also known in China as the "Queen of Diving". Guo took up diving training at the age of 8, and was later admitted to the Hebei Provincial Diving Team at 11. She became a member of the national diving team at the age of 12 and made her début at the Olympics at age 15. Despite the failure in two Olympics, she never gave up her diving dream and made painstaking efforts to improve her skills. Finally, she became the best female diver in the world by winning two gold medals in the 2004 Athens Olympic Games, and the leading member of the Chinese national women's diving team. Anyone who has watched her performance will find that this girl is displaying the charm of sport.

Lesson 3 Water Polo

Part One Listening and Speaking

Activity 1

🎧 Listen to the following conversation, and then work in pairs to act it out.

(In a water polo competition, John found an opposing player had touched the ball with two hands, breaking the rules, and he reported this to the judge. But the judge denied his report.)

A: Referee, the opposing No. 5 player touched the ball with two hands just now.

B: No, he raised both hands, but only one hand touched the ball. I saw it clearly.

A: That's because the ball hit his hands and resulted in out-of-play.

B: The ball hit his hand but it wasn't out-of-bounds.

A: I think your judgment is wrong ref.

B: I saw it very clearly.

A: All right, I hope you pay attention to the opposing No.6 player. He has a reputation of fouling when defending.

B: OK.

Words and Expressions

opposing /ə'pəʊzɪŋ/ *adj.* 对立的；相对的；对面的

break the rule 犯规

deny /dɪ'naɪ/ *v.* 拒绝；否认，否定

referee /ˌrefə'riː/ *n.* 裁判

out-of-bounds 出界

reputation /ˌrepju'teɪʃn/ *n.* 名声，声誉；荣誉

foul /faʊl/ *v.* 犯规

defend /dɪ'fend/ *v.* 防守

Activity 2

👥 Work in pairs and make conversations according to the given situations.

> **Situation 1:** The referee has just called time out. The coach is discussing defensive strategies with his team, reminding his players to pay attention to the opposing players' attack, and to do a good job in defense.
>
> **Situation 2:** Your team won the game, and everyone congratulated each other for the victory.

Part Two Reading

Passage 1

Directions: Read the passage about water polo and discuss the following questions with your partner.

Water Polo

Water polo is a water-based sport played by two teams. Each team consists of seven players, with six field players and one goalkeeper. Players cooperate with each other in the water, with the object of throwing the ball into the opposing team's goal. The winning team is the one with the highest number of goals. Water polo is a particularly challenging and fiercely competitive sport.

Water polo is thought to have originated from the United Kingdom. It is believed that in some parts of Britain in the 1860s, when children or football players swam at the beach, they competed for a football in the sea, thus forming the first water polo game. Because it involved a football, it was originally known as "aquatic football".

In 1877, England Burton Club hired William Wilson to draw up a set of rules for a water ball game. Later, these rules became the foundation for the international rules of water polo. The water polo match didn't include a goal until 1879. In 1885, the British National Amateur Swimming Association officially acknowledged water polo as a distinct event.

Water polo was first introduced to the United States in 1890, and then it widely spread to Germany, Austria, Hungary and other countries. Water polo was included as an official event in the second Olympic Games in 1900. Water Polo World

Championship was held starting in 1973, and Water Polo World Cup was first held in 1979. As for China's water polo involvement, the sport spread from Europe and America to Hong Kong and Guangdong in the mid-1920s. China's water polo team first participated in a major international competition at the 7th Asian Games in 1974, and won second place. At present, water polo is continuing to be developed, especially in Guangdong, Guangxi, Hunan, Sichuan, Fujian, and Shanghai.

Words and Expressions

goalkeeper /ˈgəʊlkiːpə(r)/ n. 守门员

cooperate /kəʊˈɒpəreɪt/ v. 合作

object /ˈɒbdʒɪkt/ n. 目标；目的；物体

goal /gəʊl/ n. 球门；得分

challenging /ˈtʃælɪndʒɪŋ/ adj. 有挑战性的

fiercely /ˈfɪəslɪ/ adv. 激烈地；凶猛地

competitive /kəmˈpetətɪv/ adj. 竞争的

originate /əˈrɪdʒɪneɪt/ v. 起源于，发源于

compete for 互相争夺

involve /ɪnˈvɒlv/ v. 涉及，包含

draw up 起草，制订

acknowledge /əkˈnɒlɪdʒ/ v. 承认，认可

participate /pɑːˈtɪsɪpeɪt/ v. 加入；参与，参加

at present 目前，现在

Questions:

1. How are the winners determined in water polo games?

2. Why was water polo originally called "aquatic football"?

3. Can you retell the history and development of water polo games?

Passage 2

Directions: Read the passage about water polo competitions at home and abroad and discuss the following questions with your partner.

Water Polo Competitions at Home and Abroad

The Water Polo World Cup is hosted by the International Swimming Federation. Participating teams include the host country and the top seven teams of the Water Polo World Championships or Olympic Games. The tournament uses the single cycle system and is held once every two years. The first Water Polo World Cup was held in Belgrade, Yugoslavia in 1979, and Hungary won the championship.

Since 1973, men's Water Polo World Championship has been organized within the FINA World Swimming Championships every two years. The first tournament was held in Belgrade, Yugoslavia. Women's water polo was added in 1986. In 2002, FINA organized the sport's first international league, the FINA Water Polo World League.

Men's water polo at the Olympics was classified as an official event in the 1900 Paris Olympics. Women's water polo became an Olympic sport at the 2000 Sydney Olympic Games. Water polo has been contested at the Asian Games since 1951. But women's water polo was added in 2000.

Water polo in China was classified as an official event in the Fifth National Games of China in 1959. As a premier national sporting event, the National Games is China's most important water polo tournament, reflecting water polo's mass fan base and the competitive level of this sport.

Words and Expressions

top /tɒp/ *n.* 最高或最重要的级别；顶部

organize /'ɔːgənaɪz/ *v.* 组织；创办

league /liːg/ *n.* 联盟

contest /kən'test, 'kɒntest/ *v.* 争夺，争取 *n.* 比赛，竞赛

premier /'premɪə(r)/ *adj.* 首要的，首位的

mass fan base 群众基础

Sports Terms

Water Polo World Cups 世界杯水球赛

single cycle system 单循制

FINA World Swimming Championships 世界游泳锦标赛

Water Polo World League 世界水球联赛

Asian Games 亚运会

The Fifth National Games of China 第五届全运会

Questions:

1. When and where did the first Water Polo World Cup take place?

2. When was water polo officially included to the Olympics?

3. Can you tell the development of water polo in our country?

Part Three Exercises

Directions: Do the following exercises.

1. Introduce the scoring system and simple rules of a water polo game.

2. Suppose you are going to interview a very famous water polo player and draft an outline for the interview.

Part Four Rules and Concepts

1. The water polo game is played in a standard 50-meter pool, and the minimum depth is 2 meters. Players have to swim or tread water during the entire game.

2. The field of play is 30 meters in length and 20 meters in width for men while the women's field is 25 meters in length and 17 meters in width. The field is marked by ropes. Two goals, 3 meters wide and 90 centimeters high, float on the water at the two ends.

3. All lines must be visible throughout the game. Suggested colors are: goal line and midline, white; 2-meter line, red; 4-meter line, yellow; 7-meter line, green.

4. The red penalty area is located at the ends of the swimming pool, behind the goal line. The distance between the pool corner, which is located by the officials' seats, is about 2 meters. When players enter this area, it means they have left the playing area. A player who is sent off has to wait in the penalty area until there's the signal to re-enter the game.

5. During a water polo competition, each team must have seven players—six field players and one goalkeeper. In addition to this, teams may have substitute field players. There can be a substitution either after a team scores or before the beginning of each period. No one may touch the ball with both hands except the

goalkeeper.

6. Matches are made up of four quarters of seven minutes. The clock stops when the ball is dead. Players can rest for two minutes between quarters, and at the same time they exchange ends of the pool.

7. The playing pool includes flags on the touchline. The red flag represents the forbidden line of the offside area (2 meters from goal); the yellow flag represents the place of a 4-meter direct free kick and forbidden line in the same foul penalty on different scales (4 meters from goal); and the white flag parallel to the goal gate represents the end line. The white flag at midfield represents the midline.

8. All players wear caps. One team must wear blue caps, the other white. The caps are numbered 1–13, and both goalies wear red caps with number 1. Referees not only use the whistle, but also hold blue and white flags to represent both sides of the competition.

9. During the game, if the ball crosses the goal line, one point is gained. After scoring, both teams' members should return to their own half, and the ball should be kicked off by the losing party in the middle of the midpoint. Neither of the two teams can possess the ball for more than 35 seconds.

10. There are two basic kinds of fouls: ordinary fouls and major fouls. The opposing party casts a free throw when ordinary fouls occur. Major fouls include: kicking or striking an opponent and committing any brutal act; interfering with the taking of a free throw; splashing water intentionally on an opponent's face; committing ordinary fouls continually with intent, and so on.

Part Five Further Reading

Dezso Gyarmati

Dezso Gyarmati was born in Hungary in 1927. He was the most successful water polo player in the history of the Olympics. He participated in five Olympics consecutively, winning gold medals with the Hungarian team in 1952, 1956 and 1964. His team received silver medals at the 1948 Olympics in London, and bronze medals at the 1960 Olympics in Rome. As a captain, Gyarmati became European champions twice, in 1954 and 1962. In the swimming pool, he was a versatile player, playing both as a forward and as a guard. He had excellent swimming technique, and his personal record for 100-meter swimming was 58.5 seconds, which led him to be known as one of the world's fastest water polo players. After retirement, he became the coach of the Hungarian national water polo team. Under his coaching, the team gained a gold medal at the 1976 Olympics in Montreal. Later, Gyarmati entered politics and was elected to parliament.

Lesson 4

Sailing

Part One Listening and Speaking

Activity 1

🎧 Listen to the following conversation, and then work in pairs to act it out.

(Peter wants to go sailing, but he's a little worried. To help him relax, John tells Peter his stories about sailing experience when he was in Qingdao last year.)

A: Hey, Peter. Have you been sailing before?

B: Not yet, have you?

A: Yeah. Last year in Qingdao, some friends and I went yachting. It was so exciting!

B: Wow, I'm sure it was! But how dangerous is it?

A: It's safer than you think, but you still have to be prepared before you go out there.

B: Really? What do I have to do?

A: Well, first, you should get some knowledge of the construction of sailboat, rules of maneuvering, and some techniques for sailing. And, of course, it is better to practice with some experts.

B: OK. That makes sense. And do I need to prepare any materials before heading out?

A: When you go sailing, you need life vests, life rings, a first aid kit, binge pump, and a bucket. You'll need some other things too, but those are the most important.

B: Oh, I see. Thank you!

Words and Expressions

sail /seɪl/ v. 乘帆船航行 n. 帆船；航行

yacht /jɒt/ v. 乘快艇；乘帆船 n. 帆船；快艇

construction /kən'strʌkʃ(ə)n/ n. 构造，结构

maneuver /mə'nuːvə/ v. 驾驶，操控

technique /tek'niːk/ n. 技术，技能

expert /'ekspɜːt/ n. 专家；能手

make sense 有道理，有意义

life vest 救生背心

life ring 救生圈

first aid kit 急救药包

binge pump 水泵

bucket /'bʌkɪt/ n. 水桶

Activity 2

👤 Work in pairs and answer the following questions.

Question 1: What etiquette should you bear in mind initially when you are boarding the yacht?

Question 2: What sailing races have been held in Qingdao, China?

Part Two Reading

Passage 1

Directions: Read the passage about sailing and discuss the following questions with your partner.

Sailing

Sailing is a water sport that relies on natural wind force to steer the ship forward. The small and light sailboat used in sailing competitions is composed of a hull, mast, tiller, centerboard, and running rigging. Due to the hull's being light and fast in speed, it is called a yacht.

The history of sailing is as long as human civilization. As a kind of sport, sailing appeared more than 1900 years ago in the poet Jill's works of ancient Rome. In the 13th century, sailing events were held in Venice regularly, but participating ships had no unified specifications and levels. Afterwards, a lot of canals were dug into low terrain, where small sailing boats were widely used for transportation or fishing in the Netherlands.

At present, sailing competitions are held all over the world and are most popular in Europe, America and Oceania. Sailing in China was first carried out in 1949, along with the development of a number of sports such as navigation. In 1958 the sailing performance game was held in the city of Wuhan's East Lake. Sailing events were carried out at the National Sailing Tournament in 1980.

Going sailing is a good way to improve health and build a strong will. When fighting with the wind and wave on the sea, people will enjoy the victory of conquering the nature as well as themselves.

Words and Expressions

rely /rɪ'laɪ/ *v.* 依靠，依赖

steer /stɪə(r)/ *v.* 驾驶；掌舵；控制
n. 操纵；指导；掌舵

civilization /ˌsɪvəlaɪ'zeɪʃn/ *n.* 文明

unified /'juːnɪfaɪd/ *adj.* 统一的，一致的；标准的

specification /ˌspesɪfɪ'keɪʃn/ *n.* 规格

canal /kə'næl/ *n.* 运河

dig /dɪg/ *v.* 开凿

carry out 开展；施行

navigation /ˌnævɪ'geɪʃn/ *n.* 航海

Sports Terms

hull /hʌl/ *n.* 船体

mast /mɑːst/ *n.* 桅杆

tiller /'tɪlə/ *n.* 舵

centerboard /'sentəˌbɔːd/ *n.* 中插板，活动船板，稳向板

running rigging 索具

sailboat /'seɪlbəʊt/ *n.* 单桅船

sailing performance game 帆船表演赛

Questions:

　　1. What kind of water sports is sailing?

　　2. Can you retell the history of sailing?

　　3. When did sailing in China develop?

Passage 2

Directions: Read the passage about the International Sailing Federation and discuss the following questions with your partner.

International Sailing Federation

The International Sailing Federation (ISAF) is recognized by the International Olympic Committee as the world governing body for the sport of sailing. It was founded in 1907 in Paris, France by UK, and is headquartered in London. The current chairman is Carlo Croce, and the general secretary is Peter Sowrey. The official language of the ISAF is English, and it is made up over 120 members from different countries or regions. In 1932, sailing was listed as a competition in the Olympic Games.

The objects of ISAF is to promote the sport of sailing regardless of race, religion, gender or political beliefs, to establish, supervise and explain rules of sailing competitions, to organize and conduct sailing events, and to protect the interests of any member of the federation. The ISAF is now most familiar to sailors for defining the Racing Rules of Sailing (RRS), which is the international standard used to control the rules of competition.

The Chinese Yachting Association, CYA for short, is the national governing body for the sport of sailing in China and is fully recognized by the International Sailing Federation.

Words and Expressions

promote /prə'məʊt/ v. 推动，促进；推广
race /reɪs/ n. 种族；比赛 v. 参加速度竞赛
gender /'dʒendə(r)/ n. 性别

supervise /'suːpəvaɪz/ v. 监督，管理；指导
sailor /'seɪlə(r)/ n. 航海者；航海家

Sports Terms

International Sailing Federation (ISAF) 国际帆船联合会
Chinese Yachting Association (CYA) 中国帆船帆板运动协会

Questions:

1. Which country founded the ISAF?

2. What are the objects of the ISAF?

3. Do you know what CYA is?

Part Three Exercises

Directions: Do the following exercises.

1. What is your opinion on the development of Chinese sailing sport? Write a composition on this topic in no less than 250 words.

2. What do you consider good or bad etiquette for members of an audience in sailing?

Part Four Rules and Concepts

1. The sailing race is conducted on the broad sea, usually 500 meters to 2000 meters from the seashore. The Olympic sailing competition usually adopts the Olympic trapezoidal route and tail wind route.

2. The start and finish lines of the race are virtual lines, which are respectively the virtual connections between the symbol mark of the flagpole at the starting point or the end point and that of the left vessel or the buoy.

3. Because of the changes in wind direction, wind speed, meteorological and hydrological conditions, the venue for the competition is not fixed. In general, it is designed according to the meteorological and hydrological conditions in the area of regulation. The layout is usually completed from 5 minutes to half an hour before the competition starts.

4. The time for a sailing competition generally ranges from 45 to 90 minutes due to different levels in sailing matches. Players can bring their own sailboat and sails.

5. There are two main forms in the race of a sailing competition: one is a group or "fleet race", and the other is a "match race". The sailing competitions in the Summer Olympics adopt a "fleet race" format.

6. When the starting signal is issued, if any part of the hull, crew or equipment crosses the start line in the direction of the first mark, it is judged as "set sail".

7. Prior to the starting signal being issued, if any part of the hull, crew or equipment is on the course side of the start line or its extension, it is called "grab air".

8. One who grabs air must return to the pre-start area to restart according to the stipulated rules of time and regulation. If there are more than one sailing that start early, and the referee cannot identify the boat that is on the course side of the start line, all the vessels of the same sailing levels are recalled for restarting.

9. The sailboat race contains a total of 11 rounds (49-rate; 16 rounds). During the first 10 rounds (49-rate; 15 rounds), scores of each sailboat are calculated according to the best 9 rounds (49-rate; 14 rounds). Each round of the ranking score is: the first gets 1 point; the second gets 2 points; the third gets 3 points; the fourth gets 4 points, and so on. The top ten sailing ships enter the finals.

10. The ranking scores of each boat in every round of the contest are added, and the worst score in the round is removed. This is the ship's total score. The boat with the lowest total score wins and others shall be ranked accordingly.

Part Five Further Reading

Olympic Champion Xu Lijia

Xu Lijia, born in 1987 in Shanghai, is a Chinese sailboat racer who won a bronze medal in women's Laser Radial class at the 2008 Summer Olympics and a gold medal in the same event at the 2012 Summer Olympics. She was also the flag bearer for China at the closing ceremony of 2012 Olympics. Xu started swimming at age 5. When she was 10, she was chosen to train for sailing. She began her international career at the age of 11 in the Optimist (OP) class and won the gold medals in the 2001 and 2002 World Championships. In 2003, Xu progressed to the Europe class (then an Olympic class) in compliance with International Sailing Federation rules. Xu Lijia was once nicknamed "Female Yao Ming" for her proficient skills and brave spirit.

2 Chapter

Ice Sports

Lesson 5 Speed Skating

Activity 1

🎧 Listen to the following conversation, and then work in pairs to act it out.

(During the competition, one athlete finds something wrong with his ice skate blade.
Now he is asking for the referee's permission to change his skates.)

A: Excuse me, sir. There is something wrong with my ice skate blade, and I need to have it checked.

B: OK. What's wrong?

A: Sorry, I'm not exactly sure what it is, but I'm afraid I need to change my skates.

B: Sure, but I'll have to check your new skates first.

A: OK. How do they look?

B: No problem. You can wear this pair for the competition.

A: Thanks a lot.

B: You're welcome. Now hurry up and get ready.

Words and Expressions

skate /skeɪt/ *n.* 冰鞋

ice skate blade 冰刀

permission /pəˈmɪʃn/ *n.* 允许，许可

check /tʃek/ *v.* 检查；核对

hurry up 快点，赶快行动

get ready 准备好；做准备

Activity 2

👤 Work in pairs and make conversations according to the given situations.

Situation 1: Before a competition, the judge considers an athlete's equipment doesn't conform with the rules and has to be changed. Now the judge is talking with the athlete.

Situation 2: An athlete who wasn't at his best during the competition threw the skates on the ground angrily. Now the coach is talking to him.

Part Two Reading

Passage 1

Directions: Read the passage about speed skating and discuss the following questions with your partner.

Speed Skating

There are generally three types of speed skating: long track speed skating, short track speed skating, and marathon speed skating. In the Olympic Games, long track speed skating is usually referred to as just "speed skating", while short track speed skating is known as "short track". Thus speed skating here means long track speed skating.

Speed skating is a competitive form of ice skating in which the competitors race each other in travelling a certain distance on skates. It demands a blend of quickness, power, and strategy. Basic techniques include straight skating, corner skating, starting technique and arm swing technique. Disciplines for speed skating are the same for both men and women: short distance (500 meters), middle distance (1000 meters), long distance (1500 meters) and all-round.

International speed skating competitions started being held at the end of the 19th century. The first was held in Amsterdam in 1889. Four years later, in 1893, the first Men's Speed Skating World Championship was held, and in 1936 the first Women's Speed Skating World Championship was held. The men's speed skating event has been part of the Olympics since the first Winter Olympic Games in 1924. In 1960, women's events were added to the Games. On June 8, 2015, mass start was listed as an official Olympic competition.

Speed skating is widely popular in sports fans, for it is beneficial to keep physical and mental health, promote metabolism, improve cardio-pulmonary function, and cultivate strong will.

Words and Expressions

track /træk/ *n.* （比赛用）跑道；轨道；轨迹

refer to 指的是；涉及；谈到

travel /'trævl/ *v.* 行走；行驶；移动 *n.* 旅行

distance /'dɪstəns/ *n.* 距离

demand /dɪ'maːnd/ *v.* 要求，需要

power /'paʊə(r)/ *n.* 力量；能量

strategy /'strætədʒɪ/ *n.* 战略，策略

fan /fæn/ *n.* 拥护者；迷

beneficial /,benɪ'fɪʃl/ *adj.* 有益的，有好处的

keep physical and mental health 保持身心健康

strong will 坚强意志

Sports Terms

long track speed skating 长距离速滑

short track speed skating 短距离速滑，短道速滑

marathon speed skating 马拉松速滑

marathon /'mærəθən/ *n.* 马拉松

straight skating 直道滑行

corner skating 弯道滑行

starting technique 起跑技术

arm swing technique 摆臂技术

short distance 短距离

middle distance 中距离

long distance 长距离

all-round 全能

mass start 团体出发

Questions:

1. Can you retell the basic techniques of speed skating?

2. Do you know the disciplines in speed skating?

3. Is mass start in speed skating an official Olympic event?

Passage 2

Directions: Read the passage about the International Skating Union and discuss the following questions with your partner.

International Skating Union

The International Skating Union (ISU) is the international governing body for competitive ice skating disciplines, including figure skating, synchronized skating, ice dancing, speed skating, and short track speed skating. It was founded in the Netherlands in 1892 and is the oldest governing international body of any winter sport. It has 85 member associations now and is headquartered in Lausanne, Switzerland. The official working languages are English, German, French and Russian. China joined the ISU in 1956.

The ISU was formed to establish standardized international rules and regulations for the skating disciplines it governs, and to organize international competitions in these disciplines. The ISU works to broaden people's interest in all its disciplines by increasing their popularity, improving their quality and increasing the number of participants throughout the world.

In addition to the Winter Olympic skating competitions, the ISU also organizes competitions of speed skating, short track speed skating and figure skating for the World Cups, European Championships, World Championships and World Youth Championships. These competitions include: the World Cup Speed Skating, the Junior World Cup Speed Skating, the European Speed Skating Championships, the World Cup Short Track Speed Skating, the World Short Track Speed Skating Championships, the World Junior Short Track Speed Skating Championships, the World Figure Skating Championships, the World Junior Figure Skating Championships, the Four Continents Figure Skating Championships, the ISU Grand Prix of Figure Skating, and so on.

Words and Expressions

govern /ˈɡʌvn/ v. 统治，控制

body /ˈbɒdɪ/ n. 组织，团体；集体

join /dʒɔɪn/ v. 参加，加入

standardized /ˈstændədaɪzd/ adj. 标准的，规范的

regulation /ˌreɡjuˈleɪʃn/ n. 规则

broaden /ˈbrɔːdn/ v. 扩展，拓宽，扩大

popularity /ˌpɒpjuˈlærətɪ/ n. 受欢迎度；普及度

throughout /θruːˈaʊt/ prep. 在……的整个期间　adv. 自始至终；到处

in addition to 除……之外，此外

Sports Terms

International Skating Union (ISU) 国际滑冰联盟

figure skating 花样滑冰

synchronized skating 同步花样滑冰

ice dancing 冰上舞蹈

World Cup Speed Skating 速度滑冰世界杯

Junior World Cup Speed Skating 青少年速度滑冰世界杯

European Speed Skating Championships 欧洲速度滑冰锦标赛

World Cup Short Track Speed Skating 短道速滑世界杯

World Short Track Speed Skating Championships 世界短道速滑锦标赛

World Junior Short Track Speed Skating Championships 世界青少年短道速滑锦标赛

World Figure Skating Championships 世界花样滑冰锦标赛

World Junior Figure Skating Championships 世界青少年花样滑冰锦标赛

Four Continents Figure Skating Championships 四大洲花样滑冰锦标赛

ISU Grand Prix of Figure Skating 国际滑联花样滑冰大奖赛

Questions:

1. Where is the ISU's headquarters?

2. What disciplines does competitive ice skating include?

3. What competitions are governed by the ISU?

Part Three Exercises

Directions: Do the following exercises.

1. Discuss the differences in equipment between short track speed skating and speed skating.

2. Discuss the differences in technique between short track speed skating and speed skating.

Part Four Rules and Concepts

1. The maximum circumference of a speed skating track is 400 meters and the minimum is 333.33 meters. The inner radius shall be no less than 25 meters and no more than 26 meters. Tracks are between 4 and 5 meters in width.

2. For short track speed skating, the circumference of the track is 111.12 meters with an inner radius of 8.25 meters.

3. The speed skater wears a nylon tight bodysuit (coat, cap, socks and gloves), and cotton or wool underclothes shall be worn to keep warm. Male athletes have to wear briefs and a guard.

4. The long blade with narrow edge shall be made of light alloy materials which are smooth, abrasion-resistant and of proper hardness.

5. The blade edge should be of uniform thickness. The two edges should be of the same height and straight with no roughness on the surface.

6. When skaters reach the exchange stretch, those in the inside lanes must change to the outside lanes, while the outside ring skaters have to change to inside lanes.

7. At the start line, all athletes must stand still between it and the preparation line when hearing "On Your Marks" and then get ready to skate after the "Ready" command. Athletes can't start skating until the starting gun goes off.

8. During the competition, athletes can surpass rivals at any time, but there are several actions that will result in skaters being disqualified such as: pushing other skaters purposely, beating the gun or skating outside of the designated track.

9. In the relay race, there are four skaters on each team. Several actions will result in skaters being disqualified, such as: pushing other skaters, beating the gun, skating outside of the designated track, surpassing illegally and being beyond the take-over zone.

10. If an athlete can't keep skating normally or falls down, not because of his own reasons, he can rest for 30 minutes and then compete again under the chief judge's permission. But for reasons such as a dirty rink or a damaged blade, the athlete will not be allowed to take part in the competition again.

Part Five Further Reading

Speed Skater Ye Qiaobo

Ye Qiaobo, born in Jilin Province in 1964, is a famous former Chinese speed skater. She has won the World Championship and claimed three Olympic medals. From 1979 to 1994, she participated in 34 various domestic and international speed skating competitions and won 52 gold medals, 36 silver medals and 12 bronze medals. At the 16th Winter Olympics in 1992, she won the silver medals both in the 500 meters event and 1000 meters competition. Her silver in the 500 meters is the first ever medal for a Chinese athlete at the Winter Olympics. In 1994, Ye went into retirement due to her injury, and she began to study in Tsinghua University. After getting her MBA degree, she set up the Qiaobo International Sports Club to help promote winter sports in the country.

(Note: It was Zhang Hong who won China's first-ever speed skating Olympic gold medal at the 2014 Sochi Olympic Winter Games.)

Lesson 6

Short Track Speed Skating

Part One Listening and Speaking

Activity 1

🎧 Listen to the following conversation, and then work in pairs to act it out.

(After winning the silver medal in the short track speed skating event, Wang Ming and his coach play the competition video and analyze it to find out which technical maneuvers need to be improved.)

A: Wang Ming, congratulations on your silver medal!

B: Thanks, coach! I don't think I was at my best in that event though. Could you help me analyze it?

A: OK. Let's take a look.

…

B: I think I need to improve my technical maneuvers.

A: Yes, and I think you need to adjust some of your tactics too.

B: Could you help me plan the tactics now?

A: Sure. In fact, I've already made a tactical plan for you! So, have a good rest and I'll see you tomorrow.

B: Thanks, coach.

Words and Expressions

silver medal 银牌	adjust /əˈdʒʌst/ v. 改进；调整，调节
analyze /ˈænəlaɪz/ v. 分析	
technical maneuver 技术动作	tactic /ˈtæktɪk/ n. 战术；策略
congratulation /kənˌɡrætʃuˈleɪʃn/ n. 祝贺	tactical /ˈtæktɪkl/ adj. 战术的

Activity 2

👥 Work in pairs and make conversations according to the given situations.

Situation 1: You have just lost a short track speed skating competition, and your coach is discussing with you about the reasons.

Situation 2: During a competition, an athlete fell off the runway and doctors came to check on him.

Part Two Reading

Passage 1

Directions: Read the passage about short track speed skating and discuss the following questions with your partner.

Short Track Speed Skating

Short track speed skating is a form of competitive ice speed skating, and is also a sister sport to long track speed skating.

Short track speed skating originated in Canada in the 1880s. At that time, many Canadian speed skating enthusiasts often went to an ice skating rink to practice, where tracks are shorter than usual for outdoor skating. Eventually indoor speed skating competitions began to be held. The first local indoor speed skating competitions were held in Montreal, Quebec City, and Winnipeg, Canada in the mid-1890s. In 1905, Canada held its first national short track speed skating competition. Throughout the early 20th century, the sport gradually spread to Europe and the rest of North America.

In 1967, the International Skating Union adopted short track speed skating, although international competitions were not held until 1976, when the first international short track speed skating competition started in Illinois, U.S. The World Championships have been held since 1981, and are now held annually as the World Short Track Speed Skating Championships.

At the 1988 Winter Olympics, short track was a demonstration sport. It was upgraded to a full Olympic sport in 1992 and has been part of the Winter Olympics since. The program was expanded from four events in 1992 to eight in 2002. The events are the same for both men and women: 500 meters, 1000 meters, 1500 meters, and the relay.

Words and Expressions

enthusiast /ɪnˈθjuːzɪæst/ n. 狂热者，爱好者

rink /rɪŋk/ n. 溜冰场，室内滑冰场

outdoor /ˈaʊtdɔː(r)/ adj. 户外的，室外的

indoor /ˈɪndɔː(r)/ adj. 室内的，屋内的

adopt /əˈdɒpt/ v. 采纳，采用

annually /ˈænjuəlɪ/ adv. 每年地；每年一次

demonstration /ˌdemənˈstreɪʃn/ n. 示范；展示，演示

upgrade /ˈʌpgreɪd/ v. 升级，提升

expand /ɪkˈspænd/ v. 扩展，扩大，扩充

relay /ˈriːleɪ/ n. （赛跑、游泳的）接力赛

Questions:

1. How was indoor short track speed skating brought out?

2. When was short track speed skating listed as an official Olympic sport?

3. What are some unsportsmanlike conducts that will result in skaters being penalized from a race?

Passage 2

Directions: Read the passage about short track speed skating competition in the Winter Olympics and discuss the following questions with your partner.

Short Track Speed Skating Competition in the Winter Olympics

When short track speed skating was officially introduced at the 1992 Winter Olympics, there were four events: 1000 meters for men, 500 meters for women and the relay events for both men and women. The event was expanded to six disciplines at the Lillehammer Olympic Games in 1994: men's and women's 500 meters, 1000 meters, and relays. Then men's and women's 1500 meters were later added at the Salt Lake City Olympics. Thus the number of gold medals offered for short track speed skating reached eight.

Though short track speed skating has been a Winter Olympic event only since 1992, competitions on short track appeared as early as 1932 at the Lake Placid Winter Olympics. All the speed skating competition forms were the same as those of today, which caused a great deal of concern among traditional Europeans. Some athletes were so strongly against these dangerous competition forms that they refused to attend.

Since 1992, this sport has been dominated by teams from Asia and North America, namely South Korea, China, Canada and the United States. By the end of 2010, those four countries have won 104 of 120 medals awarded. South Korean short track speed skaters have won a combined 37 medals. Similarly, 24 of China's 44 Winter Olympics medals are from this sport.

Words and Expressions

discipline /'dɪsəplɪn/ *n.* 项目；科目	traditional /trə'dɪʃənl/ *adj.* 传统的
cause /kɔːz/ *v.* 产生，引发，造成	attend /ə'tend/ *v.* 参加，出席
a great deal of 大量，很多	dominate /'dɒmɪneɪt/ *v.* 占优势；统治
concern /kən'sɜːn/ *n.* 担忧，担心，焦虑	award /ə'wɔːd/ *v.* 颁发，授予 *n.* 奖品
	combine /kəm'baɪn/ *v.* 联合；合并

Questions:

1. How many events were included in the short track speed skating program at the Salt Lake City Olympics? What are they?

2. Which countries dominated the short track speed skating in the Winter Olympics?

3. How many Olympic medals has China claimed in the short track speed skating?

Part Three Exercises

Directions: Do the following exercises.

1. Tell your partner the names and functions of the protective equipment for short track speed skating athletes.

2. Share your first skating experience with your partner. You can discuss your joy and worries.

Part Four Rules and Concepts

1. The rink itself is 60 meters by 30 meters with a circumference of 111.12 meters.

2. Its straightaway is no less than 7 meters in width, and 28.85 meters in length. The radius of the bend is 8 meters.

3. The safety helmet should meet the current requirements of the ASTM—be of regular shape and have no bumps.

4. The suit must meet the requirements of MU–97.1402.

5. Knee guards should be made of soft or hard materials.

6. The skate blade with closed tube and its arched root shall have a minimum radius of 10 millimeters. At least two points of the tube should be fixed on skates without any movable parts.

7. All the athletes should wear neck guards approved by skating federations.

8. The short track speed skating competition adopts the elimination system. The competition consists of preliminary, semi-final and final rounds.

9. According to the latest rule, athletes' positions are decided by drawing lots in the preliminary round, while in the semi-finals and finals, competitors' positions are decided by their scores from the previous competition. Athletes with higher scores use the inner lanes.

10. During the competition, athletes can surpass opponents at any time as long as they don't foul.

Part Five Further Reading

A Famous Short Track Speed Skater—Yang Yang

Yang Yang, born in Heilongjiang Province in 1975, is a former Chinese national short track speed skater and current IOC (International Olympic Committee) member. With 59 world championships, she has the most world championship titles of any Chinese skater. At the Salt Lake City Winter Olympics in 2002, she won the finals of women's 500 meters short track speed skating, and became the first gold medal winner in China's Winter Olympic history. Taking part in the Winter Olympics for three consecutive times, Yang Yang got five medals in total, including two gold, two silver, and one bronze. She was awarded the "Best Female Athlete" at the CCTV (China Central Television) Sports Personality of the Year 2002 and won the honor of "Sports Special Contribution" in 2011. She was voted in as a member of the International Olympic Committee in 2010. In 2012, she founded the Shanghai Feiyang Skating Centre to continue her dreams on the ice.

Lesson 7 Figure Skating

Part One Listening and Speaking

Activity 1

🎧 Listen to the following conversation, and then work in pairs to act it out.

(Peter's arm was injured by his companion's ice skate blade. Now the doctor is dressing his arm.)

A: Doctor, can you help me? I'm in a lot of pain.

B: What happened?

A: My arm was cut by an ice skate blade, and I can't stop the bleeding.

B: Let me take a look. Don't move it too much.

A: Do I have any broken bones?

B: I doubt it, but just to be safe, you should go to the hospital to have an X-ray.

A: OK.

B: It looks like a deep cut. You may also need stitches. Once I'm finished dressing your wound, head straight to the hospital. Just keep your arm in the sling and don't move it.

A: Got it. Thanks!

Words and Expressions

injured /ˈɪndʒəd/ *adj.* 受伤的

companion /kəmˈpænɪən/ *n.* 同伴，伙伴

bleed /bliːd/ *v.* 流血，出血

stitch /stɪtʃ/ *n.* 缝针

wound /wuːnd/ *n.* 伤口；受伤，伤害

sling /slɪŋ/ *n.* 悬带，绷带

Activity 2

👥 Work in pairs and answer the following questions.

Question 1: The ice arena is too dirty. How do you ask the official for a cleaning?

Question 2: Before the competition, athletes are very anxious. What can coach do to ease their worries?

Part Two Reading

Passage 1

Directions: Read the passage about figure skating and discuss the following questions with your partner.

Figure Skating

Both technical and beautiful, figure skating is a sport in which individuals or pairs of skaters perform on figure skates on ice. With prescribed movements, figure skaters generally perform two programs—short and free skate, which may include spins, jumps, lifts, throw jumps, death spirals, and other elements or moves. A panel of judges will evaluate and grade the performances based on their technical ability and artistic expression.

Figure skating originated from Britain in the 18th century and then gradually spread across Europe and North America. In 1772, Robert Jones, an Englishman, wrote *A Treatise on Skating* and published it in London. It is the first known account of figure skating. Later in 1863, American skater Jackson Haines, considered the "father of modern figure skating", combined ice skating with dancing to enrich the content and forms of figure skating. In 1868, two Americans—Daniel Mey and George Mey—performed pairs of figure skating for the first time, and four years later, in 1872, the first figure skating competition was held in Austria. In 1896, the first men's single World Figure Skating Championship was held in St. Petersburg, Russia. Ten years later, the first women's single World Figure Skating Championship was held in Davos, Switzerland. And in 1952, ice dancing entered the program officially. Figure skating became an official sport of the Winter Olympics in 1924.

Words and Expressions

skater /ˈskeɪtə(r)/ *n.* 溜冰者，滑冰者

prescribed /prɪˈskraɪbd/ *adj.* 规定的，预先设定的

element /ˈelɪmənt/ *n.* 要素；元素；成分

panel of judges 评审团，裁判团

evaluate /ɪˈvæljueɪt/ *v.* 评价，评定，评判

grade /greɪd/ *v.* 评分，分级；分类 *n.* 年级；级别

known /nəʊn/ *adj.* 已知的；著名的

account /əˈkaʊnt/ *n.* 记录；描述，记叙

enrich /ɪnˈrɪtʃ/ *v.* 丰富

content /ˈkɒntent/ *n.* 内容

enter /ˈentə(r)/ *v.* 进入；进场

Sports Terms

figure skates 花样滑冰冰鞋

short program （花样滑冰）短节目

free skate 自由滑

spin /spɪn/ *n.* 旋转

jump /dʒʌmp/ *n.* 跳跃

lift /lɪft/ *n.* 托举

throw jump 抛跳

death spiral 螺旋线

technical ability 技术水平

artistic expression 艺术表现

father of modern figure skating 现代花样滑冰之父

Questions:

1. Can you list some technical elements of figure skating?

2. How is the figure skater's performance judged and graded?

3. Who is considered the "father of modern figure skating"?

Passage 2

Directions: Read the passage about figure skating in the Winter Olympics and discuss the following questions with your partner.

Figure Skating in the Winter Olympics

Olympic sports in figure skating comprise the following four disciplines: singles (both men's singles and ladies' singles), pair skating and ice dancing. Single skating competitions include men's singles and ladies' singles, in which individual skaters perform jumps, spins, step sequences, arabesque steps and other elements. Of these disciplines, singles require the highest ability of jumping so it generally represents the highest jump difficulty of the athlete. In pair skating, a male and a female athlete need to cooperate to perform elements of single skating synchronously, and elements specific to the discipline such as throw jumps (the man "throws" the woman into a jump), overhead lifts (the woman is held above the man's head in one of various grips and positions) , pair spins (both skaters spin together about a common axis) , death spirals (the man is the pivot of the spiral) and other elements. Ice dancing is again for couples. Ice dancing differs from pairs in that it focuses on complex footwork performed in close dance holds, and must skate to the music strictly. Ice dancing lifts must not go above the shoulder.

Words and Expressions

comprise /kəm'praɪz/ v. 包括，由……组成

difficulty /'dɪfɪkəltɪ/ n. 难度；困难

synchronously /'sɪŋkrənəslɪ/ adv. 同步地

couple /'kʌpl/ n. 一对，一双；夫妇

complex /'kɒmpleks/ adj. 复杂的

Sports Terms

single skating 单人滑

men's singles 男子单人滑

ladies' singles 女子单人滑

pair skating 双人滑

step sequence 接续步

arabesque step 燕式步

overhead lift 头顶托举

pair spin 双人旋转

footwork /'fʊtwɜːk/ n. 脚法；步法

in close dance holds 近距离保持舞蹈造型

Questions:

1. How many disciplines are included in the figure skating for the Winter Olympics? What are they?

2. What are the elements specific to pair skating?

3. What are the differences between pair skating and ice dancing?

Part Three Exercises

Directions: Do the following exercises.

1. Describe briefly the main technical skills of standing on the ice.

2. Who is your favorite figure skater? Look up information online and write an essay with 200 words about his or her excellent performances.

Part Four Rules and Concepts

1. The ice arena is 56–61 meters long and 26–30 meters wide, with a 3–5 centimeters thick ice surface.

2. The most significant difference between the blades used in figure skating and hockey is the toe picks on the front of the blade.

3. The toe picks are mainly used for jumping but not for gliding and spinning.

4. The ice blade is fixed to the bottom with screws. The blades should be protected with a soft guard when not used, because the soft guard can absorb melted water and help the blades avoid being rusted.

5. When athletes are walking outside of the ice arena with blades, they have to protect the blades with a hard plastic guard in case the blades become blunt or dirtied.

6. During the competitions of singles and pairs, athletes must finish two sets of programs.

7. In the short program, individual skaters perform a series of compulsory movements, including jumps, spins and steps.

8. In the free skate or long program, athletes have a wider array of choices.

9. The competition of ice dancing usually includes three parts: at least one set of compulsory dances, one set of original dance prescribed according to annually-assigned international standard dance rhythms and one set of free dance.

10. In June 2010, the International Skating Union Congress passed a resolution to cancel compulsory dance, leaving only original dance and free dance in the ice dancing competition.

Part Five Further Reading

Figure Skating Pairs: Shen Xue and Zhao Hongbo

Shen Xue and Zhao Hongbo, both from Heilongjiang, China, are Chinese pair figure skaters, who began to work in pair in August, 1992. At the 1996 Edmonton World Figure Skating Championship, they impressed the audience with their gliding speed, difficult movements, accurate techniques and unique performance style and temperament. After their captivating performance in free skate, the entire audience burst into a thunderous standing ovation. Though their final scores only ranked 15th, their performance made a deep impression on the audience. The chairman of the French Figure Skating Association asserted that "Shen Xue and Zhao Hongbo will become world champions in the near future." In 2002, they became the first Chinese pair skating team to win a World Championship. In 2010, they are the first Chinese figure skaters to win the gold medals at the Winter Olympic Games.

Lesson 8 Ice Hockey

Listening and Speaking

Activity 1

🎧 Listen to the following conversation, and then work in pairs to act it out.

(On their way home from a hockey game, two men are discussing their impressions of the game.)

A: I thought the match was great!

B: Me too. The U.S. team played very well, both offense and defense.

A: It's such an exciting sport, but also a little violent.

B: The collisions between the players were very fierce.

A: Yeah. They often start fights because of collisions, even small ones.

B: We rarely see hockey games without fighting. I don't think the fight today was too serious though. It only happened with a few people.

A: Games like this are so much fun to watch, but I don't think I'd want to play.

B: Me neither.

Words and Expressions

ice hockey 冰球

impression /ɪm'preʃn/ *n.* 印象；看法

offense /ə'fens/ *n.* 进攻

defense /dɪ'fens/ *n.* 防卫，防护；防守

violent /'vaɪələnt/ *adj.* 暴力的；粗暴的

collision /kə'lɪʒ(ə)n/ *n.* 碰撞；冲突；（意见、看法等的）抵触

fierce /fɪəs/ *adj.* 凶猛的；猛烈的

fight /faɪt/ *n.* 打架；战斗，斗志 *v.* 打架；与……打仗，与……斗争

rarely /'reəlɪ/ *adv.* 很少；难得

serious /'sɪərɪəs/ *adj.* 严重的；严肃的

Activity 2

👤 Work in pairs and answer the following questions.

Question 1: In what way do ice hockey athletes encourage each other?

Question 2: Do you know some measures to deal with an accident in which a player's arm is injured by a hockey stick in the game?

Part Two Reading

Passage 1

Directions: Read the passage about ice hockey and discuss the following questions with your partner.

Ice Hockey

Ice hockey is a contact team sport played on ice, usually in a rink, in which two teams of skaters use their sticks to shoot a puck into their opponent's net to score points. It is a fast-paced, physical sport, most popular in areas of North America and northern and western Europe.

The earliest records of ice hockey came from 17th century Dutch publications. It was stated that gentlemen wearing skates with blades made of bones would glide with a flat circular object on the frozen river. At the beginning of the 19th century, there was a written record of Canadian Indians (Micmac Indians) playing a similar game, in which sticks and a flat circular piece of wood were used. Modern ice hockey developed in the mid-19th century in Canada. People in Kingston, Canada would play a popular game on ice, in which ice skate blades were bound to people's feet.

On December 25, 1855, an unofficial ice hockey game was held for the first time in Kingston, Canada. Beginning in 1860 Canada started to use ice hockey pucks made of rubber discs. On March 3, 1875 the first ice hockey game was officially held between the two teams of McGill University at Victoria Ice Stadium in Montreal, Canada. At that time, there were 30 members of each team on the ice. In 1879, a student from Canada's McGill University, W. F. Robertson and Professor R. F. Smith established the rules of the game jointly and regulated there should be nine members of each team. Thus hockey quickly became one of the most popular sports in Canada.

The first amateur hockey association was founded in 1885. It was at this stage of development that athletes also started using more protective gear, such as shin guards and masks for goalkeepers. Afterwards, ice hockey spread to the United States and Europe. The first European hockey club was set up in 1902 in Les Avants, Switzerland, and six years later the International Ice Hockey Federation (IIHF) was established in Paris, and later headquartered in Zurich, Switzerland. Team UK was the champion of the first session of the European Hockey Tournament held in 1910.

Seven years later, in 1917, the National Hockey League (NHL) of the United States was founded. There were only six teams until 1967. In recent years, the NHL has become a professionally and commercially successful league around the world. Its impact on ice hockey mirrors that of the NBA on basketball, and its Stanley Cup has become a legendary honor. The first professional ice hockey team, Lake's team, was founded in Michigan in the United States. Then, in 1904 the United States established the International Professional Hockey League. The International Amateur Hockey Federation was founded four years later in Europe in 1908. In the same year, the federation's first game was held in Glasgow, Scotland. UK, Bohemia, Switzerland, France and Belgium were the first five member states. Finally, in 1917, Canada established its national hockey league.

Words and Expressions

contact /'kɒntækt/ *n.* 接触；联系

stick /stɪk/ *n.* 棍，棒

popular /'pɒpjʊlə/ *adj.* 流行的，受欢迎的；大众的；普及的

record /'rekɔːd/ *n.* 记录，记载

bone /bəʊn/ *n.* 骨，骨骼

glide /glaɪd/ *v.* 滑行；滑动

circular /'sɜːkjələ(r)/ *adj.* 圆形的，环形的；环绕的

frozen /'frəʊzn/ *adj.* 冷冻的，冰冻的，结冰的

rubber /'rʌbə/ *n.* 橡胶；橡皮；合成橡胶

stadium /'steɪdɪəm/ *n.* 体育场；运动场

regulate /'regjuleɪt/ *v.* 规定；限制

amateur /'æmətə(r)/ *adj.* 业余的，非专业的

mask /mɑːsk/ *n.* 面具；口罩；面罩

professional /prə'feʃ(ə)n(ə)l/ *adj.* 专业的；职业的；职业性的

commercial /kə'mɜːʃ(ə)l/ *adj.* 商业的；盈利的；靠广告收入的

successful /sək'sesfl/ *adj.* 成功的

impact /'ɪmpækt/ *n.* 影响

legendary /'ledʒəndərɪ/ *adj.* 传说的；传奇的

honor /'ɒnə(r)/ *n.* 荣誉；名誉

Sports Terms

hockey stick 冰球球杆，冰球球棍

hockey puck 冰球

protective gear 护具

shin guard 小腿护具，护腿板

net /net/ *n.* 球网

International Ice Hockey Federation 国际冰球联盟

National Hockey League 国家冰球联盟（美国职业冰球联盟）

Stanley Cup 斯坦利杯

Questions:

1. Can you retell the origin and development of ice hockey?

2. How did ice hockey become popular in Canada?

3. Why has the NHL become a professionally and commercially successful league around the world?

Passage 2

Directions: Read the passage about the National Hockey League and discuss the following questions with your partner.

National Hockey League

The National Hockey League (NHL) is a professional hockey association composed of North American ice hockey leagues. The NHL is the world's highest level professional hockey association, and is one of the four major professional sports in North America. The teams are divided into east and west according to regions, with three subareas in each region.

The league was founded in 1917 in Montreal, Quebec, with five team members. After a series of extensions, the league draws many highly skilled players from all over the world and currently has players from approximately 20 different countries. Canadians have historically constituted the majority of the players in the league, with an increasing percentage of American and European players in recent seasons. Now it is composed of 30-member clubs: 24 in the United States and 6 in Canada. After a labor dispute that led to the cancellation of the entire 2004–2005 season, the league resumed play and held successful 2005–2006 regular games and the 2006 Stanley Cup playoff at the end of the season.

Words and Expressions

divide /dɪ'vaɪd/ v. 分开；划分

region /'riːdʒən/ n. 区域，地区

a series of 一系列的

extension /ɪk'stenʃn/ n. 扩充；延伸，延长

skilled /skɪld/ adj. 有技能的；熟练的

currently /'kʌrəntlɪ/ adv. 目前，现在

approximately /ə'prɒksɪmətlɪ/ adv. 大概，大约

historically /hɪ'stɒrɪklɪ/ adv. 历史上地，在历史上

majority /mə'dʒɒrətɪ/ n. 大部分，大多数

percentage /pə'sentɪdʒ/ n. 百分比；比率

labor dispute 劳资争议

cancellation /ˌkænsə'leɪʃ(ə)n/ n. 取消；删除

entire /ɪn'taɪə(r)/ adj. 整个的，全部的

resume /rɪ'zjuːm/ v. 重新开始，恢复；继续

Sports Terms

playoff /'pleɪɒff/ *n.* 延长赛；季后赛

season /'siːzn/ *n.* 赛季

Questions:

    1. What comprises the NHL?

    2. When and where was the NHL founded?

    3. Where were players in the NHL mainly from historically?

Part Three Exercises

Directions: Do the following exercises.

1. After you watch a wonderful ice hockey game with your friend, share your feelings and evaluate the players' performances in brief.

2. Try an ice hockey game. Wearing the ice hockey equipment, you picked up the stick and had a try with hitting the puck and scoring a goal. Now tell your friend about this experience and your feelings.

Part Four Rules and Concepts

1. The maximum size of a standard ice hockey rink is 61 meters long by 30 meters wide; the minimum is 56 meters by 26 meters. The corner radius of the circular arc is 7–8.5 meters.

2. At both ends of the rink, 4 meters away from the side wall, two parallel 5 centimeters wide red lines are drawn across the ice and extend to the edge boundary wall, which are called the goal lines.

3. The boot itself, including its toe cap, upper, sides and heelpiece, is encased in hardened materials. The long shoe tongue in front together with its tall waist can band the ankle closely so as to support the athlete and help him or her push up.

4. Originally the blade was made of steel with an iron holder. Nowadays, people use plastic for the blade holder, and the blade is made of high-quality alloy steel. This kind of blade has the advantages of resilience, and not being easy to rust.

5. The goalkeeper's ice hockey blade is quite different from other athletes'. It is made totally of metal. The blade is short and smooth with many joint points attached to the holder to prevent the puck from going through.

6. To prevent being hurt in intense rivalry, athletes wear protective gear, including a helmet, mouth guard, and guards for the shoulder, chest, waist, body, elbow, ankle and leg, as well as protective gloves and hockey pants.

7. Modern hockey gear uses light but hard plastic on the outside and soft sponge or foam padding on the inside. For the goalkeeper, there are special mouth guards, catch gloves, thickened chest protectors and thickened and widened leg pads.

8. In order to reduce the weight of the stick, sticks are now made of a carbon material. This kind of stick is lighter in weight without any change in length or width and can optimize the player's performance.

9. A game of hockey has two officials on the ice and two goal judges, two linesmen, one scorer and one time keeper. The two on-ice officials are jointly charged with controlling the whole game with each responsible for a half. Linesmen are mainly responsible for calling offside.

10. A face-off is conducted by an official standing in the center of a face-off spot. The referee drops the puck onto the ice where two center forward players "face" each other.

Part Five　Further Reading

The Greatest Hockey Player—Gretzky

Wayne Gretzky is a Canadian former professional ice hockey star. Nicknamed "The Great One", he is often labeled a global ice hockey legend with a score of 2857 points. At the age of 14, he signed up to participate in the professional league. He played 20 seasons in the National Hockey League for four teams: the Edmonton Oilers, Los Angeles Kings, St. Louis Blues and New York Rangers. He retired in 1999, and to this day he remains the leading point-scorer in NHL history. He is a former NHL coach for the Phoenix Flying Team. Currently, he is the part owner and head coach of the Phoenix Coyotes.

3
Chapter

Snow Sports

Lesson 9 Skiing

Part One Listening and Speaking

Activity 1

🎧 Listen to the following conversation, and then work in pairs to act it out.

(It's Li's first time to go skiing, and he doesn't know what to wear. John is a good skier, so Li consults him.)

A: So, how are your skiing skills?

B: Not too bad. I can ski by myself, at least. How about you?

A: It's my first time skiing, and I don't even know what to wear.

B: Oh, let me give you some tips on what to wear and what you'll need. As far as clothes go, you should wear ski boots, a ski suit, ski goggles and a ski helmet. You also need a pair of skis, ski sticks and a good pair of gloves.

A: That's a lot of stuff. I'm guessing it's expensive. Do I need to buy all of that?

B: Actually, no. There's a reception desk around the corner. You can rent everything there.

A: Sounds great. Thanks!

B: You're welcome.

Words and Expressions

ski /ski/ *n.* 滑雪橇，滑雪板 *v.* 滑雪
adj. 滑雪（用）的

skier /'skiːə(r)/ *n.* 滑雪者

tip /tɪp/ *n.* 提示

as far as... 就······而言

ski boots 滑雪靴

ski suit 滑雪服

ski goggles 滑雪镜

helmet /'helmɪt/ *n.* 面罩，头盔

glove /glʌv/ *n.* 手套

reception desk 接待台，前台接待处

rent /rent/ *v.* 出租；租用，租借
n. 租金

Activity 2

👥 Work in pairs and make conversations according to the given situations.

> **Situation 1:** You are at a reception area of the ski resort. Ask the staff of the rental agency about the equipment.
>
> **Situation 2:** A skier got injured and fell down during a competition. The doctors came to check on him.

Part Two　Reading

Passage 1

Directions: Read the passage about skiing and discuss the following questions with your partner.

Skiing

Skiing is the sport of sliding on the snowy ground with a ski board. It originated in Scandinavia. In terms of historical development, it can be classified as ancient skiing, latter-day skiing and modern skiing; in terms of skiing conditions and purposes, it includes practical skiing, athletic skiing and tourist skiing (recreation and fitness).

Practical skiing applies to such fields as forestry, border defense, hunting and transportation. Athletic skiing is a competitive sport operated in a specific environment under some competition rules. It is also a form of public skiing that has grown to meet the needs of modern people's lives and culture. Nowadays tourist skiing activities are emerging such as snowboarding, ultra short skiing, cross-country skiing, etc.

Snowboarding is performed with both feet on a broad snowboard. Ultra short skiing, which is not popular in China, is more thrilling and requires more flexible techniques. Cross-country skiing is a long distance skiing across a low mountain with hilly terrain (with flat ground, downhill and uphill covering 1/3 of the whole distance respectively).

Modern skiing mainly includes Alpine skiing, Nordic skiing and freestyle skiing. Alpine skiing gets its name from the Alpines where it originated and means to ski downhill along the slope. It contains different techniques and movements, among which straight down, cross and turn are the primary movements. Nordic skiing includes cross-country skiing and ski jumping, and gets its name from the northern European countries where it originated. Cross-country skiing is the most popular form. Freestyle skiing is a stunt performance in which the stuntman skis downhill along a rough snow slope while performing breathtaking aerial stunts like jumping back, kicking, and even somersaulting.

At present, official global skiing competition projects include Alpine skiing, Nordic skiing (cross-country skiing and ski jumping), freestyle skiing, Biathlon skiing and snowboarding.

Words and Expressions

slide /slaɪd/ *v. & n.* 滑动，滑行

purpose /'pɜːpəs/ *n.* 目的；用途

tourist /'tʊərɪst/ *adj.* 旅游的；旅行的；旅游者的

recreation /ˌriːkrɪ'eɪʃn/ *n.* 娱乐；休闲

fitness /'fɪtnəs/ *n.* 健身；健康

apply to 应用于

transportation /ˌtrænspɔː'teɪʃn/ *n.* 交通

meet the needs of 满足……的需要

thrilling /'θrɪlɪŋ/ *adj.* 刺激的；令人兴奋的；惊悚的

flexible /'fleksəbl/ *adj.* 灵活的

slope /sləʊp/ *n.* 山坡；斜坡

primary /'praɪmərɪ/ *adj.* 主要的，首要的

stunt /stʌnt/ *n.* 噱头；特技

ski board 滑雪板

practical skiing 实用类滑雪

athletic skiing 竞技类滑雪

tourist skiing 旅游类滑雪

snowboarding 单板滑雪

ultra short skiing 超短板滑雪

cross-country skiing 越野滑雪

Alpine skiing 高山滑雪

Nordic skiing 北欧滑雪

freestyle skiing 自由式滑雪

straight down 直降

cross /krɒs/ *n.* 横渡

turn /tɜːn/ *n.* 转弯

ski jumping 跳台滑雪

Biathlon skiing 冬季两项滑雪

Questions:

1. What is skiing? Where did it originate?

2. What types of skiing does modern skiing mainly include?

3. Can you list some official global skiing competition projects?

Passage 2

Directions: Read the passage about the International Ski Federation and discuss the following questions with your partner.

International Ski Federation

The International Ski Federation (FIS) is the world's highest governing body for international winter sports. It was set up in 1924 with its headquarters in Berne, Switzerland, and the current president is Gian-Franco Kasper. The working languages are English, German, French and Russian, but mainly English when an argument arises. The Chinese Skiing Association took part in the FIS in 1979.

The International Ski Federation aims to promote the development of skiing, control its orientation, and establish friendly relations between association members and athletes from all over the world. It spares no effort to encourage its members to achieve their goals. The FIS also organizes the International Skiing Championships, the World Cup, the Continents Cup and other competitions. It creates the rules and regulations, supervises their implementation, deals with any issues concerned with protests and the law and serves as an authority over any final judgment. It also aims to advance fitness-oriented recreational skiing. Furthermore, the FIS takes various measures to avoid accidents and protect the environment.

Words and Expressions

arise /əˈraɪz/ *v.* 出现；上升

spare no efforts 竭尽全力

achieve /əˈtʃiːv/ *v.* 取得，获得；实现；成功

implementation /ˌɪmplɪmenˈteɪʃ(ə)n/ *n.* 实现；履行

deal with 处理；应对

issue /ˈɪʃuː/ *n.* 问题；事件 *v.* 发给，颁发

be concerned with 与……有关；涉及

protest /ˈprəʊtest, prəˈtest/ *n. & v.* 抗议

authority /ɔːˈθɒrətɪ/ *n.* 权力；权威；权力机关

advance /ədˈvɑːns/ *v.* 促进，推动

take measure 采取措施

Questions:

1. Where is the headquarters of the FIS?

2. What are the missions of the FIS?

3. When did China take part in the FIS?

Part Three Exercises

Directions: Do the following exercises.

1. Describe to the beginners about the "dos" and "don'ts" of skiing.

2. Discuss the benefits of skiing to people's health.

Part Four Rules and Concepts

1. The playing field of ski jumping consists of the zone of departure, ski-jump ramp, transition zone 1, diving platform, transition zone 2, landing ramp and terminal zone.

2. Cross-country skiing is an event in which the athlete wears a pair of skis and ski sticks and utilizes the techniques such as climbing, downhill, turning and sliding

to slide on the snowy mountains and fields. The ranking is decided by the time of finishing the race.

3. Alpine skiing is a competitive speed skiing event in which athletes cross the gate-shaped route made by flags from the top of the mountain. The technical actions include straight downhill, diagonal glide, B-downhill, rolling downhill, snowplow downhill and plow downhill. The body gestures consist of the high, the medium and the low.

4. For the slalom, the racing route is 600–700 meters for men and 400–500 meters for women, with a 30-degree slope section covering a quarter of the whole route. The vertical drop is 140–200 meters for men and 120–180 meters for women. There are 55–75 gates and 45–60 gates for men and women respectively on the racing route.

5. Giant slalom involves skiing downhill at a high speed with continuous turns and crossing multiple gates. The racing route is 1500–2000 meters for men and more than 1000 meters for women.

6. The field of snowboarding is 936 meters long and has a slope 290 meters high, with an average slope of 18.21 degrees. The height difference is 120–200 meters.

7. There are two rounds of qualifying in the Half-pipe. The top six from the first round will go directly to the final, while others compete in the second round for the other top six spots. Then, the top twelve athletes will compete in two rounds for the final and be ranked according to their performances.

8. There are two ski jumping events: 70-meter level and 90-meter level. The referee gives a score by the posture of the two flights and adds up the posture scores and the distance scores that are given according to the distance that the athlete flies. In the end, the final score determines the ranking.

9. Nordic combined is a competitive sport consisting of ski jumping and cross-country skiing.

10. For the Nordic combined, ski jumping is held on the first day and cross-country skiing on the second. The rules require that the scores of the two be converted into final scores, and the one with higher scores ranks higher.

Part Five Further Reading

The Snow Princess—Li Nina

Li Nina, born in 1983 in Benxi, Liaoning Province, is a notable aerial skier in China who is nicknamed the "Snow Princess". Since the end of 2004, her wonderful performances have garnered her six wins in the World Cup Series. She is the first Chinese woman to win a World Cup Final Championship; first to rank world No. 1 in the aerials; and first to win the World Championship. At the 2014 Sochi Winter Olympics, Li Nina competed in the aerials of freestyle skiing. Although she only won fourth place, she still wore a sweet smile.

Lesson 10 Bobsleigh, Luge and Skeleton

Part One Listening and Speaking

Activity 1

🎧 Listen to the following conversation, and then work in groups to act it out.

(A slalom competition will begin soon, and some teammates are encouraging each other.)

A: The race will start soon. We need to try our best!

B: We're all feeling pretty confident! We can do it, right?

C: Of course. But during the race, we need to pay close attention to the position of the poles. And remember: keep control of the sledge.

A: Alright. Just follow the training rhythm, and we'll be fine.

C: Did you guys see that? Just now an athlete lost control and rolled over!

B: It won't happen to us. We must be more careful.

A: We have trained a lot. It won't be a problem for us.

C: I believe that we are the best!

A/B/C: Cheer up!

Words and Expressions

slalom /ˈslɑːləm/ *n.* 滑雪障碍赛；大回转

confident /ˈkɒnfɪd(ə)nt/ *adj.* 自信的；确信的；信心十足的

position /pəˈzɪʃ(ə)n/ *n.* 位置

keep control of 控制

sledge /sledʒ/ *n.* 雪橇

roll over 侧翻

cheer up 加油

Activity 2

👥 Work in pairs and make conversations according to the given situations.

> **Situation 1:** The audience commented on the wonderful performances of the players.
>
> **Situation 2:** In a game, the athlete fell out of the track due to his loss of control.

Part Two Reading

Passage 1

Directions: Read the passage about bobsleigh, luge and skeleton and discuss the following questions with your partner.

Bobsleigh, Luge and Skeleton

Sledge or sleigh originated in the snow-covered mountain areas of Switzerland and widely spread to Europe, North America and Asia. There are generally three types of sledges that are used for a specific sport, namely bobsleigh, luge, and skeleton. The first formal sledge competition was held by Britain in 1884. Bobsleigh first appeared in the Olympic Games in 1924. Luge was first contested at the 1964 Winter Olympics. Skeleton was added to the Winter Olympics in 2002; previously, it had been in the Olympic program only in St. Moritz, Switzerland, in 1928 and 1948.

Bobsleigh or bobsled, one of the fastest winter sports, is a team sport of two or four teammates which involves sliding down an ice track on a sledge. The sledge is made of metal, like a little boat with a streamlined hood on the front. The rudder and the steering wheel are used to control direction. A pair of rudder plates is fitted on the bottom of the front part, a pair of fixed parallel slip gauges on the back, and a brake on the rear. The sport is not for the faint-hearted, as bobsleigh crashes are potentially dangerous.

Luge is a winter sport in which one or two players ride a flat sledge while lying on the back and feet first. The sledge is made of wood with metal skateboard on the bottom. The width of a pair of paralleled skateboards is no more than 45 centimeters. Fore wings of skateboards can be flexible but are not allowed to be equipped with rudder and brake. In the Winter Olympics, there are four luge disciplines: men's singles, men's doubles, women's singles and team relay.

Although the top speeds achieved by skeleton racers are slightly slower than those of the luge competitors, in some ways the skeleton sport requires even more courage, because athletes travel headfirst and face down. Skeleton evolved from traditional bobsleigh. The first competitive skeleton race was organized between the Swiss towns of St. Moritz and Celerina. The winner received a bottle of champagne. In 1928, skeleton was competed in St. Moritz Winter Olympic Games. Twenty years later, when Winter Olympics were held there again, skeleton was contested again but never appeared until the Salt Lake City Winter Olympic Games in 2002. Since then, events for women's singles were added as well.

Words and Expressions

previously /'priːvɪəslɪ/ *adv.* 之前地；先前地；以前地

streamlined /'striːmlaɪnd/ *adj.* 流线型的；改进的，最新型的

hood /hʊd/ *n.* 罩；头巾；兜帽

wheel /wiːl/ *n.* 车轮；方向盘；转动

v. 转动，旋转

brake /breɪk/ *n.* 制动器，闸，刹车；阻碍 *v.* 刹车

rear /rɪə(r)/ *n.* 后面，后方；尾部

crash /kræʃ/ *n.* 撞击；撞车

Sports Terms

bobsleigh /'bɒbsleɪ/ *n.* 有舵雪橇，雪车

luge /luːʒ/ *n.* 无舵雪橇

skeleton /'skelɪtn/ *n.* 俯式冰橇，钢架雪车

sleigh /sleɪ/ *n.* 雪橇

ice track 冰道

rudder /'rʌdə/ *n.* 舵，船舵；飞机方向舵

steering wheel 方向盘

rudder plate 舵板

men's singles 男子单人赛

men's doubles 男子双人赛

skateboard /'skeɪtbɔːd/ *n.* 滑板

Questions:

    1. Do you know the various disciplines of sledge?

    2. What is a luge made of ?

    3. Can you tell the differences between luge and skeleton?

Passage 2

Directions: Read the passage about the International Bobsleigh and Skeleton Federation and discuss the following questions with your partner.

International Bobsleigh and Skeleton Federation

The International Bobsleigh and Skeleton Federation (IBSF), originally known by the French name Fédération Internationale de Bobsleigh et de Tobogganing (FIBT), is the international governing body of bobsleigh and skeleton, which started in northern Europe. It was founded on November 23, 1923. In June 2015, it announced a name change from FIBT to IBSF. The official languages are French, English and Germany. The headquarters of the IBSF lies in Lausanne, Switzerland.

The world's first bobsleigh club was founded in St. Moritz, Switzerland in 1897. By 1904, competitions were taking place on natural ice courses. This growth led to the creation of the FIBT in 1923 with inclusion into the International Olympic Committee (IOC) the following year, when bobsleigh was officially listed as competition in the first Winter Olympic Games. Skeleton was an Olympic sport in 1928 and 1948 when St. Moritz hosted the Games, and returned as an Olympic discipline in 2002. Women, who once had a place on the sled in five-person bobsleigh competitions in the earlier days of the sport, began officially competing in the IBSF races in 1998. The first women's bobsleigh World Championship was held in 2000 and women's bobsleigh became an Olympic sport in 2002.

Currently, the IBSF governs the following competitions: bobsleigh at the Winter Olympics, Bobsleigh World Cups, FIBT World Championships, skeleton at the Winter Olympics, etc.

announce /əˈnaʊns/ v. 宣布；公开声明	course /kɔːs/ n. 赛道；跑道；课程
	inclusion /ɪnˈkluːʒn/ n. 包括，囊括，包含

Questions:

1. When was the IBSF founded?

2. What competitions does the IBSF govern?

Part Three Exercises

Directions: Do the following exercises.

1. Talk briefly about the differences among the bobsleigh, the luge and the skeleton in their origin, development and rules.

2. Watch a sledge game and then write an essay with no less than 200 words.

Part Four Rules and Concepts

1. The sledge tracks are 1500 meters long with average slopes of 4°30′ and a maximum of 8°30′. The radius of curves is at least 20 meters, and the parapet wall of the track should be at least 50 centimeters.

2. The bobsleigh tracks are made of concrete or wood and are 1.4 meters wide. There are parapets on both sides of the tracks, with a height of 1.4 meters for the inner side and 2–7 meters for the outer.

3. The elevation difference between the start and finish of the downhill on a sledge is 700–1000 meters for men and 400–700 meters for women.

4. Any obstacles such as stones, wood, and tree roots shall not be on the racing route. If the track goes through woods, it should be at least 20 meters wide, and there shall not be any bumps or upslope on the track.

5. The elevation difference between the start and finish of the giant slalom is 400 meters for men and 300 meters for women. The track is at least 20 meters wide with at least 31 sets of gates, and the distance between gates should be no less than 6 meters.

6. The sled clothing includes a racing suit, shoulder pads, elbow guards, a helmet and special hobnailed boots.

7. The hobnails are a brush shape and are installed in a regular pattern under the boots. The length should be no more than 14 millimeters, and the space between should be no more than 3 centimeters.

8. Skeleton events are run on the same tracks as bobsleigh competitions, but the athlete lies on steel frame and saddle with head first. The skeleton weighs a maximum of 43 kilograms for men and 35 kilograms for women. As for the total weight of the skeleton and the athlete, the maximum is 115 kilograms for men and 92 kilograms for women.

9. Athletes cannot warm the runners of their sled to make them run faster. At the start of the race the runners must be within 4°C of the reference runner, which is exposed to the air for an hour beforehand.

10. The athlete must cross the finish line on the skeleton for the run to be valid, though the athlete is allowed to fall from the skeleton halfway.

Part Five Further Reading

Armin Zöggeler

Armin Zöggeler, born in 1974, is a retired Italian luger. He was nicknamed the "Iceblood Champion" because of his always cold, rational approach to the races. He made it to the medal podium in every Winter Olympic Games, from Lillehammer, Nagano, Salt Lake City, Turin, and Vancouver, to Sochi in 2014. He took part in the Winter Olympics six times consecutively and won 6 medals, of which 2 were gold. He has also won 16 medals at the FIL World Luge Championships. At the 2014 Winter Olympics opening ceremony, at age 40, Armin Zöggeler was the flag bearer of the Italian delegation, and won third place of the Luge Men's Singles. As a result of winning this bronze medal, he stood on the same podium as he had 20 years previously, becoming the first person in the Olympic history to win medals in the same sports event six consecutive times.

Lesson 11 Modern Biathlon

Activity 1

🎧 Listen to the following conversation, and then work in pairs to act it out.

(Before joining the Modern Biathlon event, Peter found that when he squatted, his thighs hurt a lot and had no strength. Now the doctor is examining him.)

A: Hello, Doctor Li!

B: Oh, Peter! What's wrong with you?

A: I think I've pulled my thigh.

B: Let me take a look at it. Does it hurt here?

A: Only slightly when I put pressure on it.

B: When you squat, does it hurt here?

A: Yes, it does, and there is no strength.

B: Oh, I know the problem. You've sprained your thigh muscle. I'll give you some spray, then you should relax for a day or two.

A: Could I participate in today's event?

B: No way, you must be joking!

A: Oh dear!

Words and Expressions

biathlon /baɪˈæθlən/ *n.* 冬季两项

squat /skwɒt/ *v. & n.* 蹲起

thigh /θaɪ/ *n.* 大腿

strength /streŋθ/ *n.* 力量；力气

pull my thigh 腿部拉伤

slightly /ˈslaɪtlɪ/ *adv.* 轻微地；稍微地

pressure /ˈpreʃə(r)/ *n.* 压力

sprain /spreɪn/ *v. & n.* 扭伤

muscle /ˈmʌs(ə)l/ *n.* 肌肉

spray /spreɪ/ *n.* 喷雾

Activity 2

👤 Work in pairs and make conversations according to the given situations.

Situation 1: If you are a biathlete and are going to share a story about how you started practicing biathlon, what story would that be?

Situation 2: You have been so exhausted in recent days that you long to ask your coach for a leave.

Part Two Reading

Passage 1

Directions: Read the passage about modern biathlon and discuss the following questions with your partner.

Modern Biathlon

Modern biathlon is a winter sport that combines cross-country skiing with shooting. Carrying rifles, athletes make one shot after every sliding distance. The one who first reaches the finish line wins. Originating in Scandinavia, modern biathlon evolved from ski hunting in ancient times. A stone sculpture from about 4000 years ago were found in Norway, showing two people chasing wild animals with skiing boards under their feet and sticks in their hands. The sport was gradually incorporated into a military training course from the Middle Ages onwards.

In 1767, Norway's ski patrol party of a frontier force held a ski shooting game—the world's first recorded modern biathlon competition. In 1912, the Norwegian army held the first ski shooting game in Oslo, named "To the War". After that, this game spread across Europe and North America and developed into a sporting event. It was listed as a demonstration event at the first Winter Olympic Games in 1924. The world's first Modern Biathlon Championship was held in 1958. In 1960, it was officially included to the Olympic Games with the name of "modern biathlon". And in 1992, modern biathlon events for women were added into the Winter Olympic Games.

In modern biathlon, there are individual, sprint, pursuit, relay and mass start events. All involve racing in laps around an undulating course. Competitors usually start at timed intervals and ski in "skating"-style against the clock, stopping to shoot at the targets. When shooting, they alternate between standing and prone (lying down) positions. Missing a target is penalized. In the individual event, there is a time penalty of one minute for each target missed. In other events, competitors must ski a 150-meter penalty loop for every target missed. The distance of the race and number of shooting phases depends on the event.

Words and Expressions

shooting /ˈʃuːtɪŋ/ *n.* 射击

rifle /ˈraɪfl/ *n.* 步枪，来福枪

make shot 射击

hunting /ˈhʌntɪŋ/ *n.* 狩猎

sculpture /ˈskʌlptʃə(r)/ *n.* 雕像；雕塑；雕刻

chase /tʃeɪs/ *v. & n.* 追捕；追逐

military training course 军事训练科目

lap /læp/ *n.* 山坳；一圈

undulate /ˈʌndjuleɪt/ *v.* 起伏，波动

interval /ˈɪntəvl/ *n.* 时间间隔；距离

against the clock 争分夺秒

target /ˈtɑːgɪt/ *n.* 目标；靶子；目的

alternate /ˈɔːltəneɪt/ *v.* 轮流，交替

penalty /ˈpenəltɪ/ *n.* 惩罚

loop /luːp/ *n.* 环；圈

Sports Terms

modern biathlon 现代冬季两项

rifle shooting 射击

individual /ˌɪndɪˈvɪdʒuəl/ *n.* 个人赛

sprint /sprɪnt/ *n.* 距离赛

pursuit /pəˈsjuːt/ *n.* 追逐赛

mass start 团体出发

standing shooting 立射

prone shooting 卧射

Questions:

1. Can you describe the origin and development of modern biathlon in your own words?

2. When was modern biathlon officially listed as a competition of the Winter Olympic Games?

3. Can you list the modern biathlon events?

Passage 2

Directions: Read the passage about the International Biathlon Union and discuss the following questions with your partner.

International Biathlon Union

The International Biathlon Union (IBU) is the international governing body of the biathlon. Its headquarters is located in Salzburg, Austria. The current president is Ander Besseberg from Norway.

The IBU was founded in 1993 as an independent association under the umbrella of the UIPMB (Union de Pentathlon Moderne et Biathlon) alongside the UIPM (Union Internationale de Pentathlon Moderne). On July 2, 1993, the biathlon was announced to be excluded from the World Federation UIPMB, which it had been part of since 1953, in order to form its own international federation. During that congress, the new federation elected their executive committee, and the 57 existing members of the UIPMB were automatically transferred to the IBU. On December 12 of the same year, the IBU was founded in Salzburg, Austria. In 1998, the IBU officially separated from the UIPMB, and in August of the same year the General Assembly International Sports Federations (GAISF) declared the IBU as a proper member. The IBU settled in Salzburg, Austria on June 1, 1999.

Competitions organized by IBU include Biathlon at the Winter Olympic Games, Biathlon World Championships for both men and women, Biathlon World Cups, the European Championships, and Junior Biathlon World Championships.

Words and Expressions

exclude /ɪk'skluːd/ *v.* 排除；逐出

congress /'kɒŋgres/ *n.* 大会；议会

elect /ɪ'lekt/ *v.* 推选，选举

executive committee 执行委员会

automatically /ˌɔːtə'mætɪklɪ/ *adv.*

自动地；机械地；无意识地

transfer /træns'fɜː/ *n.* & *v.* 转移；转让

separate /'sep(ə)reɪt/ *v.* 分开，分离

declare /dɪ'kleə(r)/ *v.* 宣布，公布；颁布

Sports Terms

International Biathlon Union (IBU) 国际冬季两项联盟

pentathlon /pen'tæθlən/ *n.* 五项运动

General Assembly International Sports Federations (GAISF)
国际单项体育联合会总会

Questions:

1. Where is the headquarters of the IBU?

2. How was the IBU separated from the UIPMB?

3. Can you list the main competitions organized by the IBU?

Part Three Exercises

Directions: Do the following exercises.

1. What abilities do you think modern biathletes should have?

2. Discuss your feelings about the modern biathlon, according to its origins and development.

Part Four Rules and Concepts

1. The target is black. After shooting the target, a white gate in front will be closed in order to identify whether it is a hit or not.

2. It's the same in broadcast—white means "hit" while black means "missed the target".

3. The target range shooting distance is 50 meters, and the goal is divided into internal and external rings.

4. When shooting in the prone position the target diameter is 45 millimeters (the inner ring); when shooting in the standing position the target diameter is 110 millimeters (the outer ring).

5. The starting area will adjust to different sizes according to different games, but the venue can accommodate at least 30 people (mass start number).

6. The penalty track is an oval level track of 150 meters long with no hills.

7. Athletes need to carry rifles during the entire process of sliding, with the muzzles pointing upward unloaded. The rifle can only be loaded with bullets after the athletes have entered the shooting position.

8. During the game, while wearing skis, holding the ski rod and carrying rifles, players must finish the entire distance by sliding along the marked track in the right direction.

9. In an individual race, competitors' starts are staggered, normally by 30 or 60 seconds.

10. Athletes are required to take five shots in an individual game and eight shots for each one each time in a relay game.

Part Five Further Reading

The King of Biathlon

Ole Einar Bjørndalen, born in 1974, is a Norwegian biathlete, often referred to by the nickname "The King of Biathlon". He is the most successful biathlete of all time at the Biathlon World Championships, having won 40 medals including 19 gold, double that of any other biathlete. He is also the most medaled Olympian in the history of the Winter Olympic Games, with 13 medals in total, including 8 gold, 4 silver and 1 bronze. He holds a record of 95 individual Biathlon World Cup victories, the most of any biathlete to date.

4
Chapter

Combat Sports and Other Events

Lesson 12 Taekwondo

Part One Listening and Speaking

Activity 1

🎧 Listen to the following conversation, and then work in pairs to act it out.

(John wants to join the taekwondo club but is a bit hesitant, not exactly knowing what it entails. The coach explains the spirit of taekwondo to convince him it is worth trying.)

A: I'd like to join the taekwondo club but I'm not sure if it's exactly what I think it is. Could you tell me something more about it?

B: Like any martial art, most people just see the fighting aspect of it, but there is actually a lot more to it.

A: I know perseverance and self-control are a part of it, but what else?

B: The true spirit of taekwondo is courtesy and integrity.

A: Courtesy? This is the first time I've heard this.

B: Yes, taekwondo makes people courteous. Training begins and ends with courtesy, and etiquette is instilled throughout the training.

A: Sounds like something everyone should do. I've decided I want to be part of this club. May I join?

B: Certainly!

Words and Expressions

taekwondo /taɪˈkwɔndəu/ *n.* 跆拳道

hesitant /ˈhezɪtənt/ *adj.* 犹豫的

spirit /ˈspɪrɪt/ *n.* 精神

convince /kənˈvɪns/ *v.* 说服；使确信

martial art 武术

perseverance /ˌpɜːsɪˈvɪərəns/ *n.* 毅力；耐性，耐力

self-control /ˌself kənˈtrəʊl/ *n.* 自我控制

courtesy /ˈkɜːtəsɪ/ *n.* 礼貌；谦恭

integrity /ɪnˈtegrətɪ/ *n.* 正直；诚实

courteous /ˈkɜːtɪəs/ *adj.* 彬彬有礼的，客气的

etiquette /ˈetɪket/ *n.* 礼节；礼仪

instill /ɪnˈstɪl/ *v.* 徐徐滴入；逐渐灌输

throughout /θruːˈaʊt/ *adv.* 到处 *prep.* 在……的整个期间

Activity 2

👥 Work in pairs and answer the following questions.

Question 1: The following words are often used by referees in taekwondo competitions. "Chung", "Hong", "Cha-ryeot", "Kyeong-rye", "Joon-bi", "Shi-jak", "Keu-man", "Kyong-go", "Gam-jeom", "Shi-gan", "Kye-sok", "Kal-yeo" and "Ha-nal, Duhl, Seht, Neht, Da-seot, Yeo-seot, II-gop, Yeo-dul, A-hop, Yeol." Do you know what they mean?

Question 2: How many points will an athlete be penalized if he/she holds, pushes, or gives his/her back to the opponent, or pretends to be injured ("Kyong-go")? How many points will an athlete be penalized if he/she deliberately throws an opponent or brings down the opponent whose feet are both off the floor, or deliberately attacks the opponent's back or face with his/her hands ("Gam-jeom")?

Part Two Reading

Passage 1

Directions: Read the passage about taekwondo and discuss the following questions with your partner.

Taekwondo

As one of the official events of the modern Olympics, taekwondo is a combat sport in which athletes mainly use their hands and feet to fight. Compared with most martial arts, it places more emphasis on kicks and punches. Taekwondo originated in the Korean peninsula and initially evolved from Tae Kyon and Hwarang during the era of Three Kingdoms in Korea. It was and still is a prevalent Korean technical art among the Korean masses. The term "taekwondo" was created by Choi Hong Hi of Korea, and this sport is regarded as the national sport of Korea.

Tae, means "to kick"; Kwon, to fight with fist; Do, represents an art of moral and ritual practice. Taekwondo is a Korean martial art influenced by the development of East Asian culture, with the martial spirit of "begin with courtesy, and end with courtesy" as its core. While competitors do use their hands, about 70% of this martial art is based on kicking. Taekwondo competition typically involves sparring, breaking, patterns, and self-defense. In the Olympic taekwondo competition, however, only sparring is performed. There are a total of 24 sets of taekwondo routines. In addition, there are weapons, grappling, wrestling lock, self-defense, and more than 10 other kinds of basic martial arts.

Currently, there are two schools of taekwondo in existence. One is the International Taekwondo Federation (ITF), which developed in North Korea and spread mainly to North America, characterized by routines involving complex and ever-changing techniques. The other is the World Taekwondo Federation (WTF), which developed in Korea and other parts of the world. It is characterized by gorgeous technical movements, highlights the flexible use of the legs, and requires players to wear complete protective gear. The WTF is used in the Olympic Games.

Words and Expressions

combat /ˈkɒmbæt/ n. 战斗；对抗

kick /kɪk/ n. & v. 踢

punch /pʌntʃ/ n. & v. 用拳重击，击打

initially /ɪˈnɪʃəlɪ/ adv. 开始地，最初地

prevalent /ˈprevələnt/ adj. 流行的；普遍的，广传的

fist /fɪst/ n. 拳头

represent /rɪprɪˈzent/ v. 代表

moral /ˈmɒrəl/ adj. 道德的；道义的

ritual /ˈrɪtʃuəl/ n. & adj. 仪式（的）

core /kɔː(r)/ n. 核心

weapon /ˈwepən/ n. 兵器；武器

school /skuːl/ n. 流派；学校

characterize /ˈkærəktəraɪz/ v. 以……为特征

ever-changing /ˈevə(r)ˈtʃeɪndʒɪŋ/ adj. 不断变化的

gorgeous /ˈgɔːdʒəs/ adj. 华丽的

highlight /ˈhaɪlaɪt/ v. 突出；强调

Sports Terms

Tae Kyon 跆跟

Hwarang 花郎道

technical art 技击术

begin with courtesy, end with

courtesy 始于礼，终于礼

sparring /'spaːrɪŋ/ *n.* 搏击；对打；

竞技

breaking /'breɪkɪŋ/ *n.* 击破

pattern /'pætn/ *n.* 套路；品势

self-defense 自卫术

grappling /'græplɪŋ/ *n.* 擒拿

wrestling lock 摔锁

schools of taekwondo 跆拳道流派

International Taekwondo Federation

(ITF) 国际跆拳道联盟

World Taekwondo Federation (WIF)

世界跆拳道联盟

flexible use of legs 灵活运用腿法

Questions:

1. What are the distinct characteristics of taekwondo?

2. What does "Tae", "Kwon", and "Do" mean respectively?

3. What are the two schools of taekwondo in existence?

Passage 2

Directions: Read the passage about world organizations of taekwondo and discuss the following questions with your partner.

World Organizations of Taekwondo

The International Taekwondo Federation (ITF) was founded by Choi Hong Hi in 1966 in Seoul, Korea. North Korea is often considered the best country in the world at developing ITF Taekwondo. The most important events organized by the ITF are the World Championships and the World Cups, which include the following disciplines: patterns, sparring, special technique, power breaking, as well as pre-arranged team sparring. In addition, other approved championships take place across the world such as the Junior and Senior World Championships, General Choi Memorial Cup Championships, Continental Championships, the ITF Open Championships, etc.

The World Taekwondo Federation (WTF) was established in 1972 in Seoul, and was recognized by the IOC in 1980. It has more than 200 nation members today. Important events hosted by the WTF include: the World Taekwondo Championships, the World Junior Taekwondo Championships, the World Taekwondo Poomsae Championships, the World Taekwondo Grand Prix Series, etc. According to the WTF, taekwondo is one of the most systematic and scientific Korean traditional martial arts, which teaches more than physical fighting skills. It is a discipline that shows ways of enhancing our spirit and life through training our body and mind.

Words and Expressions

approve /ə'pru:v/ *v.* 同意，允许

take place 发生

systematic /ˌsɪstə'mætɪk/ *adj.* 系统的

enhance /ɪn'hɑːns/ *v.* 提升，提高

physical /'fɪzɪkl/ *adj.* 身体的；物理的

Sports Terms

special technique 特技

power breaking 威力击破

pre-arranged team sparring 预约团体竞技

General Choi Memorial Cup Championships 崔泓熙将军纪念杯赛

Continental Championships 洲际锦标赛

World Taekwondo Poomsae Championships 世界跆拳道品势赛

Questions:

1. Who founded the ITF?

2. What competitions are organized by the WTF?

3. According to the WTF, what are the benefits of practicing taekwondo?

Part Three Exercises

Directions: Do the following exercises.

1. A taekwondo player was defeated in a match, and he angrily threw his helmet on the ground. The WTF gave him a lifetime ban, and expelled him from the taekwondo community. Drawing from this incident, write an essay on the topic of "Budo spirit" in no less than 250 words.

2. Discuss the relationship between taekwondo etiquette and Chinese traditional culture.

Part Four Rules and Concepts

1. The competition arena shall have a flat, square surface free from obstructions with dimensions of 8 meters in length by 8 meters in width.

2. The height of the arena shall be 0.6–1 meters above the ground. Beyond boundary lines, there shall be a slope with an angle less than 30 degrees towards the ground.

3. During the competition, the athlete wears a uniform, a belt, and a helmet to protect the head, along with armor, leggings and other protective gear.

4. The color of the armor is red or blue. Armor shall be worn outside the uniform, and the color of the helmet shall be consistent with the color of the armor. Other protective equipment includes the jockstrap, armband and leggings worn underneath the uniforms.

5. Competitors are allowed to use punches and kicks to legitimately attack the head and torso of their opponent.

6. Only the protected area between the collarbone and hip bone, and the head wrapped by a clavicle brace of the opponent, are allowed to be hit. Hitting the opponent on the back part of the head is prohibited.

7. Punches to the body score one point; rotating kicks to the body score two points; kicks to the head score three points (a countdown by the referee does not append points); rotating kicks to the head score four points.

8. Each time a player is penalized two "Kyong-go" or one "Gam-jeom", the opponent receives one point.

9. There are several methods of winning: A knockout; attaining a higher overall score; the advantage of points difference; an overtime score firstly; an advantage determination; abstaining; an opponent's disqualification from the competition; a foul penalized by the main referee.

10. In particular competitions, according to the weighing records, the lighter one wins.

Part Five Further Reading

A Legendary Figure in Taekwondo—Chen Zhong

Chen Zhong, born in 1982, is a Chinese taekwondo athlete who won the 2000 Sydney Olympics, the 2001 World Cup, the 2004 Athens Olympics and the 2007 Beijing World Championship. She has achieved the "Grand Slam" of winning the Olympic Games, the World Championship and the World Cup. On September 30, 2000, in the women's 67 kg taekwondo competition in Sydney Olympic Games, 18-year-old Chen won the first gold medal in taekwondo for China, as well as the first Olympic gold medal in the event's history. In 1994, taekwondo was officially listed as an Olympic sport, to be introduced in 2000. China set up a taekwondo national team in 1995 when a foreigner asserted that to win an Olympic gold medal of this event would require at least ten years for China. Chen's winning the gold medal shortened the whole process by five years. Chen said confidently of her abilities: "I can say that at this level there is no opponent, only myself if any."

Lesson 13 Weightlifting

Part One Listening and Speaking

Activity 1

🎧 Listen to the following conversation, and then work in pairs to act it out.

(John has just recovered from a bad injury, and he wants to be restored to his previous health as soon as possible. His coach is persuading him to calm down and resume step by step.)

A: Coach, I'm done warming up. Can I start my workout?

B: Yes, you can.

A: I feel like it has taken me a long time to get my confidence back.

B: Everything is difficult at first, especially after recovering from a bad injury. But don't worry too much about it. Regaining your confidence will take some time.

A: I'm very anxious to get back to my top level. I used to do so well in the snatch, but since my injury I feel like I've lost all my confidence.

B: Where there is pressure, there is motivation. Keep calm, keep focused, and do the exercises carefully. You need to take it one step at a time.

A: I see. Believe me, I will work hard.

B: You can do it. I know you can.

Words and Expressions

recover /rɪ'kʌvə(r)/ *v.* 恢复（健康、精力）；重新获得

restore /rɪ'stɔː(r)/ *v.* 恢复；归还

persuade /pə'sweɪd/ *v.* 说服，劝说

calm down 冷静下来

anxious /'æŋkʃəs/ *adj.* 焦虑的；担忧的

snatch /snætʃ/ *n.* 抓举

motivation /,məʊtɪ'veɪʃ(ə)n/ *n.* 动力

Activity 2

👥 Work in pairs and answer the following questions.

Question 1: Try to come up with a Chinese idiom based on the "weightlifting competition".

Question 2: Do you know the weight and color of the barbells in the Olympic weightlifting competition?

Part Two Reading

Passage 1

Directions: Read the passage about weightlifting and discuss the following questions with your partner.

Weightlifting

Weightlifting is a competitive Olympic sport that solely features strength. In the game the athlete lifts a barbell with both hands over his head, and the athlete who lifts the heaviest weights is crowned the winner. Weightlifting began in the 18th century in Europe. Initially there was a metal ball at either end of the bar. Competitors did not enjoy the advantage of adjustable weights, so victory and defeat were determined by lifting a certain weight several times. Later, an Italian named Luis Atila emptied the metal ball and added solid iron or lead shot to adjust the weight. In 1910, Casper Berg changed the metal ball into metal sheets of different weights and sizes. In 1891, the first World Weightlifting Championship was held in London, England. As for Olympic weightlifting competitions, the men's event first appeared at the 1896 Athens Olympic

Games, and the women's was first introduced at the 2000 Sydney Olympic Games.

The weightlifting program includes the snatch and clean and jerk. The snatch entails pulling with a very wide grip the barbell overhead in one single movement. The clean and jerk is more forgiving, using a narrower grip to pull the bar to the shoulders and then using the strength of the legs to push until the arms reach full upward extension.

Words and Expressions

weight /weɪt/ *n.* 重量

crown /kraʊn/ *v.* 加冕   *n.* 王冠

adjustable /əˈdʒʌstəbl/ *adj.* 可调节的

defeat /dɪˈfiːt/ *n.* 失败

size /saɪz/ *n.* 大小；尺码

grip /grɪp/ *n.* 紧抓，抓握

overhead /ˌəʊvəˈhed/ *adv.* 在头顶上

Sports Terms

weightlifting /ˈweɪtlɪftɪŋ/ *n.* 举重

barbell /ˈbɑːbel/ *n.* 杠铃

metal ball 金属球

metal sheet 金属片

clean and jerk 挺举

Questions:

1. Can you retell the development of weightlifting briefly in your own words?

2. How can we classify the weightlifting program?

Passage 2

Directions: Read the passage about the International Weightlifting Federation and discuss the following questions with your partner.

International Weightlifting Federation

The International Weightlifting Federation (IWF) was founded in 1905 and proposed by the French. There are currently 188 members, and the current IWF president is Tamas Ajan of Hungary. The IWF aims to organize and develop the sport of weightlifting, formulate weightlifting rules, manage international competitions, supervise the continental and regional activities and assist the federations of countries and regions in developing weightlifting. It has technical, coaching and research, and medical committees. The IWF funding comes from the membership fees, the television broadcasting fees and expenses paid by the organizers of the international competition. The organization publishes *World Weightlifting* monthly, which covers international competitions, World Championships, competition rules and regulations, modification of member addresses and reports from various congresses or conferences.

The IWF organizes the following main events: World Weightlifting Championships, World Youth Weightlifting Championships and Olympic weightlifting competitions. China applied to join the IWF in 1936, was recognized by the IWF in 1955, exited in 1958, and in September 1974, China's IWF membership was restored.

Words and Expressions

propose /prəˈpəʊz/ *v.* 建议；打算，计划

continental /ˌkɒntɪˈnentl/ *adj.* 大陆的；洲际的

assist /əˈsɪst/ *v.* 帮助；协助

expense /ɪkˈspens/ *n.* 费用

Questions:

1. When was IWF founded? Who is the current president?

2. What are the important competitions and events organized by IWF?

Part Three Exercises

Directions: Do the following exercises.

1. Watch a weightlifting competition and describe the differences between the snatch and the clean and jerk.

2. During a weightlifting competition, the judges' and referee's results are registered via a lighting system with a white light indicating a "successful" lift and a red light indicating a "failed" lift. When two of the three referees provide white lights, is it indicating a "successful" or "failed" lift?

Part Four Rules and Concepts

1. The weightlifting arena is square with a side length of 4 meters made of wood, plastic or any solid texture. The surface is covered with a non-slip material. The arena is no higher than 15 centimeters, and no objects are allowed to be placed around within 1 meter, including a barbell. The minimum size of the large arena is 10 meters by 10 meters.

2. Weightlifting competitions are graded by the weight of the athletes. Youth and adult men have eight divisions: 56 kg, 62 kg, 69 kg, 77 kg, 85 kg, 94 kg, 105 kg, and 105 kg and over.

3. Youth and adult women have seven divisions: 48 kg, 53 kg, 58 kg, 63 kg, 69 kg, 75 kg, and 75 kg and over.

4. The weight of each player shall be measured two hours before the competition, which lasts one hour.

5. During the competition, the snatch event takes place first, followed by a short intermission of ten minutes, and then the clean and jerk event. The number of attempts for the snatch and clean and jerk are both three, for a total of six attempts.

6. The order of the competition depends on the weight the athlete requires, the order of drawing in advance, and the number of times the athlete has attempted a lift.

7. The competitor who chooses to attempt the lowest weight goes first. If more than one competitor is successful at that weight, the competitor who chooses the smaller number in the drawing goes first. If the competitors attempted the same weight for the second or third times, then the competitor who made fewer attempts goes first. If the competitors have the same number of attempting opportunities, the competitor who went first previously goes first now.

8. The barbell is loaded incrementally and progresses to a heavier weight throughout the course of competition. Weights are set in 1 kilogram increments after each successful attempt.

9. Olympic medals are given for the heaviest weights lifted overall—the maximum lifts of both snatch and clean and jerk combined. When a tie occurs, the athlete with the lower bodyweight is declared the winner. If two athletes lift the same

total weight and have the same bodyweight, the winner is the athlete who lifted the total weight first, as the two competitors are not allowed to tie for first place in the game.

10. The time allowed for each attempt is limited to one minute. From the moment the name of the athlete is called to the moment the loader finishes loading, the time calculation begins with the ending time of the two items. The time that one competitor may attempt consecutively is restricted to two minutes. During this period, if the competitor fails to raise the barbell above his or her knees, it is deemed a failed lift.

Part Five Further Reading

Zhan Xugang

Zhan Xugang, born in Kaihua County of Quzhou City, Zhejiang Province in 1974, is a famous Chinese weightlifter. He became the first Chinese weightlifter to get two Olympic weightlifting gold medals consecutively in the Olympic history. Zhan Xugang is straightforward in nature and loves weightlifting deeply. He began practicing weightlifting at the age of 10, and at 20 he was recruited by the national weightlifting team. In the 70 kg class, he reached the world-class level. At the Atlanta Olympic Games in 1996, he won three gold medals in this event and broke three world records. Thus his sports career reached its peak. At the Sydney Olympic Games in 2000, he overcame the adverse situation of ranking fourth place in the 160 kg snatch, and went on to successfully lift 207.5 kg in the clean and jerk, which he had never done before. He lifted the same total weight of 367.5 kg as a Greek competitor Mitrou. A tie occurred, and Zhan Xugang, with the lower bodyweight, was declared the repeat champion of the event.

Lesson 14 Judo

Part One Listening and Speaking

Activity 1

🎧 Listen to the following conversation, and then work in pairs to act it out.

(The judo competition will start soon. Peter feels very nervous and needs his coach's guidance. His coach offers some advice about how to calm down.)

A: Coach, I'm a little nervous.

B: Don't worry, try to relax yourself. Your ability has improved.

A: I feel like my mind has gone blank.

B: Just take it easy. I believe you can do it. You need to believe in yourself too.

A: What can I do?

B: Now listen to me. Take a deep breath, close your eyes and tell yourself that you can do it.

A: OK. I'm trying to stay composed.

B: Come on! You're the best! Show us what you're made of.

A: I feel much better now. Thank you, coach.

Words and Expressions

nervous /ˈnɜːvəs/ *adj.* 紧张不安的；神经的

go blank 空白

take it easy 放轻松

believe in yourself 相信自己

composed /kəmˈpəʊzd/ *adj.* 镇静的；沉着的

91

Activity 2

👥 Work in pairs and answer the following questions.

> **Question 1:** Which levels of judo competition were set in the 2012 London Olympics?
>
> **Question 2:** Do you know any similarities and differences between judo and karate?

Part Two Reading

Passage 1

Directions: Read the passage about judo and discuss the following questions with your partner.

Judo

Judo is the modern art of combat that involves mainly wrestling methods and ground-based skills. The most prominent feature of judo is its competitive element, where the emphasis is on proficiency of skills rather than the contrast in strength. The game requires athletes to force an opponent to submit with an "arm lock" or "choke" on the opponent's limbs and neck. Athletes can throw an opponent down to the ground, press down until the opponent concedes defeat, or clearly throw the opponent to the ground to obtain a victory. Judo is the only Olympic sport which allows the use of suffocation or twisting of the joints to subdue the opponent.

Judo evolved from a Japanese jujitsu. In 1882, Jigoro Kano combined the essence of various jujitsu factions to create the modern judo based mainly on "nage-waza", "katama-waza", and "atemi-waza". Meanwhile, he founded the Kodokan for training judo athletes, and modern judo is the simplified word from "Japanese Kodokan Judo". It was formed in the early 1900s and became an international sports competition in the 1950s. Jigoro Kano died in 1939, and Kodokan's successor initiated reforms to help judo become a widely accepted worldwide sport. These included weight divisions used in the game and reforms of the decision of victory and defeat. Male and female judo competitions were introduced respectively in the 18th Olympic Games in 1964 and in the 25th Olympic Games in 1992.

Words and Expressions

prominent /'prɒmɪnənt/ *adj.* 突出的；卓越的

emphasis /'emfəsɪs/ *n.* 重点；强调

proficiency /prə'fɪʃnsɪ/ *n.* 精通；熟练

contrast /'kɒntrɑːst/ *n.* 对比；比照

submit /səb'mɪt/ *v.* 使屈服

limb /lɪm/ *n.* 臂；肢

concede /kən'siːd/ *v.* 承认；退让

suffocation /ˌsʌfə'keɪʃən/ *n.* 窒息

twist /twɪst/ *v.* 扭，拧

joint /dʒɔɪnt/ *n.* 关节

subdue /səb'djuː/ *v.* 制服，压制

essence /'esns/ *n.* 本质；精髓

initiate /ɪ'nɪʃɪeɪt/ *v.* 开创，发起

reform /rɪ'fɔːm/ *n.* 改革

weight division 体重分级

worldwide /'wɜːldwaɪd/ *adj.* 世界的，世界范围的

Sports Terms

wrestling /'reslɪŋ/ *n.* 格斗；摔跤

ground-based skill 地面技

arm lock 锁臂

choke /tʃəʊk/ *n.* 扼颈

jujitsu /dʒuː'dʒɪtsuː/ *n.* 柔术

Questions:

1. How can we tell the outcome of a judo competition?

2. Can you retell the development of judo?

3. When were men's and women's judo competitions officially listed as the Olympic events respectively?

Passage 2

Directions: Read the passage about the International Judo Federation and discuss the following questions with your partner.

International Judo Federation

The International Judo Federation (IJF) was founded in 1951, with its headquarters in Japan and Secretariat in South Korea. Currently its president is Marius Vizer. It has 220 members belonging to five continental federations, namely the African Judo Union (AJU), the Pan-American Judo Confederation (PJC), the Judo Union of Asia (JUA), the European Judo Union (EJU) and the Oceania Judo Union (OJU), each comprising a number of national judo associations. Russian President Vladimir Putin is the honorary president of the International Judo Federation. On October 10, 2012, he was awarded the rank of 8th dan by the IJF and became the most well-known ambassador for judo.

The IJF is responsible for organizing international competitions, hosts the World Judo Championships, and is involved in running the Olympic judo events. Since 2009, the IJF organizes yearly World Championships, Grand Prix, Grand Slams, Master Tournaments and Continental Open Tournaments.

Words and Expressions

honorary /ˈɒnərərɪ/ *adj.* 荣誉上的 | ambassador /æmˈbæsədə(r)/ *n.* 大使

Sports Terms

International Judo Federation (IJF) 国际柔道联合会

rank of 8th dan in Judo 柔道八段

Grand Slam 大满贯

Master Tournament 大师赛

Questions:

1. Who is the honorary president of the International Judo Federation and the most well-known ambassador for judo?

2. What competitions does the IJF mainly organize and conduct?

Part Three Exercises

Directions: Do the following exercises.

1. Search for relevant information and elaborate on the ranking system of judo.

2. Prepare some questions for an interview with the parents and the kids who just finished a junior judo training session. For instance, ask about their opinions on the judo sport.

Part Four Rules and Concepts

1. The arena consists of a competition area and a safe area, with tatami or suitable materials similar to tatami, usually in a green color.

2. Judo athletes wear blue or white clothing. The length of the jacket is over the lap with the left lapel over the right one. The waist belt, colored to indicate rank, is 4–5 centimeters wide.

3. The formal round time is five minutes for men and four minutes for women. There are a total of three referees. The main referee organizes the athletes onto the arena, assesses techniques, signals scores, and announces the winner. At either corner there is a corner judge to check that the fight remains within the competition area.

4. There are three ways to score in a judo contest: scoring an ippon, waza-ari, and yuko.

5. Ippon: A throw that places the opponent on his or her back with impetus and control scores an ippon. There are three conditions: "powerful", "fast" and "most of the opponent's back touching the floor". A submission is signaled by tapping the mat or the opponent at least twice with the hand or foot, or by saying "maitta" ("I surrender"). An ippon is also scored when pinning an opponent on his or her back with a recognized osaekomi-waza for 25 seconds.

6. Waza-ari: Suppress the opponent with nage-waza. There are only two conditions for meeting the requirements of an ippon. A pin lasting for less than 25 seconds but more than 20 seconds scores a waza-ari. Two scores of waza-ari equal an ippon.

7. Yuko: An athlete controls the opponent with nage-waza and throws the opponent onto the ground, but there are two insufficient conditions in the judgment of an ippon. A pin lasting for less than 20 seconds but more than 15 seconds scores a yuko. In addition, when an athlete is penalized a shido twice, the opponent gets a yuko.

8. Shido: Minor rules infractions such as using other techniques beyond the standards or walking out of the arena are penalized with a shido. Depending on the number of shidos, the opponent will get an extra point. A fourth shido makes a "foul-play defeat", resulting in the disqualification of the penalized competitor.

9. Foul out: Stretch the inside of the opponent's legs (anti-joint action), or force his or her head to hit the ground, etc. It is made when there is a serious risk of unruly behavior. The opponent scores an ippon directly.

10. If the scores of the two judokas are identical at the end of the match, the contest is resolved by the *Golden Score Rule*, a sudden death situation where the first judoka to achieve any score wins.

Part Five Further Reading

Judo Queen—Kye Sun-Hui

Kye Sun-Hui, born in Pyongyang in 1979, is a famous judoka in North Korea. Due to her tenacious style and excellent skills, she often defeats the opponent with "ippon" in a very short time, and is known as the "Queen of Judo". At the 1996 Atlanta Olympic Games, she won the 48 kg gold medal and became the youngest gold medalist in judo; at the 2000 Sydney Olympic Games, she received the 52 kg bronze medal; and at the 2004 Athens Olympic Games, she won the 57 kg silver medal. She won gold medals at the World Judo Championships in 2001, 2003, 2005 and 2007. Because of her great contributions to the sport, she was awarded the title of "labor heroine".

Lesson 15 Wrestling

Part One Listening and Speaking

Activity 1

🎧 Listen to the following conversation, and then work in pairs to act it out.

(Peter is inviting John to watch a wrestling match. They are making an appointment regarding the place and time that they will meet.)

A: Have you ever watched a wrestling match? I've got two tickets. Would you like to go with me?

B: Yes, I'd like to. I've only ever watched it on TV.

A: Great! Let's go together then. The match will be at the Capital Institute of Physical Education stadium.

B: I don't know where it is. Should we meet first and then go together?

A: Sure. You can take the No. 123 bus to Jimen Qiao West. I'll wait for you there.

B: When should we meet?

A: The match will start at seven o'clock, so we'd better meet at half past six.

B: OK. See you tonight!

Words and Expressions

appointment /ə'pɔɪntmənt/ *n.* 约定；约会

regarding /rɪ'ɡɑːdɪŋ/ *prep.* 关于；至于

ticket /'tɪkɪt/ *n.* 票

Activity 2

👥 Work in pairs and answer the following questions.

> **Question 1:** Do you know the variations of wresting?
>
> **Question 2:** Which event do you prefer to watch, taekwondo, judo or wresting? Why?

Part Two Reading

Passage 1

Directions: Read the passage about wrestling and discuss the following questions with your partner.

Wrestling

Wresting is a combat sport in which players try to grapple their opponents to the ground using a variety of skills, techniques and methods. As one of the world's oldest martial arts, wrestling has a long history. Records in ancient Greece, Egypt, China and Japan said that wrestling occupied a prominent place in these countries. Modern wrestling is thought to have originated in Greece. At the ancient Olympic Games, wrestling competition, brutal in many aspects, served as the focal sport.

Currently, international wrestling has two variations: Greco-Roman style and freestyle, and athletes compete in a division determined by their body mass. In Greco-Roman style, it is forbidden to hold the opponent below the belt, to make trips, and to actively use the legs in the execution of any action. By contrast, freestyle allows the use of the wrestler's or his or her opponent's legs in offense and defense.

Greco-Roman wrestling appeared in the first modern Olympic Games in Athens in 1896. Since 1908, the sport has been in every Summer Olympics. Freestyle wrestling became an Olympic event in 1904. Women's freestyle wrestling was added to the Summer Olympics in 2004. Now wrestlers not only compete in the Olympic Games, but they also appear in all kinds of large-scale fighting games, such as Ultimate Fighting Championship (UFC), Ultimate Fighting, Strike Force, etc.

Words and Expressions

grapple /ˈgræpl/ *v.* 扭打；格斗

occupy /ˈɒkjupaɪ/ *v.* 占据；居住；占有

ancient /ˈeɪnʃənt/ *adj.* 古老的

brutal /ˈbruːtl/ *adj.* 残忍的，野蛮的

focal /ˈfəʊkl/ *adj.* 焦点的

variation /ˌveərɪˈeɪʃn/ *n.* 变化；变异，变种

body mass 体重

forbid /fəˈbɪd/ *v.* 禁止

make trip 绊腿

Sports Terms

Greco-Roman style wrestling 古典式摔跤

freestyle wrestling 自由式摔跤

wrestler /ˈreslə(r)/ *n.* 摔跤选手

Ultimate Fighting Championship (UFC) 终极格斗冠军赛

Questions:

1. Can you describe the sport of wrestling in your own words?

2. Do you know the differences between the Greco-Roman style wrestling and freestyle wrestling?

Passage 2

Directions: Read the passage about the United World Wrestling and discuss the following questions with your partner.

United World Wrestling

United World Wrestling (UWW) is the international governing body for the sport of amateur wrestling. It was formerly known as the International Federation of Associated Wrestling Styles (FILA), founded in 1912 in Antwerp, Belgium, and having assumed its current name in September 2014. Its duties include setting rules and regulations and holding international competitions in the following wrestling styles: Greco-Roman wrestling, freestyle wrestling for men and women, as well as others. The flagship event of the UWW is the World Wrestling Championships.

The UWW is the body responsible for supervising Olympic wrestling competitions. Besides the Summer Olympics, there are also various international competitions such as the Commonwealth Games, the Pan-American Games, the Continental Championships and Continental Cups, etc. Competitions are graded by weight: 48 kg, 52 kg, 57 kg, 62 kg, 68 kg, 74 kg, 82 kg, 90 kg, 100 kg and over. The Olympic Games also use the same grading criteria.

China joined the federation in 1954, exited in 1958, and in 1979 restored its membership.

Words and Expressions

assume /əˈsjuːm/ v. 假定；承担

flagship /ˈflæɡʃɪp/ n. 旗舰；佼佼者

criteria /kraɪˈtɪərɪə/ n. 标准；条件

Sports Terms

United World Wrestling (UWW) 国际摔跤联合会

Commonwealth Games 英联邦运动会

Pan-American Games 泛美运动会

Continental Cups 洲际杯赛

Questions:

1. What are the major responsibilities of the UWW?

2. Can you list the main competitions organized by the UWW?

Part Three Exercises

Directions: Do the following exercises.

1. Give a brief description of the characteristics of Chinese-style wrestling.

2. In February 2013, the International Olympic Committee voted to remove the wrestling from the 2020 Summer Olympics onwards. However, on 8 September, 2013, the IOC announced that wrestling would return to the Summer Olympics in 2020. Look for the background information and write an essay in no less than 250 words on the reasons behind this incident.

Part Four Rules and Concepts

1. The Olympics allow two different kinds of wrestling: the Greco-Roman and freestyle.

2. Falls are scored in wrestling.

3. The Greco-Roman style uses standing holds. Wrestlers are not allowed to trip or grab one another below the belt.

4. The freestyle uses multiple prone holds. Compared with the Greco-Roman style, it is much freer, but it is also restricted in some aspects.

5. In freestyle wrestling, kicking and choking are against the rules, but tripping and tackling are allowed.

6. The weight of all levels of athletes is measured the day before the match, and the process lasts for half an hour. After the weight of all levels of athletes is measured, they choose their own lottery numbers. Based on the chosen numbers, they have their own pairings.

7. If there are one or several players who do not participate in weight measuring or are overweight, then the athletes' numbers will be rearranged according to the principle of ascending sequence of numbers after the weight measuring.

8. Grouping and pairing will be done according to the numbers athletes choose. Pairs are arranged in the order of drawing such as: number 1 competes with number 2, number 3 competes with number 4, number 5 competes with number 6, and so on.

9. According to the number of competitors, they are divided into two groups for elimination games. The last winner of each group will take part in the final championship.

10. Athletes who only lost to the competitors of the final participate in the repechage to compete for the third through eighth place of the game; the rest of the competitors will be eliminated, and their final ranking will be arranged according to the obtained ranking.

Part Five Further Reading

Alexander Karelin

Alexander Karelin was born in Siberia of the Soviet Union in 1967. He is a PhD holder and is considered to be the greatest modern Greco-Roman wrestler. With the nickname "Russian Bear", he has only lost two matches in all of his 887 Greco-Roman wrestling competitions. In the history of the modern Olympic Games, he is the only one to have won the gold medal in the men's 130 kg Greco-Roman wrestling competition for three consecutive times. At the World Wrestling Championships and European Wrestling Championships, he has won 9 and 12 gold medals respectively. He officially retired after the 2000 Olympic Games. In 2001, the IOC President Juan Antonio Samaranch awarded him an Olympic Order.

Lesson 16

Bicycle

Part One Listening and Speaking

Activity 1

🎧 Listen to the following conversation, and then work in pairs to act it out.

(The roll-call for BMX is beginning. There are installation errors in Tim's timing block. The referee is helping him to correct it.)

A: Your attention please! All athletes for the mountain bike cross-country rally should go to the roll area for roll-call.

B: Hey ref, have I installed the time sensor correctly?

C: No, not yet. It needs to be installed according to the rally rules.

B: How about now? Is it right?

C: Yes.

B: OK. Do I need to put my bib number on both sides of my outfit?

C: Yes. Make sure your outfit is within the dress code, and wear a bib number on the front and back.

B: OK. Thanks!

> **Words and Expressions**
>
> **roll-call** 检录
>
> **BMX (bicycle motocross)** 自行车越野赛
>
> **Your attention please!** 请注意
>
> **roll area** 检录处
>
> **install** /ɪnˈstɔːl/ *v.* 安装；设置
>
> **time sensor** 计时块
>
> **bib number** 号码布
>
> **outfit** /ˈaʊtfɪt/ *n.* 一套服装，套装；
> 全套装备
>
> **dress code** 着装要求

103

Activity 2

👥 Work in pairs and answer the following questions.

> **Question 1:** Before the race, the athlete's bike should be inspected. If it is not qualified, how should it be dealt with?
>
> **Question 2:** If a player is severely injured in a race, is he or she required to quit the race and get treatment?

Part Two Reading

Passage 1

Directions: Read the passage about cycling and discuss the following questions with your partner.

Cycling

The bike, also known as the bicycle or cycle, usually refers to two-wheeled small land vehicle. Cycling is the sport of using the bicycle as a speed competition tool. Since 1896, cycling has become an official competition in the Olympic Games. Current cycling events include the track cycling race, road cycling race, mountain biking race and BMX (bicycle motocross).

Track cycling is performed on the racing field called velodrome. The velodrome track is a closed, ellipse circuit, with a circumference of 250 meters, a width of 5–9 meters, and a curving slope of 25–45 degrees. Cyclists take the dead flywheel bikes without installing transmission and brakes. With the exception of the 1912 Olympics, track cycling has been featured in every modern Olympic Games.

Road bicycle racing began in the 19th century in Europe. The first official race was held in St. Cloud Park of Paris on May 31, 1868, and the world's first women's cycling race was held in 1888 in the Sydney suburb of Ashfield. Nowadays it is the most widespread form of cycling. The most prestigious cycling race is the Tour de France.

Mountain biking is the sport of riding bicycles over tough terrain. It generally has several categories, including cross-country and downhill. The distance for a cross-country mountain race is generally 30–50 kilometers. Downhill racing involves cycling down a rugged mountainside at a high speed to the bottom.

BMX racing is a type of off-road bicycle racing on purpose-built tracks. Although it resembles adult racing on children's toys, in fact the small bikes allow not only rough-terrain racing but also freestyle events on flat terrain, where riders perform stunts. BMX racing was selected as an Olympic sport for the 2008 Beijing Games.

Cycling in China came from Europe around the year 1913. The development of the sport is supported by current competitions such as the Tour of Qinghai Lake International Road Cycling Race, the Tour of Hainan International Road Cycling Race, and various track races and mountain races.

Words and Expressions

vehicle /'viːəkl/ *n.* 车辆；交通工具

ellipse /ɪ'lɪps/ *n.* 椭圆形

circuit /'sɜːkɪt/ *n.* 圈；巡回

prestigious /pre'stɪdʒəs/ *adj.* 享有声望的

terrain /tə'reɪn/ *n.* 地带，地形

off-road /ɒf-rəʊd/ *adj.* 越野的

Sports Terms

track cycling race 场地自行车赛

road cycling race 公路自行车赛

mountain biking race 山地自行车赛

velodrome /'veləɪdrəʊm/ *n.* （单车）比赛场

cyclist /'saɪklɪst/ 骑行者；自行车赛选手

Tour de France 环法自行车大赛

cross-country mountain race 越野赛

downhill race 降速赛

Tour of Qinghai Lake International Road Cycling Race 环青海湖国际公路自行车赛

Tour of Hainan International Road Cycling Race 环海南岛国际公路自行车赛

Questions:

1. What is cycling?

2. Can you list some cycling events?

3. Can you name some cycling competitions that take place in China?

Passage 2

Directions: Read the passage about International Cycling Union and discuss the following questions with your partner.

International Cycling Union

The International Cycling Union (UCI) is the world governing body for sports cycling and oversees international competitive cycling events. It was established in 1900 in Paris, and is based in Aigle, Switzerland. The official languages are English and French. China joined the UCI in 1939, exited in 1958, and in 1979 restored its membership.

The major responsibilities of the UCI are: issuing racing licenses to riders, managing the classification of races and the points ranking system in various cycling disciplines including mountain biking, road and track cycling, BMX racing, trials, indoor cycling, for both men and women, amateurs and professionals. Major competitions organized by the UCI are the World Championships and World Cups under various disciplines.

The winner of a UCI World Championship is awarded a rainbow jersey, white with five colored bands on the chest: from the bottom up the colors are green, yellow, black, red and blue; the same colors that appear in the rings on the Olympic flag. This tradition is applied to all disciplines of cycling.

Words and Expressions

license /'laɪsns/ n. 证件

band /bænd/ n. 带；环

from the bottom up 从下往上

Sports Terms

International Cycling Union (UCI) 国际自行车联盟

trial /'traɪəl/ n. 预选赛

indoor cycling 室内自行车赛

rainbow jersey 彩虹战衣

Questions:

　　1. When was the UCI founded?

　　2. What are the UCI's responsibilities?

　　3. Do you know why the winner of a UCI World Championship should wear a rainbow jersey?

Part Three Exercises

Directions: Do the following exercises.

1. Watch a video clip of an Olympic cycling competition. Write a passage about the match in no less than 250 words. The passage should particularly highlight the emotion and performance of the players.

2. What is your opinion on the development of cycling in China? Share your opinions with your partner.

Part Four Rules and Concepts

1. Track cycling race: At the Olympic Games, the men's events include the time trial, the individual sprint (three laps), 4000-meter individual pursuit race and the team pursuit race, and the points race. Women's events include a sprint, 500-meter individual time trial race, points race and 3000-meter individual pursuit race.

2. The individual pursuit is a track cycling event where two cyclists start respectively from the opposite sides of the track at the same time when the gun goes off, chasing each other in a prescribed distance, usually 4 kilometers for men and 3 kilometers for women. If one player catches his or her opponent or manages to get side-by-side with him or her, the race is effectively over. Otherwise, the one crossing the finish line in the shortest possible time wins. The winner shall join in the next round of the competition.

3. In the team pursuit race, each team has 4 players that participate in the competition. As with the individual pursuit, the objective is to cover the distance in the fastest time or to catch and overtake the other team. The position of the third rider is pivotal because final times are measured as this team member's front wheel crosses

the finish line.

4. In the time trial, players start from the same starting point one by one with equal intervals, and they draw lots to determine the starting sequence. The ranking shall be judged by their separate times in reaching the destination. The less time it takes, the higher the ranking is. If players get the same score, they shall share the rank with each other.

5. In the points race, the starting sequence shall be decided by drawing lots. A person is appointed to be the first rider. When the competition starts, the players follow the first rider to ride a circle. When they reach the starting point, a gun goes off to indicate the beginning of the competition. A sprint is held every ten laps. The top four players shall be scored, earning 5, 3, 2, and 1 points. In addition, any riders managing to lap the main field are awarded an extra 20 points. The ranking of the players shall be decided by the total score in the competition.

6. Road cycling race: a round-trip route is selected in the race, and the road needs to have uphill and downhill sections. The starting point is also the ending point in most cases. The competitors go to the meeting place for roll-call.

7. During the road cycling, all the players start from the starting line collectively. The ranking shall be judged by their separate times in reaching the destination.

8. In the road cycling, players can cooperate with each other for some help, such as the exchange of food, beverage and accessories, but they can't push each other. If the bicycle breaks down, the player can get help from the team's equipment in the car or from the asylum car, or get help from the fixed maintenance station of each racing period.

9. Mountain biking race: According to the rules, each circle is 4–5 kilometers in general. The race time is usually not more than 90 minutes. The organizing committee of the general assembly usually chooses a better player to ride a lap so it can calculate the time to make performance predictions, and then according to the forecasting data it can determine the number of laps in the competition.

10. If it takes a top women's MTB player 30 minutes to ride a lap, then the organizing committee of the game shall set the distance covered by a race at four laps, so that the best total match time is likely to be 2 hours normally.

Part Five Further Reading

Prince of Bicycle—Wong Kam-po

Wong Kam-po is a Hong Kong cyclist. He was born in 1973 and was given the title "Prince of Bicycle" by the Hong Kong media. He was also nicknamed the "Tiger of Asia" by Japanese cycling circles.

At the age of 17, Wong Kam-po joined the Hong Kong cycling team and began his career as a cyclist. He has been awarded a number of medals in the major cycling events, and he was the first cyclist from Hong Kong to be crowned the world champion. Most typically, he is famous for winning the gold medal twice in the Asian Games road cycling competition. In 2007 UCI Track World Championship, he won the first world champion for China in the race of 15-kilometer Pursuit. At the 2012 Olympic Games in London, in the men's road cycling race, Wong Kam-po came in 37th place, with a final sprint of 5 hours 46 minutes and 37 seconds. At this point he ended his Olympic career. He has become synonymous with Hong Kong sports because of his five appearances at the Olympic Games, representing the spirit of self-improvement in Hong Kong.

Shooting

Lesson 17

Listening and Speaking

Activity 1

🎧 Listen to the following conversation, and then work in pairs to act it out.

(The shooting event will begin soon. The coach is encouraging Li Ming to be confident.)

A: Li Ming, have you finished your practice shooting?

B: Yes, I have.

A: Has your gun been examined by the judges?

B: Yes, and they said it met all the requirements.

A: How do you feel about the contest this afternoon?

B: I feel very confident, actually. And I think I should be able to score 585 points.

A: Believe in yourself, and keep calm. Just treat the contest as if you were in training.

B: Thanks, coach. I'll keep that in mind and try my best.

Words and Expressions

gun /gʌn/ *n.* 枪	**requirement** /rɪˈkwaɪəmənt/ *n.* 要求
examine /ɪgˈzæmɪn/ *v.* 检验，检查	**keep in mind** 牢记

Activity 2

👥 Work in pairs and answer the following questions.

> **Question 1:** When the game ends, the referee requires players to stop shooting. Are the bullet clips required to be removed or not?
>
> **Question 2:** In the event that a bullet doesn't fire after 8-second shooting, should the athlete raise his/ her hand to give a signal or not?

Part Two Reading

Passage 1

Directions: Read the passage about shooting and discuss the following questions with your partner.

Shooting

Shooting is a competitive sport in which a shooter with a gun attempts to fire accurately on a set goal and hit the target. Balance, concentration, eye-hand coordination, mental focus, time sense and other qualities are important requirements for players in shooting under pressure.

The basic disciplines of shooting in Olympic Games are rifle, pistol, running target, and shotgun. Each of them includes multiple events, categorized by the type of firearm, targets, and distances at which the targets are shot. The shooter's skills are referred to as marksmanship.

Firearms were originally used for hunting and military purposes. Now, shooting is taken as a recreational activity. Shooting was included firstly in the modern Olympic Games in 1896 in Athens. The International Shooting Sport Federation was founded in 1907. America, China, Russia and Germany are leading the world in shooting. Up until 2012, Chinese shooting athletes have won 21 gold medals in the Olympic Games. In the 23rd Olympic Games in 1984, Xu Haifeng, a Chinese shooter athlete, won the first Olympic gold medal for China.

Words and Expressions

fire /'faɪə(r)/ v. 开枪射击

accurately /'ækjərətlɪ/ adv. 精准地，准确地

balance /'bæləns/ n. 平衡

concentration /ˌkɒnsn'treɪʃn/ n. 集中；专心

coordination /kəʊˌɔːdɪ'neɪʃn/ n. 协调

firearm /'faɪərɑːm/ n. 枪支

Sports Terms

shooter /'ʃuːtə/ n. 射手；射击运动员

pistol /'pɪstl/ n. 手枪

moving target 移动靶

shotgun /'ʃɒtgʌn/ n. 飞碟

marksmanship /'mɑːksmənʃɪp/ n. 射击术，枪法

Questions:

1. What is your understanding about shooting?

2. What are the disciplines of shooting?

3. What qualities should a good shooter have?

Passage 2

Directions: Read the passage about the International Shooting Sport Federation and discuss the following questions with your partner.

International Shooting Sport Federation

The International Shooting Sport Federation (ISSF) is the governing body of the Olympic shooting events in rifle, pistol and shotgun disciplines, and of several other shooting sports events. It was founded in 1907 as the International Shooting Union. Its headquarters is in Munich, and the president Mr. Olegario Vazquez Rana is a Mexican. Now there are 154 association members, belonging to five continental federations, namely Africa, America, Asia, Europe and Oceania. The official languages in the ISSF are German, English, French, Russian, and Spanish. The working language is English. The Chinese Shooting Association joined the ISSF in 1954.

The ISSF is mainly responsible for establishing technical regulations, issuing referee licenses, and assisting the International Olympic Committee in organizing shooting competitions in the Olympic Games. Moreover, its job involves technical supervision, organizing the World Shooting Championships every four years, promoting and developing teaching plans and methods, and rewarding outstanding individuals who contribute to the ISSF.

The main events organized by the ISSF consist of shooting games in the Olympic Games, Paralympic Games, the World Championships and the World Cups.

Sports Terms

International Shooting Sport Federation (ISSF) 国际射击运动联合会

technical regulation 技术规则

referee license 裁判执照

technical supervision 技术监督

Paralympic Games 残奥会

Questions:

1. When was the ISSF founded?

2. What are the responsibilities of the ISSF?

3. What competitions does the ISSF organize?

Part Three Exercises

Directions: Do the following exercises.

1. Write an interview outline about the Olympic champion Cai Yalin.

2. Watch a shooting match and write a review about it in approximately 250 words.

Part Four Rules and Concepts

1. Shooting includes four categories: rifle, pistol, running target, and shotgun, and each discipline contains qualification and final rounds. The top eight or six players in the qualification round qualify for the final rounds. The score in the qualification

round is added to the final score, and the winner is the shooter with the best aggregate score. Ties are resolved by shooting additional shots.

2. Pistol disciplines consist of 10-meter, 25-meter and 50-meter events. Players use guns with a single arm, stand and shoot without relying. The score of each shot in qualifying involves 10 rings, 9 rings, 8 rings, etc. In the final, the score zones are divided into 10 decimals, so that each final shot may earn up to 10.9 points.

3. Rifle is divided into 10-meter and 50-meter events, and the player shoots in the prone, standing or kneeling position. The method of calculating scores is the same as that of the pistol discipline.

4. Clay target shooting, also known as clay pigeon shooting, is a sport whereby a person shoots at a saucer-shaped flying target with a double-barrel shotgun. In the past, live pigeons were used as targets. The targets are now made of a clay-mixture material such as asphalt or gypsum. In the match, according to fixed directions, clay targets are thrown by a machine and the shooter successively shoots the targets at different positions. Smashing the target is a hit, and the player with the most hits is the winner.

5. In running target events, players use a small bore rifle in stance towards the moving target across a distance of 50 meters. Previously the moving target was often a running pig, so it is also called a bobbing target. In 1900, it was listed as one of the Olympic events. In the later running target games, the original bobbing target was gradually changed into the target similar to that of the 10 meters air rifle.

6. Standard targets in rifles and pistols consist of 10 target rings, ranging from 1 to 10 rings. The target loop in the outside ring is 1 point, and the target core is 10 points. Olympic pistol and rifle disciplines have adopted electronic targets recognized by the International Shooting Sport Federation (ISSF).

7. In the clay target shooting matches, the diameter of the target is 110 millimeters with a thickness of 25–26 millimeters. It weighs 105 grams and contains bright colors such as white, yellow or orange. Flash targets must be used in the final.

8. Rifle shooters must comply with the regulations on dress required by the ISSF, including a shooting jacket, pants, shoes, shooting gloves and shooting belt. Before the game, clothing must be inspected to ensure that it conforms to the rules. Pistol

shooters don't need special clothing. They are allowed to wear special shooting shoes made of fabric leather or fiber products with hard soles for stability. The clay target shooter must wear shooting clothing marked with an ISSF official belt, which is 250 millimeters long and 30 millimeters wide with yellow trimmed in black. The belt must be permanently sewn under the tip of the elbow in the horizontal position so that the referee can observe whether the shooters break any rules at the moment of shooting.

9. Rifles can be classified into three categories: the air rifle, small bore rifle and shotgun. The air rifle is for 10-meter events, the small bore rifle for 50-meter events, and the shotgun is used for events in clay pigeon shooting.

10. The pistol is classified as either an air pistol or a small caliber pistol. The air pistol is for 10-meter events, and the small caliber pistol is for 25-meter and 50-meter events. The bullets used for 10-meter pistol and rifle are 4.5 millimeters while bullets in 25-meter and 50-meter events are 5.6 millimeters. For the events in clay pigeon shooting, players usually use No. 12 shotgun shells, with a loading amount of less than 24.5 grams.

Part Five Further Reading

Olympic Champion—Xu Haifeng

Xu Haifeng, born in 1957, was a famous shooter and leading figure for the Chinese shooting team. He was the men's 60 pistol slow shooting champion at the 23rd Olympic Games in 1984, as well as the first Chinese gold medal winner in the Olympic history.

Xu made significant contributions to the sport of shooting in China, enjoying very high prestige and popularity in China's shooting community. He never showed off for it, but instead silently worked hard throughout his shooting career. He demanded of himself: "Be a good man before you shoot well." At the same time, he also warned himself: "Be satisfied with treatment and honor, but never be satisfied with your career and work."

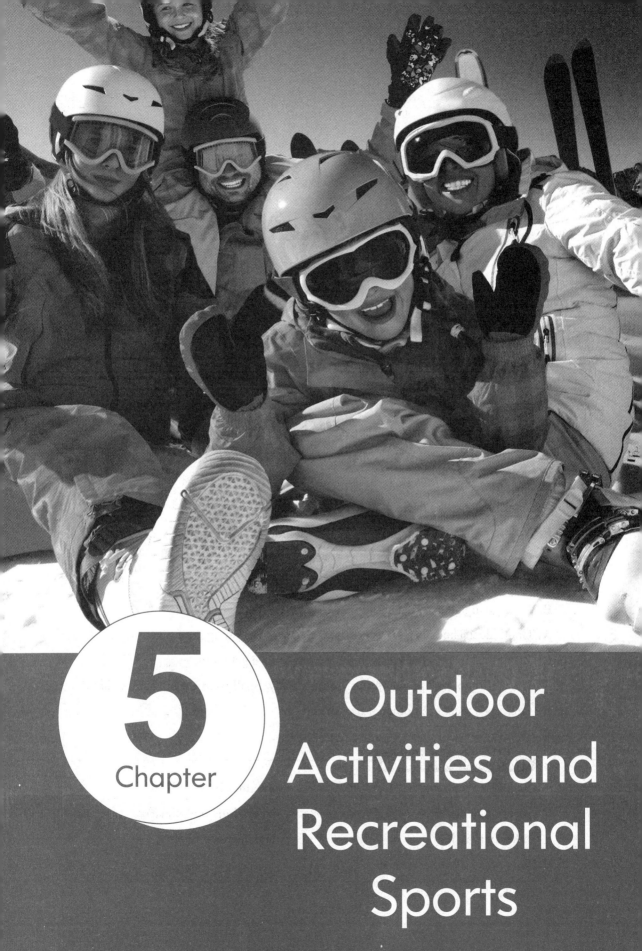

5 Chapter

Outdoor Activities and Recreational Sports

Lesson 18 Outdoor Activities

Activity 1

🎧 Listen to the following conversation, and then work in pairs to act it out.

(Zhang and Li are neighbors. They meet each other outdoors one morning and realize the weather is very pleasant. Zhang suggests their two families go for an outing by bicycles with their children.)

A: What a sunny day today!

B: You're right! We shouldn't spend all day indoors. There's plenty to do outside. Do you have any suggestion?

A: I'd like to take a trip to the outskirts and breathe some fresh air.

B: Let's go together! What about bike riding?

A: Good idea! The kids have been looking forward to riding their bikes.

B: Bring the kites, so the kids can fly them when we get there.

A: Great! I'll go back now and start getting ready. Shall we meet in about an hour?

B: OK! Let's meet each other at the gate.

Words and Expressions

neighbor /'neɪbə(r)/ *n.* 邻居，邻里

plenty /'plentɪ/ *pron.* 许多；大量

take a trip 去旅行

outskirt /'aʊtskəːt/ *n.* 郊外

breathe /briːð/ *v.* 呼吸

fresh /freʃ/ *adj.* 新鲜的

look forward to 期盼

Activity 2

👥 Work in pairs and make conversations according to the given situations.

> **Situation 1:** A newly joined outdoor enthusiast wants to buy a pair of professional outdoor mountaineering shoes. As a senior outdoor enthusiast, please offer him some suggestions.
>
> **Situation 2:** You and your friends are on an outing and are ready to sleep in the open. One of your friends doesn't know how to install a tent. Please help him accomplish this task.

Part Two Reading

Passage 1

Directions: Read the passage about outdoor activities and discuss the following questions with your partner.

Outdoor Activities

An outdoor activity is a program of group events that are held in natural sites such as mountaineering, rock climbing, cliff drop, camping, picnic, orienteering and stream adventures, etc. To challenge themselves and embrace the nature, participants climb different geomorphic mountains or ridges without any equipment or with some specialized outfits. Most outdoor activities are extreme sports, being explorative, challenging and thrilling in nature.

Outdoor activities can be dated back to as early as the 18th century in Europe. In May, 1760, de Saussure, the well-known French scientist, in order to do research on alpine plants, posted a notice in Chamonix at the foot of the Alps, saying "whoever could climb the summit of Mount Blanc or provide the route for it will be rewarded with a large amount of money." It was not until June 1786, 26 years later, that a doctor named Vaccaro in Chamonix tore off the notice. After two months' preparation, with the company of Barma, a mining worker of the local area in search of berg crystals, on August 6, 1786, Vaccaro first climbed the peak of Mount Blanc, with an altitude of 4810 meters, which is the highest mountain in Western Europe. Later in 1787, a mountaineering team led by de Saussure and guided by Barma climbed the peak again, which symbolized the beginning of modern mountaineering.

Words and Expressions

program /'prəʊɡræm/ *n.* 项目群；程序

adventure /əd'ventʃə/ *n.* 探险；冒险，奇遇

challenge /'tʃælɪndʒ/ *v. & n.* 挑战

explorative /ɪk'splɔrətɪv/ *adj.* 探险性的

notice /'nəʊtɪs/ *n.* 告示

summit /'sʌmɪt/ *n.* 顶峰；顶点

route /ruːt/ *n.* 路线，路径

reward /rɪ'wɔːd/ *v.* 奖赏，奖励

tear off 揭下

company /'kʌmpənɪ/ *n.* 陪同；公司

peak /piːk/ *n.* 山峰；顶端

altitude /'æltɪtjuːd/ *n.* 高度；海拔

symbolize /'sɪmbəlaɪz/ *v.* 象征

Sports Terms

outdoor activity 户外运动

natural site 自然场地

mountaineering /ˌmaʊntə'nɪərɪŋ/ *n.* 登山，登山运动，爬山

rock climbing 攀岩

cliff drop 悬崖速降

camping /'kæmpɪŋ/ *n.* 野外露营

picnic /'pɪknɪk/ *n.* 野炊

orienteering /ˌɔːrɪən'tɪərɪŋ/ *n.* 定向运动，定向越野

stream adventure 溪流探险

extreme sports 极限运动

Questions:

1. Based on your own experiences, can you talk about outdoor activities that you know?

2. What are the characteristics of outdoor activities?

3. How did outdoor activities originate?

Passage 2

Directions: Read the passage about X Games and discuss the following questions with your partner.

X Games

The extreme sport originated in Europe and North America in the 1960s. Now it has already developed into a new sports activity including dozens of competitive events. It advocates "pursuing oneself and challenging oneself," and its culture has

already influenced young people's life philosophy—in particular, that of "seeking for free space, exploring the unknown and creating personal value."

The X Games is the most influential and highest-level traditional festival in extreme sports. It was created and is organized by ESPN (Entertainment and Sports Programming Network), a U.S. based global cable company, once a year.

The inaugural X Games were held in the summer of 1995 in Newport, Rhode Island. Participants competed to win bronze, silver, and gold medals, as well as prize money. The competition often features new tricks such as Tony Hawk's 900 in skateboarding, Travis Pastrana's double backflip in freestyle motocross, Heath Frisby's first ever snowmobile front flip in Snowmobile Best Trick, and Torstein Horgmo's first landed triple flip in a snowboard competition, etc. Concurrent with the competitions is the "X Fest" sports and music festival, which offers live music, athlete autograph sessions and other interactive elements.

After years of development, X Games has become one of the most popular multiple-project extreme sports festivals around the world. The games are broadcast live on television.

Words and Expressions

advocate /ˈædvəkeɪt/ *v.* 主张；提倡，倡导

pursue /pəˈsjuː/ *v.* 追求

philosophy /fɪˈlɒsəfɪ/ *n.* 哲学

seek for 寻求，追寻

explore /ɪkˈsplɔː(r)/ *v.* 探索，探寻

personal value 自我价值

influential /ˌɪnfluˈenʃl/ *adj.* 有影响力的

festival /ˈfestɪvl/ *n.* 节日；盛会

inaugural /ɪˈnɔːgjərəl/ *adj.* 创始的，首次的；就任的；开幕的

prize money 奖金

trick /trɪk/ *n.* 技巧；窍门；花招

live /laɪv/ *adj.* 现场的；活的

broadcast /ˈbrɔːdkɑːst/ *v.* 广播；播放

interactive /ˌɪntərˈæktɪv/ *adj.* 互动的

Sports Terms

X Games 世界极限运动会

double backflip 后空翻两周

motocross /'məʊtəkrɒs/ *n.* 摩托车越野赛

snowmobile /'snəʊməbiːl/ *n.* 机动雪橇

front flip 前空翻

triple flip 三转空翻

Questions:

　　1. What do you think about the saying "pursuing oneself and challenging oneself"?

　　2. Who organizes X Games?

　　3. What are the competitions of X Games?

Part Three Exercises

Directions: Do the following exercises.

1. Make a plan for outdoor activities with the motif of "Life is a movement."

2. Talk about your favorite outdoor activity.

Part Four Rules and Concepts

1. Rock climbing can be divided into two types: free climbing and aid climbing. The former doesn't need any supportive equipment, only the participant's own physical strength. The latter needs the aid of some specialized outfits. Rock climbing is considered by many to be a thrilling and challenging sports activity.

2. Ice climbing is a sports activity of climbing icefalls, frozen waterfalls, etc. that needs the aid of some outfits and equipment. Ice can be broadly divided into alpine ice and water ice.

3. BASE jumping is an extreme sport of parachuting from a cliff or other structures. BASE is an acronym that stands for four categories of objects from which one can jump: building, antenna, span and earth.

4. River trekking is an explorative sport of hiking from the sources of rivers to the tops of mountains. It goes over every geomorphic obstacles between the upstream and downstream of canyons and streams. The greatest feature and joy of it lies in continually getting across waterfalls and whirlpools one after another, and advancing through the rapids and against the current.

5. Surfing is a water sport in which athletes traverse the upsurging waves by using a surfboard. The surfer needs to be equipped with a surfboard and safety ropes tied to his feet.

6. Bungee jumping is a sport that involves jumping from a high platform with one end of a bungee rope tied to the player's body or ankles and the other end tied to the high platform, which usually ranges from tens of meters to over a hundred meters high.

7. Camping is an outdoor recreational activity. Participants leave cities to spend time outdoors, and live in tents in more natural areas during the night. Campers are usually in pursuit of activities which provide enjoyment, such as hiking, fishing and swimming. To be regarded as "camping", a minimum of one night must be spent outdoors.

8. Skiing is a winter sport in which the participant uses skis to glide on. It is mainly comprised of Nordic, Alpine and Telemark skiing.

9. Drifting is a recreational activity in which the drifter advances downstream in calm or turbulent rivers using a rubber boat or bamboo raft.

10. Hiking is considered to be a leisure activity in which the participant walks a long distance in suburban, rural or mountainous areas. Because hiking is relatively simple, without too much emphasis on skills and equipment, it is regarded as the most typical and common leisure activity.

Part Five Further Reading

Felix Baumgartner

Felix Baumgartner was born in 1969 in Salzburg, Austria. He is a famous Austrian parachutist and extreme sports enthusiast. He has challenged the records of high altitude jumps many times and broken many records in altitude and free fall. He is praised by his fans as "fearless Felix".

When he was a little boy, he often dreamed about flying in the sky. In 1999 he claimed the world record for the highest parachute jump from a building, the Petronas Towers in Kuala Lumpur, Malaysia. On July 20, 2003, Baumgartner became the first person to skydive across the English Channel using a specially-made carbon fiber wing. On December 12, 2007, he successfully jumped from the 91st floor observation deck of the then tallest building in the world, Taipei 101, setting a new BASE jumping record once again.

On October 14, 2012, Felix Baumgartner rose to 39 kilometers in the sky by balloons. He jumped down with a parachute and landed successfully. In doing this, he created two world records: the highest altitude by balloons of any human being (39 kilometers), and the highest speed of free fall of any human body (1357 kilometers per hour).

Lesson 19 Orienteering

Part One Listening and Speaking

Activity 1

🎧 Listen to the following conversation, and then work in pairs to act it out.

(The orienteering competition is about to begin. The coach is requesting the captain to check all the equipment before commencing.)

A: Captain, tell everyone that they must check whether they've got everything needed for the competition before setting off.

B: We have checked several times, coach.

A: Also, you should look at the map carefully while running, and make sure you choose the shortest and safest route. And of course, go in the right direction.

B: Can we choose the more dangerous route if it is the shortest?

A: No, you can't. Safety comes first.

B: Got it, coach!

A: And do keep in mind: To avoid missing any control points or wasting time searching for the same one, you should eliminate the control point after punching it.

B: Got it. Don't worry.

Words and Expressions

captain /'kæptɪn/ *n.* 队长

commence /kə'mens/ *v.* 开始

set off 出发

direction /dɪ'rekʃn/ *n.* 方向

safety comes first 安全第一

avoid /ə'vɔɪd/ *v.* 避免

miss /mɪs/ *v.* 遗漏

control point 点标

waste /weɪst/ *v.* 耽误；浪费

eliminate /ɪ'lɪmɪneɪt/ *v.* 消除；排除

punch /pʌntʃ/ *v.* 打印记；做标记

Activity 2

👤 Work in pairs and answer the following questions.

Question 1: What are the functions of the map and compass in orienteering?

Question 2: Do you know the six factors of a map?

Part Two Reading

Passage 1

Directions: Read the passage about orienteering and discuss the following questions with your partner.

Orienteering

In orienteering, competitors use a map and compass to find the control points marked on the map, and the one who finds and punches all the points in the quickest time wins. Normally, orienteering is held in forests, suburbs, urban parks or a campus.

Orienteering, originally a form of military training, started in Sweden. In 1895, orienteering sports were held in the military camps of Stockholm (Sweden) and Oslo (Norway), which symbolized the beginning of orienteering sports. In 1932, the first international orienteering competition was held.

Nowadays, orienteering has grown from a single form of military training into a group of comprehensive sports activities for common people, which include various competitive events and entertainment activities. There are such common forms of orienteering as foot orienteering, relay orienteering, 100-meter orienteering, ski orienteering, night orienteering, line orienteering, O-Ringen 5-days, school orienteering, Trim orienteering, and so on.

Basic techniques are required in orienteering, such as setting a map and thumbing, the use of a compass, handrail, collecting catching features and attack points, pacing and aiming off. Orienteering is also one of the formal competitive events of the International Military Sports Council, and military forces from more than ten nations are involved in each military orienteering.

Words and Expressions

compass /'kʌmpəs/ *n.* 指南针

mark /mɑːk/ *v.* 做标志，做记号

suburb /'sʌbɜːb/ *n.* 郊区，郊外

urban /'ɜːbən/ *adj.* 城市的，都市的

campus /'kæmpəs/ *n.* 校园

military /'mɪlɪtrɪ/ *adj.* 军事的

comprehensive /ˌkɒmprɪ'hensɪv/ *adj.* 综合的

entertainment /ˌentə'teɪnmənt/ *n.* 娱乐

Sports Terms

foot orienteering 徒步定向

relay orienteering 接力定向

100-meter orienteering 百米定向

ski orienteering 滑雪定向

night orienteering 夜间定向

line orienteering 专线定向

O-Ringen 5-days 五日定向

school orienteering 校园定向

Trim orienteering 特里拇定向

set a map and thumbing 地图正置及拇指辅行法

handrail /'hændreɪl/ *n.* 扶手法；借线法

collect catching features 搜集途中所遇特征

attack point 攻击点

pacing 数步测距

aiming off 目标偏测

International Military Sports Council 国际军体理事会

Questions:

    1. In what places can orienteering be held?

    2. Do you know any orienteering disciplines?

    3. Can you list some techniques used in orienteering?

Passage 2

Directions: Read the passage about the International Orienteering Federation and discuss the following questions with your partner.

International Orienteering Federation

The International Orienteering Federation (IOF) is the international governing body of the sport of orienteering. Its head office is located in Helsinki, Finland. The official language of the IOF is English. In 1992, the Chinese Orienteering Federation joined the IOF.

The IOF governs four orienteering disciplines, including foot orienteering, mountain bike orienteering, ski orienteering, and trail orienteering. It aims to spread the sport of orienteering and promote its development.

The IOF was founded on May 21, 1961, in Copenhagen, Denmark. By 1969, the IOF represented 16 countries, including its first two non-European member federations Japan and Canada, and in 1977 the IOF was recognized by the International Olympic Committee. As of 2013, the membership of the IOF comprises 79 orienteering federations.

The IOF is governed by an elected council consisting of a president, a senior vice president, two vice presidents, and seven other council members. Day-to-day operations of the IOF are the responsibility of the IOF secretary general. In addition, several standing commissions of the IOF are responsible for the development of the sport worldwide. These commissions include Foot Orienteering, MTB Orienteering, Ski Orienteering, Trail Orienteering, Environment, IT, Map, Medical, and Rules.

International Orienteering Federation (IOF) 国际定向越野联合会

mountain bike orienteering 山地车定向越野

trail orienteering 轮椅定向越野

Questions:

1. When was the IOF founded and where is its headquarters?

2. What disciplines are governed by the IOF?

Part Three Exercises

Directions: Do the following exercises.

1. Write a proposal on encouraging college students to take part in orienteering sports. It should focus on the advantages of orienteering, such as keeping one's body strong and healthy, and cultivating the ability to think and solve problems.

2. Why is orienteering a form of sports activity with no age and gender limits?

Part Four Rules and Concepts

1. The orienteering course is marked in purple or red on a map. A triangle is used to indicate the start and a double circle indicates the finish. Circles are used to show the control points.

2. Control points are marked in the terrain by white and orange flags.

3. The winner is normally the competitor who completes the course in the shortest time.

4. If a competitor missed or wrongly located the position of a control point, his or her score would be invalid.

5. The punishment of warning will be given to the competitor for the following conducts: competitors enter the warm-up area without any permission, not causing any consequence; competitors prematurely obtain a map and set off in the start

area; competitors accept assistance from other people; competitors offer assistance to other people; competitors intentionally run with or behind other competitors during the event in order to profit from their skill; competitors don't properly wear the number cloth.

6. In a competition, competitors' scores will be deemed invalid for the following conducts: competitors use others' ID; competitors travel by transport; the preponderance of evidence shows that competitors made prior investigation of the competition area; competitors do not visit all the checkpoints; competitors are not able to report to the finish by the announced closing time of the finish.

7. The following conducts will lead to competitor's disqualification: Competitors cheat in the competition; competitors intentionally impede other competitors' progress; competitors intentionally damage control points, punches, and other competition facilities on the course; competitors forge scores by technique or any other means; competitors do not wear the number cloth provided by the organization; competitors lose their control cards.

8. Competitors who are not able to finish the competition because of injury will have their results posted as "Sporting Withdrawal", and they should notify the nearest judge.

9. If competitors withdraw before the start of the competition, the team leader or coach should notify the judge at the start.

10. Competitors who unduly damage property on the course shall be given punishments based on seriousness of the circumstances.

Part Five Further Reading

Minna Kauppi

Minna Kauppi, born on November 25, 1982, in Asikkala, Finland, is a well-known Finnish female orienteer. Kauppi is an eight-time World Champion, including five golds from relays. In 2010, Minna Kauppi was honored as the "Best Athlete of the Year" in Finland. She became the first orienteer to win this title in Finnish history since the beginning of this event in 1947.

When she was young, Minna Kauppi was introduced to a wide array of sports along with her siblings. At the age of 8, she discovered orienteering and became interested in it. In addition to track and field and cross-country skiing, she also played tennis and did gymnastics. However, it became clear to her that she was more of a runner or a skier type.

Until her late-teens, she was almost certain that she would become a cross-country skier. The secrets of orienteering seemed too difficult for her to understand at that time, and her legs seemed to move too fast for her skills. But around the age of 18, she realized that orienteering wasn't that difficult after all, and as her older siblings had already been chosen to be orienteers, it was easy for her to follow them.

The first years of real training started around that same time. She determined that she would qualify for the next Junior World Orienteering Championship, and she did. To everyone's surprise, she actually came home with two bronze medals. After leaving the junior playground, she easily made it onto the women's national team. In 2005, Minna Kauppi received her first individual gold in middle distance in the Open Nordic Orienteering Championship. After this, she won various world championships one by one and became a legendary figure in the world of orienteering.

Lesson 20 Outward Bound

Part One Listening and Speaking

Activity 1

🎧 Listen to the following conversation, and then work in pairs to act it out.

(In an Outward Bound training session, there is a wide gap in John's path. He is too nervous to step over it. Now the coach is encouraging him to be brave and overcome his fear.)

A: Sir, I'm afraid I cannot step over such a wide gap.

B: Just try. How do you know you can't manage it if you don't even try?

A: Such a wide gap. I can't do that.

B: Success and failure are just one step away. Step over it bravely. I believe you!

A: Give me a few more minutes. I need to calm down myself.

B: OK. Now listen to me. Take a deep breath, extend your arms horizontally and naturally, keep your balance, push forward from your back foot, lean forward and step over it with a stride.

A: I made it! I don't believe I should do it!

B: Yes, well done! You are very brave.

> ### Words and Expressions
>
> | | |
> |---|---|
> | **Outward Bound** 拓展运动 | **extend** /ɪk'stend/ *v.* 伸展；延伸 |
> | **gap** /gæp/ *n.* 沟壑；缝隙 | **horizontally** /ˌhɒrɪ'zɒntəlɪ/ *adv.* 水平地 |
> | **step over** 跨越 | **push forward** 向前蹬 |
> | **brave** /'breɪv/ *adj.* 勇敢的 | **lean forward** 向前倾 |
> | **overcome** /ˌəʊvə'kʌm/ *v.* 克服；战胜 | **stride** /straɪd/ *n.& v.* 跨大步 |
> | **take a deep breath** 深呼吸 | |

Activity 2

👤 Work in pairs and answer the following questions.

> **Question 1:** Have you ever taken part in the Outward Bound? Share your experience with your partner.
>
> **Question 2:** What characteristics do the Outward Bound drills have?

Part Two Reading

Passage 1

Directions: Read the passage about Outward Bound and discuss the following questions with your partner.

Outward Bound

Outward Bound (OB) is an international, non-profit, independent, outdoor education organization with approximately 40 schools around the world and 200,000 participants per year. Outward Bound programs aim to foster the personal growth and social skills of participants by challenging expeditions in the outdoors.

Outward Bound is also called Survival Training. The name derived from the idea that a small boat bore off the tranquil harbor irrevocably, headed on a journey into the unknown and took up challenges one after another. Outward Bound originated in England during the Second World War, with the aim of enhancing young sailors' survival skills after a ship struck a reef in the sea. Then its popularity spread little by little. Its training extended from initially sailors to other soldiers, students, workers of industry and commerce, etc. The training objective also extends from simple physical agility and survival training to psychological training, personality training, management training, etc.

Currently the events of Outward Bound cover three types: aquatic events, outdoor events and field events. Outward Bound often makes full use of such natural environments as high mountains and lofty hills, expansive oceans and great rivers, as well as specialized training venues and facilities. These all aim to enhance one's mind, cultivate one's taste, improve one's personality and mold the team's spirit by means of well-designed events.

Words and Expressions

non-profit /nɒn-'prɒfɪt/ *adj.* 非营利的

foster /'fɒstə(r)/ *v.* 培养，培育

expedition /ˌekspə'dɪʃn/ *n.* 远征；探险

survival /sə'vaɪvl/ *n.* 生存；求生

bear off 驶离

tranquil /'træŋkwɪl/ *adj.* 平静的；安静的

harbor /'hɑːbə(r)/ *n.* 港口

irrevocably /ɪ'revəkəblɪ/ *adv.* 义无反顾地

take up 开始从事；占据

strike /straɪk/ *v.* 冲撞，撞击；打击

physical agility 体能

psychological training 心理训练

personality training 人格训练

management training 管理训练

make full use of 充分利用

high mountains and lofty hills 崇山峻岭

expansive oceans and great rivers 翰海大川

venue /'venjuː/ *n.* 会场；场地

facility /fə'sɪlətɪ/ *n.* 设施；装备

enhance one's mind 磨炼意志

cultivate one's taste 陶冶情操

improve one's personality 完善人格

mold the team's spirit 熔炼团队

Questions:

1. What is the objective of Outdoor Bound?

2. What is the origin of Outdoor Bound?

3. Do you know different types of Outdoor Bound?

Passage 2

Directions: Read the passage about organizations of Outward Bound and discuss the following questions with your partner.

Organizations of Outward Bound

Outward Bound is an innovative educational idea put forth by Kurt Hahn, a famous German educator, who taught young British sailors the vital survival skills necessary during World War II. In 1946, the Outward Bound Trust was established in England with the purpose of expanding the concept of Outward Bound and raising funds for creating OB schools. In 1961, Joshua Miner brought the ideas of Outward Bound into the United States, and founded the first OB School in the U.S. In 1964, Outward Bound Inc. was founded in America. It is the largest and oldest non-profit organization in the world that focuses on experiential education. Now OB training centers and schools have spread across the globe.

The National Outdoor Leadership School (NOLS) was founded in 1965 by Paul Petzoldt, a world-famous mountaineer. It is a non-profit outdoor education school based in the United States dedicated to teaching environmental ethics, technical outdoors skills, wilderness medicine, risk management and judgment, and leadership and teamwork. NOLS has trained more than 280,000 students.

Outward Bound Hong Kong (OBHK) was established in 1970, making it the first outdoor education organization within China. In the 1960s, it was noted that Hong Kong lacked a well-rounded education. OBHK was seen as a short term and intensive character training organization for youth who were leaving school or university. Today, it provides training on key elements of success including leadership, communication, integrity, team work and the like, and remains at the forefront of outdoor experiential education in Asia.

Words and Expressions

innovative /'ɪnəvetɪv/ adj. 创新的，革新的

put forth 提出；发表

vital /'vaɪtl/ adj. 重要的，关键的

raise /reɪz/ v. 筹集，募集

fund /fʌnd/ n. 资金

experiential education 体验教学，体验教育

ethic /'eθɪk/ n. 伦理；道德标准

wilderness /'wɪldənəs/ n. 野外，荒原

risk management 风险管理

leadership /'liːdəʃɪp/ n. 领导力

well-rounded /wel'raʊndɪd/ adj. 全方位的；全能的；多才多艺的

intensive /ɪn'tensɪv/ adj. 集中的；密集的

forefront /'fɔːfrʌnt/ n. 前沿；最前端

Sports Terms

Outward Bound Trust 外展训练信托基金会

Outward Bound Inc. 外展训练法人组织

National Outdoor Leadership School (NOLS) 美国户外领队学校

Outward Bound Hong Kong (OBHK) 香港外展训练学校

Questions:

1. How was the first Outdoor Bound school founded?

2. What are the aims of NOLS and OBHK respectively?

Part Three Exercises

Directions: Do the following exercises.

1. Make a plan for an Outward Bound training with the theme of "Enhancing Cooperation, Communication and Cohesion."

2. Discuss your understanding of why some schools choose to open Outward Bound courses.

Part Four Rules and Concepts

1. Fly wins Luding bridge: Personal challenge. Simulating the Red Army's fighting for Luding bridge bravely, the trainee stands at ten meters' height and strides across a soft bridge with each plank being half a meter apart. The trainee relies on oneself for balance.

2. Horizontal bar in the sky: Personal challenge. The trainee climbs to the top of an independent pole, stands on the small round platform, leaps forward and catches hold of the dangling triangle bar.

3. Precipices and cliffs: Personal or cooperative event. The trainee climbs from one side to the other of a steep cliff without any gripper equipment.

4. Trust Suplex: Personal psychological challenge and teamwork event. A team member stands on a 1.4-meter-high platform in turn and falls on his back into the net of his team members' arms.

5. Getting water in the minefield: Teamwork event. There is a basin of water in a pool that is 5 meters in diameter. The trainee gets treasure to save the lives of all team members with a rope and without touching the water.

6. Tramcar: Team motivation event. Team members are properly divided into several groups. Each group stand on a plank and advance together by pulling themselves forward with ropes in hand.

7. Simulation grid: Teamwork event. With everyone's cooperation, all the team members attempt to cross a net within the required time. However, no parts of people's bodies can touch the net, and each grid mesh can only be used once.

8. High ladder: Cooperative event. The two trainees cooperate with each other and climb up to the highest point of the high ladder with safety protection.

9. Combined bridge: Teamwork event. One or two people form a group and climb up to the 9-meter-high hanger plate that includes three pieces. Four to six people under every hanger plate control the rope in order to keep the hanger plates balanced. The climber steps on every hanger plate until he reaches the other side successfully by his own efforts and other people's cooperation.

10. Interdependence in the sky: Cooperative event. Two trainees attempt to reach the other side crosswise on two steel cables face-to-face and hand-by-hand.

Part Five Further Reading

Boatman and Philosopher

Once, a philosopher was crossing a river by boat. Although the boatman was very old, he rowed the boat with might and main all the time. It seemed very hard, hence the philosopher asked the boatman, "Old gentleman, have you ever learned philosophy?" The old man answered, "Sorry, I haven't." The philosopher spread out his hands and said, "What a pity! You have lost 50 percent of your life." After a while, seeing the old man so painstaking, he then said, "Have you ever learned Mathematics?" The old boatman said, "Sorry, sir, I haven't." The philosopher then said, "What a pity! You have lost 80 percent of your life." Just at this moment, a big wave overturned the boat, and the two men fell into the water. The boatman saw the philosopher struggling with such great effort, then said, "Sir, have you ever learned swimming?" The philosopher said no. The old boatman said helplessly, "It is such a great pity. You will lose 100 percent of your life."

Knowledge alone can't help you deal with real life's danger. Although everyone says, "Knowledge is power," pure knowledge itself can't produce power. Only when the knowledge is turned into people's means of production or labor skills, can it exert its function.

Lesson 21 Darts

Part One Listening and Speaking

Activity 1

🎧 Listen to the following conversation, and then work in pairs to act it out.

(Peter and John are both available. Peter suggests playing darts to kill time. John agrees with him immediately.)

A: How about playing the game of darts?

B: Good! I'm an ace at darts. I can hit anything.

A: Really? Let's get it on then.

B: What type? Magnetic darts or pin darts?

A: Players all use pin darts in international games, so let's use these.

B: Nearest to the bull's-eye starts?

A: Yeah. You throw first.

B: OK. No problem.

Words and Expressions

available /əˈveɪləbl/ *adj.* 空闲的

play dart 玩飞镖

dart /dɑːt/ *n.* 飞镖

kill time 打发时间

ace /eɪs/ *n.* 高手；能手

magnetic dart 磁性飞镖

pin dart 针式飞镖

bull's-eye /ˈbʊlz-aɪ/ *n.* 靶心

139

Activity 2

👥 Work in pairs and answer the following questions.

> **Question 1:** Can you illustrate some ceremonial language in darts games?
>
> **Question 2:** Can you explain the types of popular darts games?

Part Two Reading

Passage 1

Directions: Read the passage about darts and discuss the following questions with your partner.

Darts

Darts are thin and long spears with a metal front and tail end that players throw towards the target. Focusing on precise casting, this competitive game is good for keeping healthy and entertaining. It originated in the United Kingdom. According to records, Roman legions were sent to distant Britain by the Roman emperor. The rainy climate in Britain was not suitable for outside activities, so soldiers threw their arrows at the board made from oak in the shed. This activity gradually evolved into the sport of modern darts.

In 1896, the British carpenter Brian Gamlin invented the modern dart board partition system, and promoted the popularity of darts in the UK. It then became a very popular sport in British bars, and gradually developed into a fashionable indoor recreational activity around the world.

Darts appeared in China in the 1980s. Thanks in part to the in-depth development of China's national fitness campaign, darts was officially listed as a sports project in 1999, and from then on darts became popular everywhere. In 1999, 2000 and 2001, three national darts competitions were held consecutively, and a large number of outstanding professionals emerged.

Words and Expressions

precise /prɪˈsaɪs/ *adj.* 精准的，准确的

cast /kɑːst/ *v.* 投掷；抛

bar /bɑː(r)/ *n.* 酒吧；酒馆

fashionable /ˈfæʃnəbl/ *adj.* 时髦的，时尚的

outstanding /aʊtˈstændɪŋ/ *adj.* 杰出的，卓越的

emerge /ɪˈmɜːdʒ/ *v.* 涌现，产生，出现

Sports Terms

arrow /ˈærəʊ/ *n.* 箭

dart board 镖盘

partition system 分区系统

national fitness campaign 全民健身运动

Questions:

1. Have you ever watched darts matches? How do you think about it?

2. How did modern darts come into being?

3. Do you think that the teenagers should be encouraged to play darts? Why or why not?

Passage 2

Directions: Read the passage about the World Darts Federation and discuss the following questions with your partner.

World Darts Federation

The World Darts Federation (WDF) is the official world sport governing body and tournament organizers for the game of darts. It was formed in 1974 by representatives of the original 15 founding members. Membership is open to the national organizing body for darts in all nations. The WDF encourages the promotion of the sport of darts among and between those bodies, in an effort to gain international recognition for darts as a major sport.

The WDF stages the WDF World Cup, as well as continental championships such as the WDF Americas Cup, the WDF Asia-Pacific Cup and the WDF Europe Cup. The country that is first in the overall best result in the three events—singles, pairs, teams becomes the world champion. Winners of any of the events in the World Cup can also call themselves the official World Champion. By contrast, winners of continental championships can call themselves the official champion of their own areas.

One of the WDF national members is the British Darts Organization (BDO). It is the official darts body for Britain, the leading darts country. It stages the Lakeside World Professional Darts Championship (PDC), which is a recognized WDF major tournament.

Words and Expressions

promotion /prə'məʊʃn/ *n.* 提升；推广

gain /geɪn/ *v.* 赢得；获得

recognition /ˌrekəg'nɪʃn/ *n.* 认同，认可

stage /steɪdʒ/ *v.* 举行；上演 *n.* 舞台

Sports Terms

World Darts Federation (WDF) 世界飞镖联盟

British Darts Organization (BDO) 英国飞镖组织

World Professional Darts Championship (PDC) 世界职业飞镖锦标赛

Questions:

1. Can you describe the WDF briefly in your own words?

2. What is the major tournament of the WDF?

Part Three Exercises

Directions: Do the following exercises.

1. Write an introduction for a college student darts team in no less than 150 words.

2. Suppose you were the darts game scorekeeper, what knowledge should you master in advance?

Part Four Rules and Concepts

1. There are many different ways to play darts, and the rules of the game can vary, but the basic rule is the same.

2. Each turn consists of three darts.

3. Darts that bounce off or fall out of the dartboard can't score and will not be re-thrown.

4. Darts is a game that can be played between two players or between two teams. Both sides' team members take turns to throw.

5. Throwing nine times before the start of the game is usually part of the pre-match warm-up, and the team whose dart is closest to the bull's-eye starts first.

6. Each player throws three darts and then retrieves their darts.

7. If the player's feet or shoes cross the throw line or if the player accidentally stumbles over and releases the darts, the points are not counted, and there is no chance to throw again.

8. Darts must remain for more than 5 seconds in the dartboard. If the darts fall off or thrust into other darts, then the point is not counted.

9. Athletes may come to the dartboard to confirm the location of the darts at any time, but no one can touch them during a turn.

10. No one can stand within 2 feet of the darts players for courtesy and safety.

Part Five Further Reading

Phil Taylor

Phil Douglas Taylor, born in Stoke-on-Trent, England in 1960, is a legendary figure in the international darts world. Nicknamed "The Power", he has won over 200 professional tournaments including 16 world championships. He won eight consecutive world championships from 1995 to 2002 and reached 14 consecutive finals from 1994 to 2007. No darts player has a winning record in matches against him.

Taylor was an unknown blue-collar worker before the age of 26. Later he met the most important person in his life—Eric Bristol, one of the most famous darts players of the 1980s. In 1990, Taylor qualified for the World Darts Championship for the first time. In 1998 he won his sixth world championship and broke the record of Eric Bristol, a five-time world champion, and became the first player to win the championship in four consecutive years. Taylor said he wanted to win more titles, so that in the future no one could surpass him, just like Peter Shilton's surprising 1000 play football league record.

Lesson 22

Fishing

Part One Listening and Speaking

Activity 1

🎧 Listen to the following conversation, and then work in pairs to act it out.

(John and his friends will go fishing tomorrow. Peter also wants to join them, but he is a little worried about the dangers of fishing.)

A: I've heard that you will go fishing tomorrow?

B: Yes. It's fishing season now. I've waited all year, and I can't wait any longer!

A: Fishing is a good leisure activity. Can I tag along with you?

B: Sure, welcome to our angling team.

A: But I've heard that fishing can be dangerous. Is that true?

B: Don't worry! With many people around, there is no danger at all.

A: Will there be snakes in the area? I'm afraid of snakes.

B: We have protective measures in advance, so we'll try to avoid the grassland.

A: Thanks! I feel better about it now. I'll go to prepare my fishing gear.

Words and Expressions

go fishing 去垂钓，去钓鱼
leisure /ˈleʒə/ *n.* 休闲放松
angling /ˈæŋglɪŋ/ *n.* 垂钓
snake /sneɪk/ *n.* 蛇

protective measure 防护措施
in advance 预先，事前，提前
grassland /ˈɡrɑːslænd/ *n.* 草丛
fishing gear 渔具

Activity 2

👥 Work in pairs and answer the following questions.

> **Question 1:** Do you think that the fish is a poikilotherm?
>
> **Question 2:** Are the baits used for fishing all the same?

Part Two Reading

Passage 1

Directions: Read the passage about fishing and discuss the following questions with your partner.

Fishing

Fishing is the activity of catching fish in the wild, and its implication has a sense of enticement and cheating. According to the purpose, fishing can be classified into commercial fishing, recreational fishing and sport fishing. Commercial fishers fish for profit while recreational and sport fishers fish for pleasure and competition.

Sport fishing or recreational fishing has rules and laws that limit the way in which fish may be caught; typically, these prohibit the use of nets and the catching of fish with hooks not in the mouth. The most common form of sport fishing is done with a rod, line, hooks and baits. The practice of catching or attempting to catch fish with a hook is generally known as angling. In angling, it is sometimes expected or required that fish be returned to the water (catch and release). The primary reward for sport fishing is the challenge of finding and catching the fish rather than the culinary or financial value of the fish's flesh.

Fishing can be traced back to the production activities of our ancient ancestors, and it gradually evolved into a kind of fun, elegant, and healthy activity. It is not just a leisure activity for after dinner. With a love of nature, people sit by the water like children and enjoy the pleasures brought by a fishing rod, and even a quick-tempered man will likely become "quiet as a pussy".

Words and Expressions

implication /ˌɪmplɪˈkeɪʃn/ *n.* 含意；寓意

enticement /ɪnˈtaɪsmənt/ *n.* 引诱

profit /ˈprɒfɪt/ *n.* 利益；利润

prohibit /prəˈhɪbɪt/ *v.* 禁止；严禁

flesh /fleʃ/ *n.* 肉

trace /treɪs/ *v.* 追溯；追踪

ancestor /ˈænsestə(r)/ *n.* 祖先

quiet as a pussy 静如处子

Sports Terms

net /net/ *n.* 网；渔网

hook /hʊk/ *n.* 鱼钩

rod /rɒd/ *n.* 钓竿

bait /beɪt/ *n.* 鱼饵

catch and release 钓后即放

Questions:

1. Have you ever been to fishing? How do you think about it?

2. What tools does fishing need?

3. Can you elaborate on the phrase "quiet as a pussy"?

Passage 2

Directions: Read the passage about the International Confederation of Sport Fishing and discuss the following questions with your partner.

International Confederation of Sport Fishing

The International Confederation of Sport Fishing (CIPS) is an international organization representing a number of international federations concerned with angling sports. It was founded in Rome, Italy in 1952. It works to enhance communication among fishing fans from different countries and improve their reputation by holding international fishing competitions. Currently, there are 138 national federations from 69 countries belonging to the CIPS.

The CIPS is a confederation of the following international federations: the International Fresh Water Sport Fishing Federation, International Sea Sport Fishing Federation, the International Fly Sport Fishing Federation and the International Casting Sport Fishing Federation. These organizations hold dozens of fishing tournaments

each year respectively, and they have absolute authority in the global fishing industry. The tournament launched by the CIPS has become the Olympic Games of the fishing industry. The Chinese fishing team took part in the 50th and 51st World Freshwater Angling Championships in Slovakia and Belgium respectively in 2003 and 2004. Since then, China has formally stepped onto the international sport fishing stage.

Words and Expressions

confederation /kənˌfedəˈreɪʃn/ *n.* 同盟；组织联盟

fresh water 淡水

absolute /ˈæbsəluːt/ *adj.* 绝对的；完全的

launch /lɔːntʃ/ *v.* 发起；发动

Sports Terms

International Confederation of Sport Fishing (CIPS) 国际钓鱼运动联合会

International Fresh Water Sport Fishing Federation 国际（淡水）钓鱼运动组织

International Sea Sport Fishing Federation 国际海钓运动组织

International Fly Sport Fishing Federation 国际飞钓运动组织

International Casting Sport Fishing Federation 国际抛竿钓运动组织

fishing industry 垂钓行业

World Freshwater Angling Championships 世界淡水钓鱼锦标赛

Questions:

  1. When was the CIPS founded? Where is it headquartered?

  2. What federations are managed by CIPS?

Part Three Exercises

Directions: Do the following exercises.

1. Write an expository on the fishing scene entitled "Sunset Fishing" in no less than 250 words.

2. Nowadays, many people revel in fishing activities. Please share your views and understanding on this phenomenon.

Part Four Rules and Concepts

1. Streams, rivers, canals and lakes can all serve as the venue for sport fishing. The coast along the venue must be able to be fully used. The depth of the water must be at least 1.5 meters, and the depth of each division should be uniform for as far as possible, with a minimum width of 25 meters. Between the designated fishing divisions should be a 1-meter-wide neutral zone.

2. Before the whistle, all players' hooks and floats are not allowed into the water. After the end of the competition is signaled by the whistle, any fish that are no longer in the net are not calculated.

3. The fish must remain in the net, and the players may continue to fish.

4. All players must not use their hands to throw bait or any utility model. All athletes' bait diameters shall not be more than 2 centimeters. All players in the game may not mix the bait, and if there is any violation of this provision, the match result will be canceled.

5. All players in the game may not conspire or fish maliciously. If there is any violation of this provision, the match result will be canceled.

6. All players' casting direction should be in front of the rod rest, and should not interfere with players on either side. If there is any violation of this provision, the match result will be canceled.

7. The side players are not allowed to cast slanted to improve their performance, and if there is any violation of this provision, the match result will be canceled.

8. Competitors can fly fish or catch the fish into the dip net. The testing of fishing equipment is not allowed in the game pool and must remain in the named location.

9. If any wrong numbers or series number is found, after confirmation, the match results of both sides will be canceled.

10. The results are calculated and ranked according to the number of or total weight of the fish.

Part Five Further Reading

The Father of Chinese Fishing

Who is the most widely recognized fisherman in China? It is likely to be Jiang Ziya of the Shang Dynasty. Jiang Ziya was an ancient Chinese military strategist who helped King Wen and King Wu of Zhou overthrow the Shang Dynasty. Before he met King Wen, he was said to have spent years of his exile fishing, but his methods of fishing were particularly strange with a straight hook, or no bait, or with his hook dangling above the water. The truth is that he was fishing for a Lord, not a fish. Later, King Wen appointed him as prime minister and he was known as "Taigong", or "the Grand Duke". The degree to which this qualifies as a myth is open to question, but "Grand Duke Jiang fishes—those who are willing jump at the bait" is a derived idiom meaning to "put one's own head in the noose".

Lesson 23 Chess

Part One Listening and Speaking

Activity 1

🎧 Listen to the following conversation, and then work in pairs to act it out.

(Xiao Li meets his friend Xiao Zhao on his way to a community chess and card room. Then they start to discuss how to find a good chess partner.)

A: Are you going to play Chinese chess with Mr. Wang again today?

B: No, I don't think so. He only plays with Mr. Zhang these days because Mr. Zhang plays better than him.

A: Oh. Well, that's not a bad idea. You can figure out your strengths and weaknesses when you play with a stronger person.

B: I see, but then who do the best chess players play with?

A: The really good chess players don't want to play with bad players. It's not challenging enough. And since it's not easy for them to find suitable opponents, they usually play against themselves.

B: Against themselves? Why?

A: Because you can think of yourself as an opponent. This forces you to think carefully about what could happen after you make your move.

B: Oh, I get it now! So I guess I'll start looking for chess partners who are better than me.

150

Words and Expressions

play chess 弈棋	strength /streŋθ/ *n.* 优势；力量
figure out 想出，理解	weakness /'wiːknɪs/ *n.* 缺点，弱势

Activity 2

👥 Work in pairs and answer the following questions.

Question 1: In which years were chess, weiqi, and Chinese chess classified as events in the Asian Games?

Question 2: Chess is one of the world's most ancient combat games, as famous as Chinese chess, weiqi, and Japanese shogi. Can you explain the origin of Chinese chess?

Part Two Reading

Passage 1

Directions: Read the passage about chess and cards and discuss the following questions with your partner.

Chess and Cards

Chess and cards is the general term for the chess and card entertainment projects. Chinese chess, weiqi and chess have all been listed as sports competitions, as well as Mongolian chess (Sha tar), gomoku, Chinese checkers, checkers, Jungle chess, Flying chess, etc. In addition, bridge, poker, and mahjong are also the most popular public recreational projects.

Chess and cards is a competitive, entertaining, and skillful activity requiring commitment, strategy, and fair play. It is governed by a set of rules or customs, and is a mind game where the outcome is determined mainly by mental skill, rather than by pure chance. Chess is recognized as a sport by the International Olympic Committee. Card games are mostly folk games whose rules vary by region, culture, and person.

Words and Expressions

commitment /kəˈmɪtmənt/ *n.* 专注；
承诺

fair play 公平竞争

chance /tʃɑːns/ *n.* 机会，时机

folk /fəʊk/ *adj.* 民间的，民俗的

Sports Terms

chess and cards 棋牌

Chinese chess 中国象棋

Weiqi 围棋

chess /tʃes/ *n.* 国际象棋

Mongolian chess 蒙古象棋

gomoku 五子棋

Chinese checkers 跳棋

checkers /ˈtʃekəz/ *n.* 国际跳棋

Jungle chess 斗兽棋

Flying chess 飞行棋

bridge /brɪdʒ/ *n.* 桥牌

poker /ˈpəʊkə/ *n.* 扑克

mahjong /mɑːˈdʒɔŋ/ *n.* 麻将

Questions:

1. Can you list some chess programs?

2. What are the benefits of playing chess?

Passage 2

Directions: Read the passage about the World Chess Federation and discuss the following questions with your partner.

World Chess Federation

The World Chess Federation (FIDE from its French acronym) is an international organization that connects the various national chess federations around the world and acts as the governing body of international chess competitions. It is founded in Paris in 1924, and is based in Athens, Greece. Chess was listed as an official competition in the Olympic Games in 1924, and in 1999, the FIDE was recognized by the International Olympic Committee as an international federation.

The FIDE is responsible for the calculation of the player's rank (Elo ratings), and uses these as the basis on which it awards titles for achievement in competitive play: FIDE Master, International Master, International Grandmaster and women's versions

of those titles. It also awards Master and Grandmaster titles for achievement in problem composing and solving.

Important competitions that the FIDE holds or that members of the FIDE authorize include: the World Chess Championship (overall and for women and juniors), regional championships, and the Chess Olympiad, etc.

Words and Expressions

connect /kəˈnekt/ v. 联系；连接

calculation /ˌkælkjuˈleɪʃn/ n. 计算

rank /ræŋk/ v.& n. 排名

title /ˈtaɪt(ə)l/ n. 头衔

authorize /ˈɔːθəraɪz/ v. 授权，委托；批准

Sports Terms

World Chess Federation (FIDE) 世界国际象棋联合会

Elo rating 等级分

FIDE Master 国际棋联大师

International Master 国际大师

International Grandmaster 国际特级大师

World Chess Championship 国际象棋世界冠军赛

World Chess Olympiad 世界国际象棋奥林匹克团体锦标赛

Questions:

1. When was the FIDE founded? Where is its headquarters?

2. What are the titles awarded by the FIDE to the chess players?

3. What competitions are organized by the FIDE or the members of the FIDE?

Part Three Exercises

Directions: Do the following exercises.

1. Chess is a "battle of wits" and is a kind of useful, intellectual recreational exercise. Based on your understanding, write an essay on playing chess in no less than 250 words.

2. What kind of chess and card games do you like to play in your spare time? Give your reasons.

Part Four Rules and Concepts

1. A square board, 8 by 8 lines, with 64 squares arranged in two colors (dark and light) is used in chess.

2. The dark square is named a "black" square and the light square is named a "white" square. Chess pieces move in these squares.

3. There are 32 pieces, which are divided into two groups—black and white. Each player controls one group. The armies are the same and are divided into six types: one king (K), one queen (Q), two rooks (R), two bishops (B), two knights (N) and eight pawns (P).

4. The white army goes first, followed by the black. The two sides take turns playing chess and move one piece at a time until either someone's king is captured, or the game ends in a draw.

5. In Weiqi, each board has 19 by 19 grid of lines. There are a total of 361 points, with nine dots on the board, known as "stars". In the official game, there are 180 black and 180 white pieces.

6. Each side holds a color, and black goes first, followed by white.

7. The objective of playing Weiqi is to surround a larger total area of the board with one's points than the opponent.

8. The board of Chinese chess consists of 9 vertical lines and 10 horizontal lines. Pieces are placed on the intersections known as points. Each player in turn moves one piece from the point it occupies to another point.

9. The color of the Chinese chess pieces is usually divided into black and red, with 16 pieces on each side.

10. For one game, as long as one side's general is captured, the other side wins.

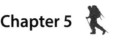

Part Five Further Reading

Zhu Chen

Zhu Chen, born in Wenzhou, Zhejiang Province in 1976, is the recipient of both the Women Grandmaster and Men Grandmaster titles. She is the first chess player who wins the championship in the junior and adult competitions in the world. In 1988, Zhu won the World Girls Under-12 Championship in Romania. In 1994 and 1996, she won the World Junior Girls Chess Championship twice, setting the record of 12 points in 13 games. In 1998, the team of Zhu Chen, Xie Jun, Wang Lei, and Wang Pin topped the World Chess Olympiad, and won the women's team championship. Chinese women for the first time had broken the "encirclement" of Europe and had become the champions. In 2001, Zhu Chen won the World Women's Individual Championship. She is the second world chess champion after Xie Jun.

附 录　参考译文

第一章

水上运动

第 **1** 课 游泳

第一部分 听和说

活动 1

🎧 听下面的对话，然后两人一组将其表演出来。

（彼得游泳时腿抽筋，他向救生员大喊求救。）

A: 快来，救生员！

B: 你怎么了？

A: 我腿抽筋了。

B: 不要乱动，我来帮你。上体靠在我身上，脚后跟向前蹬。好点了吗？

A: 好多了。

B: 我现在把你送上岸，休息一会儿就会好的。

A: 非常感谢！

活动 2

👥 两人一组，回答下列问题。

问题 1：游泳时感觉头晕恶心，该怎么办？

问题 2：游泳时耳朵灌进一些水，如何处理？

第二部分 阅读

文章 1

阅读下面这篇关于游泳运动的文章，讨论文后的思考题。

游泳

游泳一直是最受大众喜爱的娱乐休闲活动之一。在有些国家，游泳是教育大纲中的必修课程。游泳的起源很早，据史料记载，生活在沿海地区的古代人通过观察和模仿鱼类、青蛙等动物在水中游泳的动作，逐渐学会了游泳。

现代游泳运动起源于 19 世纪的英国。1828 年，英国在利物浦乔治码头修造了第一个室内游泳池。1837 年，英国举办了最早的游泳比赛。1869 年，游泳作为一项专门的运动项目正式确立下来，并随之传入各英国殖民地，继而传遍全世界。1896 年，第一届夏季奥运会在希腊雅典召开，游泳被列入正式竞赛项目。

游泳分为实用游泳、竞技游泳和花样游泳三大类。实用游泳在军事、生产、生活服务上使用价值较大，主要有侧泳、潜泳、反蛙泳、踩水、救护、武装泅渡等形式。竞技游泳是指有特定技术要求，按竞赛规则进行的游泳项目。竞技游泳主要有四种泳姿：自由泳（爬泳）、蛙泳、仰泳（背泳）、蝶泳。游泳比赛可采用上述任一泳姿进行，但个人混合泳需包括这四种泳姿。花样游泳，又称"艺术游泳"，是集舞蹈、体操、游泳等于一体的竞技体育项目，分为单人游泳、双人游泳和集体游泳三大类。由于它的动作优美，又有音乐配合，因此有"水上芭蕾"之称。

思考题：

　　1. 古代人们是如何学会游泳的？

　　2. 现代游泳运动起源于哪个国家？

　　3. 你能说出竞技游泳的分类吗？

文章 2

阅读下面这篇关于国际游泳联合会的文章，讨论文后的思考题。

国际游泳联合会

国际游泳联合会，简称国际泳联，是国际奥委会认定的管理水上赛事的国际组织。1908 年在英国伦敦成立，总部设在瑞士的洛桑，现任主席为胡利奥·马廖内。国际泳联正式用语为英语和法语，工作用语为英语。

　　国际游泳联合会所管理的运动项目包括游泳、跳水、花样游泳、水球和公开水域游泳。负责主办的赛事包括奥运会游泳比赛、世界锦标赛（1973 年始）、世界杯赛（1979 年始）、世界短池锦标赛（1993 年始）、跳水大奖赛（1994 年始），跳水世界杯中增加花样跳水项目（1994 年始），在世界水球锦标赛中增加少年女子水球比赛（1995 年始）。中国在中华人民共和国成立前即为国际泳联会员，1958 年退出，1980 年 7 月恢复会员资格。

思考题：

1. 国际泳联总部地点在哪？现任主席是谁？
2. 国际泳联管理的水上项目有哪些？
3. 你能否列举出国际泳联组织的主要赛事？

第三部分　练习

请完成以下练习。

1. 你的朋友今天进行了游泳练习，请向他讲解游泳后该如何恢复。

   （提示：由于游泳非常消耗体力，因此在游泳结束后要大量补水，并且多补充蛋白质，运动结束后的拉伸也是必要的。）

2. 你最喜爱的游泳名将是谁？讲述他／她的故事，写一篇不少于 150 词的短文。

   （提示：可以从游泳名将的成绩、如何刻苦训练、技术特点等方面进行介绍，说明你喜爱的原因。）

第四部分　规则与概念

1. 国际标准游泳池长 50 米，宽至少 21 米，深 1.8 米以上。设 8 条泳道，每条泳道宽 2.5 米，分道线由直径 5 ～ 10 厘米的单个浮标连接而成。

2. 比赛时，运动员必须站在出发台上做好出发姿势（仰泳除外）。出发台高出水面 50 ～ 75 厘米，台面积为 50 厘米 ×50 厘米。

3. 在游泳比赛中，任何一个运动员在出发时如果有抢跳行为都会被取消比赛资格。

4. 自由泳、蛙泳、蝶泳及个人混合泳的比赛，运动员必须从出发台起跳出发，仰泳项目在水中出发。

5. 在自由泳和仰泳比赛中，运动员到达终点时可以只用一只手触壁，但在蛙泳和蝶泳比赛中，必须使用双手同时触壁。所有距离在 50 米以上的游泳比赛都必须在途中折返。

6. 转身时，自由泳和仰泳允许运动员使用身体的任何部分触及池壁，即运动员可以在水下转身后，用脚去蹬池壁。

7. 在个人混合泳中，从仰泳泳姿转换到蛙泳时，运动员必须保持仰泳的姿势直到触及池壁。

8. 游泳运动员的比赛时间和地点都由一个电子系统自动决定。运动员出发时，出发台上的压力板将记录数据。

9. 每条泳道两边的墙上都有触摸板，当运动员触壁时会有记录。由于触摸板和出发台是互连的，因此裁判可以判断参加接力比赛的运动员是否是在其队友触壁以后才入水的。

10. 接力比赛中，如果任何一个运动员在其队友触壁 0.03 秒之前离开出发台，这个队将被自动取消比赛资格。

第五部分 拓展阅读

迈克尔·菲尔普斯

迈克尔·菲尔普斯，1985 年 6 月 30 日出生于马里兰州巴尔的摩市，美国退役游泳运动员，男子 200 米蝶泳、200 米个人混合泳和 400 米个人混合泳三项世界纪录的保持者，奥运冠军，罕见的游泳奇才。2004 年雅典奥运会上一人获得 6 枚游泳金牌；2008 年北京奥运会，他以 8 枚金牌的成绩打破了传奇运动员马克·施皮茨在 1972 年慕尼黑奥运会所创造的 7 金纪录，成为在同一届奥林匹克运动会中获得金牌最多的运动员。2012 年伦敦奥运会后，菲尔普斯成为奥运会历史上获得金牌数（18 枚）及总奖牌数（22 枚）最多的运动员。2012 年 8 月，菲尔普斯宣布正式退役。

第 ②课 跳水

第一部分 听和说

活动 1

🎧 听下面的对话，然后两人一组将其表演出来。

（彼得和约翰是跳水队队员。他们在进行赛前适应性训练，纠正彼此错误。）

A: 马上就要比赛了，今天我们练习什么呢?

B: 按比赛要求，我们做一次适应性训练吧。

A: 好的。

B: 你的节奏很好，但步幅较大，会影响起跳效果的。

A: 是的呀! 每次起跳时都不是很顺畅。

B: 我觉得你最后一步应该步幅小一点，有助于起跳发力。

A: 知道了! 非常感谢!

B: 那我们反复多练习几次，直至完美。

A: 好!

活动 2

👥 两人一组，根据以下所给情景设计对话。

> 情景 1: 在跳水训练时，有一名运动员无法完成动作，教练建议他先使用陆上辅助器材。
>
> 情景 2: 某一队员在训练中大腿拉伤，医生对他进行了紧急处理，并建议他休息几天再训练。

第二部分 阅读

文章 1

阅读下面这篇关于跳水运动的文章，讨论文后的思考题。

跳水

　　跳水运动是人类在同自然界斗争中，伴随着游泳技能的发展而产生的一个运动项目。在伦敦博物馆里，一只陶质花瓶上描绘着一群头朝下作跳水姿势的男孩子，这是迄今为止见到的关于跳水运动最早的图像。

　　我国宋朝时出现一种跳水运动，当时叫"水秋千"。表演者借秋千使身体凌空而起，在空中完成各种动作之后，直接跳入水中。它动作惊险、姿态优美，类似现代的花样跳水。

　　现代跳水运动始于 20 世纪。1900 年第二届奥运会上，瑞典运动员表演了跳水；1904 年跳水成为奥运会正式比赛项目。竞技跳水分跳台跳水和跳板跳水两类。跳台跳水在无弹性的平台上进行，跳台距水面高度分为 5 米、7.5 米和 10 米三种。奥运会、世界锦标赛、世界杯赛限用 10 米跳台。跳板跳水是在一端固定、另一端有弹性的板上进行，跳板离水面的高度有 1 米和 3 米两种。

　　跳水根据起跳动作的方向和结构，可分为向前、向后、向内、反身、转体五组。每组均有规定动作和自选动作，每个动作又有不同的难度系数。根据跳水空中姿势，可以分为直体、屈体、抱膝、翻腾兼转体。运动员跳水时，动作简单，难度系数就低；动作复杂，难度系数就高。裁判员根据运动员的助跑（即走板、跑台）、起跳、空中动作和入水动作来评定分数。

思考题:

　　1. 在古代中国，跳水运动是如何产生的？

　　2. 竞技跳水运动分成哪两类？

　　3. 跳水运动员的表现是如何评分的？

文章 2

阅读下面这篇关于中国游泳协会的文章，讨论文后的思考题。

中国游泳协会

中国游泳协会是负责中国水上运动的全国性运动协会，成立于 1956 年，总部设在北京，首任主席李梦华。中国游泳协会是中国奥林匹克委员会承认的运动组织，是代表中国参加国际游泳联合会、亚洲游泳联合会的唯一合法组织。中国泳协管辖游泳、跳水、花样游泳、水球、公开水域比赛五个分项，下设教练、科研、裁判、少儿训练指导、长距离游泳、老年人游泳、冬泳和救生等专项委员会。中国游泳协会举办的全国性赛事有：全国游泳锦标赛、全国花样游泳锦标赛、全国跳水锦标赛、全国水球锦标赛、全国青年水球比赛，等等。

思考题：

1. 中国游泳协会管辖哪些分项比赛？
2. 中国游泳协会举办的全国性比赛有哪些？

第三部分 练习

请完成以下练习。

1. 假设你将要采访一位非常有名的跳水运动员，现在请起草一份采访提纲。
2. 观看一段跳水比赛视频，讨论运动员的姿势、动作和比分。

第四部分 规则与概念

1. 跳水姿势包括向前跳水、向后跳水、向内跳水、反身跳水、臂立跳水及转体跳水。跳水时的身体姿势有直体、屈体、团身及自由姿势。
2. 裁判对跳水运动员的助跑、起跳、腾空、空中姿势和入水进行分析与评分，继而得出总成绩。
3. 评判入水动作优劣的标准有两个：入水角度和水花溅起的大小。入水时脚尖绷直，角度应近乎垂直；溅起的水花越小越好。
4. 跳水动作开始时，运动员应保持身体直立，头部正直，脚跟并拢，两臂伸直贴于身体两侧。

5. 踏跳步之前的助跑应该不少于 3 步。

6. 向后起跳时，不允许运动员在正式起跳前把脚抬离跳板。

7. 每组跳水动作都有自己的号码，以表示动作组别和翻腾转体的周数。

8. 1 ~ 4 组动作组别的号码均采用 3 位数。第一个数代表动作组别；第二个数代表飞身动作（如果第二位数是"0"，则表示没有飞身动作）；第三个数代表翻腾周数（以"1"为半周，"2"为一周，"3"为一周半，以此类推）。例如，"201"，表示第二组动作：向后跳水翻转半周；"305"，表示第三组动作：反身翻腾两周半。

9. 第 5 组转体动作采用 4 位数。第一位数表示第 5 组（特指转体跳水）；第二位数表示翻腾的方向；第三位数表示翻腾周数；第四位数表示转体周数，计算方法同前。例如，"5136"这个动作中，"5"表示第 5 组转体跳水，"1"表示用第 1 组向前跳水的方向完成翻腾转体，"3"表示翻腾一周半，"6"表示转体三周。再如"5337"这个动作，是指第 5 组转体动作，采用第 3 组反身跳水方向完成翻腾转体，翻腾一周半，转体三周半。

10. 第 6 组臂立动作也采用 3 位数。第一位数表示第 6 组（特指臂立跳水）；第二位数表示臂立跳水的方向；第三位数表示翻腾周数（计算方法同上）。例如"614"动作中，"6"表示第 6 组臂立跳水，"1"表示采用第一组向前跳水方向翻腾，"4"表示翻腾两周。再如"632"，是指第 6 组的臂立跳水动作，用反身跳水方向翻腾一周。

第五部分 拓展阅读

跳水皇后

郭晶晶，1981 年出生，河北保定人，中国著名跳水运动员，曾获得 4 枚奥运会金牌，五次世锦赛个人 / 双人三米板冠军，素有"跳水皇后"美称。郭晶晶 8 岁开始从事跳水训练，11 岁入河北省跳水队，12 岁入选国家跳水队，15 岁首次参加奥运会。在经历连续两届奥运会失败后，她始终怀揣跳水之梦，苦练技术，终于在 2004 年雅典奥运会夺得两枚金牌，成为跳水世界的女一号、中国跳水的领军人物。看过郭晶晶跳水的人，会发现这个女孩展示着体育的魅力。

第 ③ 课 水球

第一部分 听和说

活动 1

🎧 听下面的对话，然后两人一组将其表演出来。

（在一场水球比赛中，约翰发现对方队员双手触球犯规，向裁判报告。但裁判否决了他的报告。）

A: 裁判，对方 5 号队员刚才双手触球了。

B: 不是的，他双手虽然都举起来了，但只是单手触球，我看得很清楚。

A: 那也是打到他的手出界了。

B: 这个球是打到了他的手，但是没有出界。

A: 我认为您的判断有问题。

B: 我看得很清楚。

A: 那好吧。我希望您注意一下对方 6 号，他防守时有很严重的犯规。

B: 好的。

活动 2

👥 两人一组，根据以下所给情景设计对话。

> ○ 情景 1: 裁判刚刚暂停了比赛。教练在跟他的队员讨论防守策略，提醒
> ○   队员注意对方队员的进攻，做好防守。
> ○ 情景 2: 你们队赢了比赛，大家互相祝贺。

第二部分 阅读

文章 1

阅读下面这篇关于水球运动的文章，讨论文后的思考题。

水球

水球运动是在水中进行的两队对抗的球类运动。比赛时每队上场 7 人，包括守门员 1 人。运动员在水中互相配合，以将球投入对方球门得分，得分最多者胜。水球运动是一项极富挑战又具有激烈对抗性的运动。

水球运动起源于英国。据传在 19 世纪 60 年代英国一些地方，孩子们或足球运动员在海滩游泳时，将足球抛在海上互相争夺，由此形成了最初的水球游戏。由于它与足球有联系，故最早称为"水中足球"。

1877 年，英格兰伯顿俱乐部聘请威尔森为水球比赛拟定规则。后来，这一规则成为国际水球比赛规则的基础。到 1879 年出现了有球门的水球比赛。1885年，英国国家业余游泳协会正式承认水球为一项独立的比赛项目。

1890 年水球首先传入美国，后又逐渐在德国、奥地利、匈牙利等国家广泛开展。在 1900 年第二届奥运会上，水球列入正式比赛项目。1973 年起，水球世界锦标赛首次举办，1979 年又开始举办世界杯水球赛。中国的水球运动，在 20世纪 20 年代中期由欧美传入香港和广东。1974 年第七届亚运会上，中国水球队首次参加大型国际水球比赛，获得第二名。目前，我国水球运动开展较好的地区有广东、广西、湖南、四川、福建、上海。

思考题：

1. 水球比赛中，依据什么判定比赛胜负？
2. 为什么最初称水球为"水中足球"？
3. 你能简要描述水球的历史和发展历程吗？

文章 2

阅读下面这篇关于国内外水球大赛的文章，讨论文后的思考题。

国内外水球大赛

世界杯水球赛由国际游泳联合会主办，参加者是东道主和世界锦标赛或奥运会比赛的前七名，采用单循制，每两年举行一届。第一届世界杯水球赛于 1979 年在南斯拉夫贝尔格莱德举行，匈牙利队获冠军。

世界游泳锦标赛男子水球比赛，自 1973 年由国际游泳联合会创办，首届比赛在南斯拉夫贝尔格莱德举行，每两年举行一届。自 1986 年起始设女子项目。2002 年，国际游泳联合会创办首届世界水球联赛。

奥运会水球比赛，男子水球于 1900 年巴黎奥运会上被列为正式比赛项目，女子水球在 2000 年悉尼奥运会上被列为正式比赛项目。在亚洲，男子水球比赛于 1951 年第一届亚运会上被列为比赛项目，直到 2000 年才加入女子水球比赛。

我国水球项目于 1959 年第五届全运会被列为正式比赛项目，这是中国水球最重要的国内水平比赛，反映水球运动的群众基础和竞技水平。

思考题:

1. 首届世界杯水球赛的时间和地点是什么？
2. 你知道哪一年将水球设为奥运会正式比赛项目吗？
3. 你能简要介绍水球运动在我国的发展吗？

第三部分 练习

请完成以下练习。

1. 请介绍一下水球比赛的计分方法和简单规则。
2. 假定你要采访一位著名的水球运动员。请拟定一个采访提纲。

第四部分 规则与概念

1. 水球比赛是在标准的 50 米游泳池中进行，水深至少 2 米。比赛期间运动员一直游泳或踩水。
2. 男子比赛场地是 30 米长，20 米宽；女子比赛场地是 25 米长，17 米宽。比赛区均用绳索标示。3 米宽、90 厘米高的两个球门漂浮在两端的水面上。
3. 所有标线在整场比赛中须清晰可见。规定的颜色是：出球门线和中心线——白色，两米线——红色，四米线——黄色，七米线——绿色。
4. 红色的处罚区位于泳池的两端，在球门线后面，距离正对比赛官员席的池角大约两米。球员进入该区即意味着该球员离开了比赛区，被罚球员在处罚区等待重新进场比赛的信号。

5. 水球比赛时，每队上场 7 人，包括守门员 1 人。场外替补队员 6 人，任何一方得分后或每节比赛开始前均可换人。除守门员外，任何人不得用双手触球。

6. 比赛分 4 节进行，每节 7 分钟，死球时停表。两节间休息两分钟，同时双方交换场地。

7. 比赛场地边线上设置小旗。红旗表示越位区域的禁线（离球门 2 米处）。黄旗表示判罚 4 米直接任意球地点和同一犯规动作不同判罚尺度的禁线（离球门 4 米）。与球门平行的白旗表示端线。中场白旗表示中线。

8. 参赛运动员需戴泳帽。一队戴蓝色帽子，另一队戴白色。帽子上有 1 ~ 13 的号码，双方守门员均戴 1 号红色帽子。裁判员除使用哨子外，还要手持蓝、白旗以表示比赛双方。

9. 比赛时，以球体越过球门线为得分。得分后，双方队员应回到本方半场，由失分一方队员在中线的中心点开球。比赛中，一方控球时间不得超过 35 秒。

10. 水球比赛中的犯规有一般犯规和严重犯规之分。一般犯规由对方掷任意球。严重犯规包括：踢或打对方队员，做出任何粗暴行动；干扰掷任意球；有意向对方队员脸上泼水；连续有意地发生一般犯规等。

第五部分 拓展阅读

德兹索·乔尔玛蒂

德兹索·乔尔玛蒂，匈牙利人，1927 年出生，被誉为奥运史上最成功的水球运动员。他曾连续五次参加奥运会，于 1952 年、1956 年和 1964 年获奥运会水球金牌，1948 年伦敦奥运会获水球银牌，1960 年罗马奥运会获铜牌。作为队长，他于 1954 年和 1962 年两次夺得欧洲锦标赛冠军。在游泳池里，他技术全面，既能打前锋，又能打后卫；尤其是拥有出色的游泳技术，百米游泳个人记录为 58.5 秒，是世界上速度最快的水球运动员之一。退役后，他成为匈牙利国家水球队教练，并带队参加了 1976 年蒙特利尔奥运会，夺得金牌。后来，乔尔玛蒂开始从政，并当选国会议员。

第 **4** 课 帆船

第一部分 听和说

活动 1

🎧 听下面的对话，然后两人一组将其表演出来。

（彼得想去玩帆船，但是有些害怕。为了让他放轻松，约翰向他讲述了自己去年在青岛玩帆船的经历。）

A: 彼得，你玩过帆船吗？

B: 没有呢，你呢？

A: 我玩过。去年在青岛，我和朋友玩儿过一次帆船，好刺激！

B: 一定很好玩。危险吗？

A: 没有想象的那么危险，只不过出发前需要做好充足的准备。

B: 是吗？我需要做哪些准备呢？

A: 首先，你得了解帆船构造、帆船驾驶规则和一些技术要领。当然，最好能找人练习一下。

B: 好的，有道理。我去之前需要准备什么东西吗？

A: 出发前，你要提前准备好救生背心、救生圈、急救药包、水泵、水桶等物品。你还需要一些别的，但这些是最重要的。

B: 知道了，谢谢。

活动 2

👤 两人一组，回答下列问题。

> 问题 1：初次登帆船需要注意哪些登船礼仪？
>
> 问题 2：我国青岛举办过哪些帆船比赛？

第二部分 阅读

文章 1

阅读下面这篇关于帆船运动的文章，讨论文后的思考题。

帆船运动

帆船运动是依靠自然风力作用于帆上，使驾驭船只前进的一项水上运动。比赛用的帆船是由船体、桅杆、舵、稳向板、索具等部件构成的小而轻的单桅船。由于船体轻、航速快，因此又名"快艇"。

帆船历史同人类文明史一样悠久。作为一种运动项目，最早见于 1900 多年以前古罗马诗人吉尔的作品中。13 世纪，威尼斯开始定期举行帆船比赛，但比赛船只没有统一的规格和级别。后来，荷兰因地势很低而开凿了很多运河，人们普遍使用小帆船运输或捕鱼。

目前，世界各地普遍开展帆船运动，欧洲、美洲和大洋洲开展得较为广泛。我国帆船运动是在 1949 年以后随着航海等多项运动而开展的，1958 年在武汉东湖举行过一次帆船表演赛，1980 年举行了全国帆船锦标赛。

从事帆船运动能够增强体质，锻炼意志。在大海上与风浪斗争，人们沉浸在战胜自然、挑战自我的喜悦之中。

思考题：

　　1. 帆船运动是一种什么样的水上运动？

　　2. 你能否简述一下帆船运动的历史？

　　3. 我国帆船运动是从哪年开始开展的？

文章 2

阅读下面这篇关于国际帆船联合会的文章，讨论文后的思考题。

国际帆船联合会

国际帆船联合会，简称国际帆联，是国际奥委会承认的世界帆船比赛的管理机构。1907 年成立于法国巴黎，创始国是英国，总部设在英国伦敦。现任主席卡罗·克罗齐，秘书长彼得·索里。国际帆联正式用语为英语，现有逾 120 个会员国（或地区）。帆船运动于 1932 年进入奥运会。

国际帆联的任务包括：不分种族、宗教、性别或政治信仰，推动帆船运动发展；制定、监督和解释帆船比赛的规则；管理、举办各种帆船赛事；保护会员的权益。对帆船选手来说，最熟悉的莫过于国际帆联制定的《国际帆船竞赛规则》，这是帆船赛事的国际通用标准规则。

中国帆船帆板运动协会，简称"中国帆协"，是中国帆船运动的国家管理机构，也是国际帆船联合会承认的运动协会。

思考题：

1. 哪个国家创建了国际帆船联合会？
2. 国际帆联的任务有哪些？
3. 中国帆协是一个什么样的组织？

第三部分 练习

请完成以下练习。

1. 你对中国帆船运动的发展有何看法？请就此话题写一篇不少于 250 词的作文。

2. 你如何理解帆船比赛的观赛礼仪？

第四部分 规则与概念

1. 帆船比赛要求在开阔的海面上进行，距海岸应有 0.5 ～ 2 公里。奥运会的帆船比赛通常采用奥林匹克梯形航线和迎尾风航线。

2. 比赛的起航线、终点线均为虚拟线，分别是起点船、终点船上的标志旗杆与其左侧船或浮标的标志旗杆之间的虚拟连线。

3. 由于风向、风速、气象、水文等条件的不断变化，竞赛场地不是固定不变的，通常是在规定的区域里按照气象水文情况进行布设，且布设工作一般在距比赛起航半小时至 5 分钟前完成。

4. 不同级别的帆船比赛用时不同，一般在 45 ～ 90 分钟之间。运动员可以自带船和帆。

5. 帆船比赛主要有两种比赛形式，一种为集体出发的"船队比赛"，另一种为两条船之间一对一的"对抗赛"。奥运会帆船比赛都是采用"船队比赛"的方式。

6. 起航信号发出后，赛船的船体、船员或装备的任何部分在通向第一标的航向时，触及起航线，即算"起航"。

7. 起航信号发出前，赛船的船体、装备或船员身体的任何部分触及起航线或其延长线，判为"抢航"。

8. 抢航者要在规定的时间内按规则规定的方式返回到起航准备区重新起航。如果有较多的帆船抢航，裁判员无法辨明抢航帆船时，则全部召回该级别所有帆船，重新起航。

9. 帆船竞赛共进行 11 轮（49 人级 16 轮），前 10 轮（49 人级前 15 轮）选其中最好的 9 轮（49 人级 14 轮）成绩来计算每条帆船的名次。每一轮名次的得分为：第一名得 1 分，第二名得 2 分，第三名得 3 分，第四名得 4 分，以此类推。前十名的船进入决赛。

10. 每条帆船在每一轮比赛中的名次得分相加，其中去掉一轮最差的成绩，就是该船的总成绩。总成绩得分越少者名次越靠前。

第五部分 拓展阅读

奥运冠军徐莉佳

徐莉佳，1987 年出生于上海，中国帆船赛运动员，2008 年奥运会女子帆船激光镭迪尔级铜牌，2012 年奥运会帆船激光镭迪尔级冠军，2012 年奥运会闭幕式中国代表团的旗手。徐莉佳 5 岁开始学习游泳，10 岁开始从事帆船训练，仅 11 岁进军国际 OP 级别帆船比赛，并于 2001 年、2002 年连续两年夺取世锦赛女子 OP 级帆船比赛冠军。2003 年，徐莉佳按照国际帆船联合会的规定，由小级别的 OP 级帆船改练欧洲级帆船。由于她技术娴熟、勇敢无畏，一度被比作"女姚明"。

冰上运动

第 **5** 课 速度滑冰

第一部分 听和说

活动 1

🎧 听下面的对话，然后两人一组将其表演出来。

（比赛中，一名运动员发现他的冰刀有问题。现在他正向裁判申请更换冰鞋。）

A: 裁判，您好！我的冰刀有些问题，我想检查一下。

B: 可以。出什么问题了？

A: 不好意思，我不清楚问题出在哪，请允许我更换冰鞋。

B: 可以更换，但我需要先检查一下你的新冰鞋。

A: 您看新冰鞋可以吗？

B: 没有问题，你可以穿这双冰鞋参加比赛。

A: 非常感谢。

B: 不客气，赶紧准备比赛吧！

活动 2

👥 两人一组，根据以下所给情景设计对话。

> 情景 1：比赛前，裁判认为一名运动员的装备不符合规定，需要更换。
> 现在，裁判正在与运动员交涉。
>
> 情景 2：比赛中运动员发挥失常，赛后生气地将冰鞋狠狠摔在地上。教
> 练正在开导他。

第二部分 阅读

文章 1

阅读下面这篇关于速度滑冰运动的文章，讨论文后的思考题。

速度滑冰

速度滑冰通常包括三种：长距离速度滑冰、短距离速度滑冰和马拉松速度滑冰。在奥运会比赛中，长距离速滑一般指"速度滑冰"，短距离速滑一般指"短道速滑"。因此本课中的速度滑冰指的是长距离速度滑冰。

速度滑冰是一项竞技冰上体育运动。运动员穿着冰鞋在规定距离的冰上滑行，快者取胜。它需要运动员的速度、力量以及战略战术。速度滑冰基本技术包括直道滑行、弯道滑行、起跑技术和摆臂技术。比赛项目包括短距离（500米）、中距离（1000米）、长距离（1500米）和全能四种，每种均分男、女组。

国际性速滑比赛始于19世纪末。1889年，在阿姆斯特丹举行了第一届国际速滑比赛。1893年，举办了第一届世界男子速滑锦标赛；1936年，举办了第一届世界女子速滑锦标赛。1924年，第一届冬季奥运会始设男子速滑比赛项目；1960年冬奥会上增加了女子速滑比赛项目。2015年6月8日，速度滑冰集体出发列入冬奥会正式比赛项目。

从事速滑运动有益于保持身心健康，促进新陈代谢，提高心肺功能，培养坚强意志，因此受到运动爱好者的广泛追捧。

思考题：

    1. 你能复述一下速度滑冰的基本技术吗？

    2. 你知道速度滑冰比赛项目有哪些吗？

    3. 速度滑冰集体出发是冬奥会正式比赛项目吗？

文章 2

阅读下面这篇关于国际滑冰联盟的文章，讨论文后的思考题。

国际滑冰联盟

国际滑冰联盟是竞技冰上运动项目的国际管理机构，负责花样滑冰、同步花样滑冰、冰上舞蹈、速滑、短道速滑等运动的开展。1892年在荷兰成立，是最早的冬季运动项目的国际管理组织。现有会员协会 85 个，总部设于瑞士洛桑，正式工作语言为英语、德语、法语和俄语。中国于 1956 年加入国际滑联。

国际滑联的成立意在为其监管范围内的滑冰项目建立规范的国际规则和章程，组织各项目的国际比赛；其任务是通过普及滑冰运动，提升运动质量，增加滑冰参与者数量，以提高人们对于滑冰运动的兴趣。

除冬季奥运会的滑冰比赛外，国际滑联的主要比赛还有速度滑冰、短道速滑和花样滑冰的世界杯赛、欧洲锦标赛、世界锦标赛、世界青年锦标赛等。具体包括：速度滑冰世界杯、青少年速度滑冰世界杯、欧洲速度滑冰锦标赛、短道速滑世界杯、世界短道速滑锦标赛、世界青少年短道速滑锦标赛、世界花样滑冰锦标赛、世界青少年花样滑冰锦标赛、四大洲花样滑冰锦标赛、国际滑联花样滑冰大奖赛等。

思考题：

1. 国际滑联总部设在哪里？

2. 竞技滑冰项目包括哪些？

3. 国际滑联举办的比赛有哪些？

第三部分　练习

请完成以下练习。

1. 谈谈短道速滑和速度滑冰所需装备的不同之处。

2. 谈谈短道速滑和速度滑冰在技术规则要求的不同之处。

第四部分　规则与概念

1. 速滑跑道最大周长为 400 米，最小为 333.33 米，内弯道半径不能小于 25 米或大于 26 米，每条跑道宽 4 ~ 5 米。

2. 短道速滑跑道周长 111.12 米，内弯道半径 8.25 米。

3. 速滑运动员穿尼龙紧身全连服 (衣、裤、帽、袜、手套连在一起)。为保暖需穿贴身的棉毛内衣。男运动员还要穿三角短裤和护身。

4. 速滑冰刀刀长刃窄，用滑度好、耐磨、硬度适宜的轻合金材料制成。

5. 冰刀刀刃厚薄要均匀，两刀刃高度要相同，刀刃要笔直，没有凹凸不平等毛病。

6. 内道起跑的运动员，滑行到换道区时应换到外道，外道运动员要换到内道。

7. 起跑时，在"各就各位"口令下达后，运动员要在起跑线与预备线之间静止站好；"预备"口令下达后，立即做好起跑姿势。鸣枪前运动员不准活动，保持静止，枪响后即起跑。

8. 在比赛过程中，运动员可随时越过对手，但如使用不法手段，如：故意推挤其他对手、偷跑、滑出跑道等，都会被取消比赛资格。

9. 在接力赛中，每队有4位运动员，运动员故意推挤其他对手、偷跑、滑出跑道、非法超越、超越接棒区都是不法行为，会被取消比赛资格。

10. 运动员在比赛中由于不属于自身的原因而影响了正常滑跑或摔倒时，经裁判长允许，可以休息30分钟后，重新参加该项比赛；但因冰场不洁或冰刀损坏，则不能重新比赛。

第五部分 拓展阅读

速滑运动员叶乔波

叶乔波，1964年出生，吉林人，前中国著名女子速度滑冰运动员，曾夺得世锦赛冠军和3枚奥运会奖牌。从1979年到1994年间，她共参加34场国内外速度滑冰比赛，获得金牌52枚、银牌36枚、铜牌12枚。在1992年第十六届冬季奥林匹克运动会上，叶乔波获得500米和1000米速滑两枚银牌，为中国在冬奥会历史上赢得了首枚奖牌。1994年，由于伤病，叶乔波退役，并进入清华大学学习。在取得MBA学位之后，叶乔波创办了乔波冰雪世界俱乐部，以促进国家冰雪运动的发展。

（注：中国冬奥会史上首枚速滑金牌由张虹在2014年索契冬奥会上夺得。）

第 **6** 课 短道速滑

第一部分 听和说

活动 1

🎧 *听下面的对话，然后两人一组将其表演出来。*

（短道速滑比赛获得银牌后，王明和教练一起观看比赛录像，分析哪些技术动作需要完善。）

A: 王明，祝贺你获得短道速滑比赛亚军。

B: 谢谢教练！我认为自己还没有发挥出最好水平。您能帮我分析分析吗？

A: 我们来看看比赛录像吧。

……

B: 我觉得技术动作需要改进。

A: 是的，改进技术的同时还需要重新制定战术。

B: 您现在能帮我制定战术吗？

A: 放心吧，王明，我早已为你制定好了！好好休息，明天见。

B: 谢谢教练！

活动 2

👤 *两人一组，根据以下所给情景设计对话。*

> 情景 1：你刚刚输掉一场短道速滑比赛，教练正在给你分析原因。
>
> 情景 2：比赛中运动员摔出跑道，医生来查看情况。

第二部分 阅读

文章 1

阅读下面这篇关于短道速滑运动的文章，讨论文后的思考题。

短道速滑

短道速滑是一项竞技性冰上速滑运动，是长距离速滑的姐妹项目。

短道速滑于 19 世纪 80 年代起源于加拿大，当时加拿大的一些速度滑冰爱好者常到滑道比户外滑冰较短的室内冰场上练习。最终，室内速度滑冰比赛开始举行。及至 19 世纪 90 年代中期，加拿大的蒙特利尔、魁北克、温尼伯等城市相继出现室内速度滑冰比赛。1905 年加拿大首次举行全国短道速滑比赛。20 世纪早期，这项运动逐渐在欧美国家广泛开展。

1967 年，国际滑冰联盟采纳了短道速滑项目，然而直到 1976 年才首次在美国伊利诺伊州举行国际短道速滑赛。1981 年起举办世界短道速滑锦标赛，每年一届。

在 1988 年举办的冬季奥运会上，短道速滑作为表演项目亮相。1992 年，短道速滑成为冬季奥运会的正式比赛项目，并延续至今。从 1992 年到 2002 年，短道速滑项目由 4 个扩展为 8 个，分别为男子 / 女子 500 米、1000 米、1500 米、男子 / 女子接力。

思考题：

1. 室内短道速滑运动是如何产生的？
2. 短道速滑哪年被列为冬奥会正式比赛项目？
3. 赛场上，哪些缺乏运动精神的行为可能导致运动员比赛出局？

文章 2

阅读下面这篇关于奥运会短道速滑比赛的文章，讨论文后的思考题。

奥运会短道速滑比赛

1992 年，短道速滑正式成为冬奥会比赛项目，但只设立了男子 1000 米、女子 500 米和男女接力 4 个项目。1994 年利勒哈默尔冬奥会上，短道速滑项目扩充为男女 500 米、男女 1000 米和男女接力 6 个小项。之后在盐湖城冬奥会上，进一步增加了男女 1500 米比赛，从而使冬奥赛上短道速滑金牌总数达到 8 枚。

短道速滑虽然在 1992 年才成为冬奥会项目，但在短道上的比赛形式早在 1932 年的普莱西德湖冬奥会上就出现了。当时举行的所有速度滑冰比赛都采用了与今天短道速滑类似的形式进行，这引起了传统的欧洲人的担忧。短道竞赛有危险，一些运动员对此非常反感，因而拒绝参加这种形式的比赛。

自 1992 年以来，短道速滑一直是韩国、中国、加拿大、美国这四个国家的优势项目，截至 2010 年，这 4 个国家已总揽了冬奥会短道速滑全部 120 枚奖牌中的 104 枚。韩国在冬奥会短道速滑项目上共斩获 37 枚奖牌，中国共获得的 44 枚冬奥会奖牌中也有 24 枚来自短道速滑项目。

思考题：

1. 盐湖城冬奥会上的短道速滑比赛有多少个小项？都是什么？
2. 哪些国家在冬奥会速滑比赛上有领先优势？
3. 中国在冬奥会短道速滑这一项目上共获得了多少枚奥运奖牌？

第三部分 练习

请完成以下练习。

1. 请向同伴介绍短道速滑运动员身上的护具名称与作用。
2. 与你的同伴分享你第一次滑冰的经历，比如你可以谈谈当时的担心与喜悦。

第四部分 规则与概念

1. 比赛场地的大小为 30 米 ×60 米，场地周长 111.12 米。
2. 直道宽不小于 7 米，长 28.85 米。弯道半径 8 米。
3. 短道速滑安全头盔应符合现行的 ASTM 标准。头盔必须有规则的形状，不能有突起。
4. 安全比赛服应符合 97.1402 号 MU 型。
5. 护膝应由软垫或硬壳制成。
6. 冰刀管必须是封闭的，刀根必须是圆弧形，最小半径为 10 毫米。刀管最少有两点固定在鞋上，没有可动的部分。

7. 所有运动员必须佩戴滑冰协会批准使用的护颈。

8. 短道速滑比赛采用淘汰制，以预赛、半决赛、决赛的方式进行。

9. 最新规则规定，预赛站位通过抽签决定，之后的半决赛、决赛按照上一轮比赛的成绩确定站位，成绩好的站内道。

10. 比赛途中，在不犯规的前提下，运动员可以随时超越对手。

第五部分 拓展阅读

短道速滑名将杨扬

　　杨扬，1975 年出生，黑龙江人，前中国女子短道速滑队运动员，现为国际奥委会委员。共获得 59 个世界冠军，是中国获得世界冠军最多的速滑运动员。在 2002 年盐湖城冬奥会上，杨扬获得女子 500 米短道速滑决赛冠军，实现中国冬奥会史上金牌"零"的突破。她连续三次参加奥运会，将五枚奖牌收入囊中，其中 2 金 2 银 1 铜。杨扬曾获 2002 年 CCTV 体坛风云人物"年度最佳女运动员"、2011 年 CCTV 体坛风云人物"年度体坛特别贡献奖"等荣誉。2010 年当选国际奥委会委员。2012 年创办上海飞扬冰上运动中心，延续自己的冰上梦想。

第 **7** 课 花样滑冰

第一部分 听和说

活动 1

🎧 听下面的对话，然后两人一组将其表演出来。

（彼得的胳膊被同伴的冰刀划伤。现在医生正在给他包扎。）

A: 医生，快帮帮我，太疼了。

B: 你怎么了？

A: 冰刀划伤了我的胳膊，血一直流，止不住。

B: 我看看，你不要动。

A: 不会伤到骨头吧？

B: 不好说，为安全起见，一会儿送你到医院拍片检查。

A: 好的。

B: 伤口看起来很深，你可能需要缝针。我给你包扎伤口后，你直接去医院。把手臂放在这个绷带上，不要乱动。

A: 明白，谢谢。

活动 2

👥 两人一组，回答下列问题。

> 问题 1：冰场太脏了，如何向裁判员请求清理冰场？
>
> 问题 2：赛前，运动员非常紧张，教练员如何给运动员舒缓压力？

第二部分 阅读

文章 1

阅读下面这篇关于花样滑冰运动的文章，讨论文后的思考题。

花样滑冰

花样滑冰，既优美又极具技术难度，是由一人或两人穿着花样滑冰冰鞋在冰上表演的体育运动。花样滑冰项目分为短节目和自由滑两部分，表演者预先以技术动作为基础编排好动作，并完成旋转、跳跃、托举、抛跳、螺旋线等一系列动作要素和步伐。裁判组将根据选手的技术水平和艺术表现评估打分。

花样滑冰起源于 18 世纪的英国，后在欧美国家逐渐传播开来。1772 年，英国人罗伯特·琼斯撰写的《论滑冰》在伦敦出版，这是已知的第一部有关花样滑冰的记录。1863 年，被誉为"现代花滑之父"的美国人杰克逊·海因斯将滑冰运动与舞蹈艺术融为一体，丰富了花样滑冰的内容和形式。1868 年，美国的丹尼尔·梅伊和乔治·梅伊首次表演了双人滑。1872 年，奥地利首次举办了花样滑冰比赛。1896 年，首届世界男子单人花样滑冰锦标赛在俄国圣彼得堡举行；1906 年，首届世界女子单人花样滑冰锦标赛在瑞士达沃斯举行；1952 年，冰上舞蹈正式成为花样滑冰的比赛项目之一。花样滑冰于 1924 年正式成为冬季奥运会比赛项目。

思考题：

1. 你能列举一些花样滑冰的技术动作吗？
2. 花样滑冰运动员的表现是如何评判和打分的？
3. 谁被誉为"现代花滑之父"？

文章 2

阅读下面这篇关于奥运会花样滑冰项目的文章，讨论文后的思考题。

奥运会花样滑冰项目

奥运会花样滑冰正式比赛项目共有 4 个：单人滑（分男子和女子两项）、双人滑与冰上舞蹈。单人滑包括男子单人滑与女子单人滑两项，技术动作要素包括跳跃、旋转、接续步、燕式步等其他动作步伐。单人滑对跳跃的要求最高，因此单人滑通常代表了选手能达到的最高跳跃难度。双人滑要求一位男选手和一位女选手配合，在冰上表演同步的单人滑动作，以及双人滑特有的动作：抛跳（男选手"抛掷"女选手跳跃）、头顶托举（男选手将摆成某种造型的女选手高举过头）、双人旋转（两位选手同时绕一个共同轴心旋转）、螺旋线（男选手是螺旋转的轴）等。冰上舞蹈也是要求双人配合。冰舞与双人滑的主要区别在于冰舞要求两名选手在近距离保持国际标准舞造型的同时，要紧扣音乐节拍表演复杂多样的步法，而且托举不能过肩。

思考题：

> 1. 奥运会花样滑冰比赛项目有几个？都是什么？
> 2. 双人滑独有的动作有哪些？
> 3. 冰舞与双人滑的主要区别是什么？

第三部分　练习

请完成以下练习。

1. 请简述冰上站立的技术要领。
2. 你最喜欢的花样滑冰运动员是谁？查阅相关资料，写一篇 200 词左右的短文，介绍他 / 她的事迹。

第四部分　规则与概念

1. 花样滑冰的冰场长 56～61 米，宽 26～30 米，冰的厚度不少于 3～5 厘米。
2. 花样滑冰的冰刀与冰球冰刀最显著的不同在于前者前端有"刀齿"。
3. 刀齿主要用在跳跃中，不应用在滑行和旋转中。
4. 冰刀以螺丝固定在冰鞋的鞋底。选手不穿冰鞋时，要用软套保护冰刀，它可以吸收残留的融水，防止冰刀生锈。
5. 选手穿着冰鞋在冰场外行走时，要在冰刀外套上硬塑料的保护套，这是为了避免冰刀被地面磨钝或沾上灰尘杂质。
6. 在花样滑冰的单人滑与双人滑比赛中，选手必须完成两套节目。
7. 在短节目中，每个选手必须完成一系列必选动作，包括跳跃、旋转和步法。

8. 在自由滑／长节目中，选手选择动作有更大的自由度。

9. 冰上舞蹈的比赛通常包括三个部分：至少一套规定舞、一套每年指定采用一种国际标准舞节奏的创编舞、一套选手自己选择的自由舞。

10. 2010 年 6 月，国际滑联大会通过决议，在今后的冰上舞蹈比赛中取消规定舞，只保留创编舞和自由舞。

第五部分 拓展阅读

花样滑冰双人滑选手——申雪／赵宏博

申雪和赵宏博，同为黑龙江人，是中国花样滑冰双人滑选手。1992 年 8 月，二人开始配对练习双人滑。1996 年，在加拿大埃德蒙顿举办的世界花样滑冰锦标赛上，申雪／赵宏博以滑行速度快、动作难度高、冰上技术精确的优势，加上特有的表演风格和气质，令在场的观众耳目一新。当两人结束了自由滑表演后，现场观众按捺不住激动的心情，全场起立，爆发出了长时间、雷鸣般的掌声，场面极为壮观。虽然他们最终只获得了总分第 15 名，却给人们留下了极其深刻的印象。法国花样滑冰协会主席当时断言："申雪和赵宏博在不远的将来一定会成为世界冠军！"2002 年世界花样滑冰锦标赛，申雪和赵宏博夺得中国在双人滑项目上的首个世界冠军。2010 年，他们又摘得中国在冬奥会双人滑项目上的首个世界冠军。

第 8 课 冰球

第一部分 听和说

活动 1

🎧 听下面的对话，然后两人一组将其表演出来。

（回家路上，两个人讨论刚看完的冰球比赛。）

A: 今天冰球比赛好精彩！

B: 是啊，美国冰球队发挥得很出色，无论是防守还是进攻。

A: 冰球真是一项刺激的运动项目，但有些粗暴。

B: 运动员之间的各种冲撞十分激烈。

A: 是啊，这样造成冰球比赛经常发生打架斗殴的情况，即便是很小的摩擦也不例外。

B: 很少看见冰球比赛中没有打架的，今天还不算是严重，只有个别队员打起来了。

A: 这样的比赛看看很刺激，但我可不想去打冰球了。

B: 我也这样认为。

活动 2

👥 两人一组，回答下列问题。

> 问题 1：冰球比赛中，运动员以何种方式相互鼓励加油？
>
> 问题 2：冰球比赛中，运动员手臂被球棍打到的处理方式有哪些？

第二部分 阅读

文章 1

阅读下面这篇关于冰球运动的文章，讨论文后的思考题。

冰球

　　冰球是一种在冰上进行的接触性的集体运动项目，通常在冰场进行，两方冰球运动员使用冰球杆将冰球打入对方球网得分。这是一项速度快、力量猛的对抗性运动，在北美、欧洲的北部和西部地区都很流行。

　　最早的关于冰球的记录见于 17 世纪荷兰的出版物，上面记载绅士们脚穿绑有骨头磨成的刀刃的冰鞋，在结冰的河面上带着一个圆饼滑行。在 19 世纪初期，有记载加拿大的印第安人（密克马克族）在进行一种类似的游戏，他们使用的是棍棒和木质的圆饼。现代冰球运动发源于 19 世纪的加拿大。加拿大金斯顿流行一种冰上游戏，参加游戏者足绑冰刀前行。

　　1855 年 12 月 25 日，加拿大金斯顿首次举行非正式的冰球比赛。1860 年，人们开始使用橡胶制成的盘形冰球。1875 年 3 月 3 日，加拿大蒙特利尔的维多利亚冰场第一次正式举办冰球赛，这场比赛在麦克吉尔大学的两支队伍间进行。当时，每支球队有 30 名队员在场上。1879 年麦克吉尔大学的学生罗伯逊和史密斯教授共同制定了冰球比赛规则，规定每队比赛人数为 9 人。冰球在加拿大迅速成为最流行的项目。

　　1885 年，第一个业余冰球协会成立。发展到这个阶段，运动员开始使用更多的护具以保证自身的安全，比如守门员就用上了护腿板，并戴上了面罩。之后，冰球运动传到美国及欧洲大陆。1902 年欧洲第一个冰球俱乐部在瑞士的莱萨旺成立。1908 年，国际冰球联盟在巴黎成立，总部设在瑞士苏黎世。1910 年举行第一届欧洲冰球锦标赛，英国获得冠军。

　　七年后，1917 年，美国国家冰球联盟成立，直到 1967 年只有 6 支球队参赛。近些年，美国冰球联盟已经成为世界上职业化和商业化十分成功的联赛，其对冰球的影响和 NBA 之于世界篮球相似，而"斯坦利杯"也成为具有传奇色彩的荣誉。第一支职业冰球队——蒂湖队，在美国密歇根州成立。1904 年美国成立了国际职业冰球联盟。1908 年，欧洲成立国际业余冰球联合会，此联合会的首次比赛同年在苏格兰格拉斯哥举行，英国、波希米亚、瑞士、法国和比利时为最初的 5 个会员国。1917 年，加拿大成立了国家冰球联盟。

思考题:

1. 你能说说冰球的起源与发展吗?

2. 冰球如何成为加拿大最流行的体育项目?

3. 为什么说美国国家冰球联盟是世界上职业化和商业化十分成功的联盟组织?

文章 2

阅读下面这篇关于美国国家冰球联盟的文章,讨论文后的思考题。

美国国家冰球联盟

美国国家冰球联盟是由北美冰球队伍所组成的职业运动联盟,它是全世界最高级别的职业冰球联盟,为北美四大职业运动之一。队伍共分成东、西两个大区,每个大区各分为三个分区。

美国国家冰球联盟于 1917 年在魁北克蒙特利尔成立,成立之初只有 5 支队伍。在一系列的扩充之后,联盟囊括了来自 20 多个国家的顶级球员。加拿大球员一直是联盟主力,但是最近的赛季中,美国和欧洲球员数量也在不断增加。现在联盟共有 30 支球队,24 支位于美国,6 支位于加拿大。整个 2004—2005 球季因劳资争议球员大罢工而取消,之后联盟成功进行了 2005—2006 赛季的例行赛和 2006 "斯坦利杯" 季后赛。

思考题:

1. 美国国家冰球联盟的队伍是如何组成的?

2. 美国国家冰球联盟成立时间? 在哪个城市?

3. 历史上美国国家冰球联盟的球员主要来自哪个国家?

第三部分 练习

请完成以下练习。

1. 你和朋友观看了一场精彩的冰球比赛,现在分享你的感受,简单评价球员的发挥。

   (提示:你可以对某一个进球、某一个球员的进攻或者防守,以及守门员的发挥进行评价。)

2. 试试打冰球的感觉。你穿上了冰球运动员的装备，拿起了球棍，试着击球和射门。现在对你的朋友讲述这个经历以及你的感受。

（提示：你可以描述运动员的装备都有哪些，以及击球的感觉。）

第四部分 规则与概念

1. 标准冰球场地最大规格为长 61 米，宽 30 米；最小规格为长 56 米，宽 26 米；四角圆弧的半径为 7 ~ 8.5 米。

2. 在冰场两端各距端墙 4 米、横贯冰场并延伸到边线界墙，画出宽 5 厘米的两条平行红线为球门线。

3. 球鞋为高腰型，鞋头、鞋帮、两踝、后跟等外层均为硬质。前面的长鞋舌加上硬实的高腰可将腿踝箍紧，帮助运动员支持和用力。

4. 球刀原为铁托钢刃，现多采用全塑刀托，优质合金钢刀刃，具有抗击打、不易生锈等优点。

5. 守门员冰刀与运动员冰刀有较大区别，它全为金属制作，刀身矮而平，刀刃与刀托有多处连接以防漏球。

6. 为防止在紧张激烈的对抗中受伤，运动员全身穿戴护具。护具包括头盔、面罩、护肩、护胸、护腰、护身、护肘、护踝、护腿、手套、裤衩等。

7. 现代冰球护具一般多采用轻体硬质塑料外壳，内衬海绵或泡沫塑料软垫。守门员戴有特制的面罩、手套，加厚的护胸及加厚加宽的护腿。

8. 为了减轻重量，现已有碳素材料所制的球杆，在长宽不变的情况下重量减轻，更容易让选手发挥。

9. 冰球比赛的裁判人员包括两名场上裁判员、两名监门员（球门裁判员）、两名边线裁判员、一名记分员和一名计时员。两位场上裁判员共同控制整个比赛，各负责一个半场。边线裁判员主要负责当有人越位时打出信号。

10. 比赛在争球圈内开球。裁判员站在争球圈中心位置，把球落在两个相对而立的中锋之间。

第五部分　拓展阅读

伟大冰球手——格雷茨基

　　韦恩·格雷茨基，前加拿大职业冰球明星，得到 2857 分的"伟大冰球手"，全球冰球界传奇人物。14 岁时签约参加职业联赛。在美国国家冰球联盟征战了 20 个赛季，曾为埃德蒙顿炼油者冰球队、洛杉矶国王队、圣路易蓝调队和纽约巡游者冰球队效过力，至今保持美国职业冰球最高进球纪录，于 1999 年退役。格雷茨基曾任美国国家冰球联盟菲尼克斯飞人队教练，目前是凤凰城郊狼冰球队的任事股东和主教练。

第三章 雪上运动

第9课 滑雪

第一部分 听和说

活动 1

🎧 听下面的对话，然后两人一组将其表演出来。

（李第一次去滑雪，不知道该穿什么。约翰滑雪滑得很棒，所以李向他征询意见。）

A: 你的滑雪技术怎么样？

B: 还可以，自己能够独立滑行。你呢？

A: 我是第一次滑雪，都不清楚滑雪时穿戴什么呢。

B: 哦，那我告诉你要准备些什么。滑雪时要穿滑雪靴和滑雪服，戴上滑雪镜和滑雪头盔。还得有滑雪板、滑雪杖和一副手套。

A: 这么多啊！我想一定得花不少钱。全都得买吗？

B: 不用的，拐角那儿的接待处什么装备都出租。

A: 知道了。谢谢你！

B: 不必客气！

活动 2

👤 两人一组，根据以下所给情景设计对话。

情景 1：你在滑雪场接待区，向装备租借处的工作人员询问租借滑雪用品事宜。

情景 2：一个滑雪者在比赛中滑倒并受了伤，医生前来检查。

第二部分 阅读

文章 1

阅读下面这篇关于滑雪运动的文章，讨论文后的思考题。

滑雪运动

滑雪是指利用滑雪板在雪地滑行的一种体育运动。滑雪运动起源于斯堪的纳维亚国家。从历史沿革角度分类，滑雪可划分为古代滑雪、近代滑雪和现代滑雪；从滑行的条件和参与的目的，可分为实用类滑雪、竞技类滑雪和旅游类（娱乐、健身）滑雪。

实用滑雪用于林业、边防、狩猎、交通等领域。竞技滑雪是将滑雪提升为在特定的环境条件下，以比赛为目的的竞技运动，是适应现代人们生活、文化需求而发展起来的大众性滑雪。当前还出现了单板滑雪、超短板滑雪、越野滑雪等旅游滑雪。

单板滑雪是双脚同踏一只宽大的雪板。超短板滑雪更具有刺激性，技术更灵活，在中国尚未普遍开展。越野滑雪是在低山丘岭地带（平地、下坡、上坡各占约 1/3）的长距离滑行。

现代滑雪运动主要有阿尔卑斯山式、北欧式和自由式。阿尔卑斯山式滑雪由滑降运动源于阿尔卑斯山而得名，是指沿雪坡滑降的滑雪运动，包括了各式技巧和动作，其中三组最基本的动作是直降、横渡和转弯。北欧式滑雪包括了越野滑雪和跳台滑雪，其名称的由来是因为这种运动起源于北欧国家。越野滑雪是最大众化的滑雪方式。自由式滑雪其实是一种特技表演，表演者从陡峭而崎岖不平的雪坡向下滑降，同时表演后跳、踢腿，甚至翻跟头等其他惊险的空中特技。

目前，世界上正规滑雪比赛类型有：高山滑雪、北欧滑雪（越野滑雪、跳台滑雪）、自由式滑雪、冬季两项滑雪、单板滑雪等。

思考题：

1. 什么是滑雪运动？它起源于哪个国家？
2. 现代滑雪运动主要有哪几种形式？
3. 世界上正规的滑雪比赛类型主要有哪些？

文章 2

阅读下面这篇关于国际滑雪联合会的文章，讨论文后的思考题。

国际滑雪联合会

国际滑雪联合会，简称国际滑联，是冬季运动的国际最高管理机构。1924年成立，总部设在瑞士伯尔尼，现任主席是卡斯珀。工作用语为英、德、法、俄语，出现争议时，以英语为准。中国滑雪协会于 1979 年加入国际滑雪联合会。

国际滑雪联合会的任务是促进滑雪运动的发展并把握其方向，在协会会员间及各国运动员之间建立和保持友好关系，全力支持协会会员实现其目标。此外，国际滑雪联合会组织世界滑雪锦标赛、世界杯和大洲杯赛以及联合会批准的其他比赛，制定并监督规则的执行，作为终审机关处理与联合会比赛及规则有关的抗议与法律问题，促进以增进健康为目的的娱乐滑雪。国际滑雪联合会还采取各种措施，避免事故发生，保护环境。

思考题：

1. 国际滑雪联合会总部设在哪里？
2. 国际滑雪联合会的任务是什么？
3. 中国滑雪协会哪一年加入国际滑雪联合会的？

第三部分 练习

请完成以下练习。

1. 请向初学者介绍滑雪时应注意的事项。

    （提示：上雪道前，应该将髋、膝、踝、腕等多处关节活动开。先从初级道开始练习，逐渐升级到高级道。）

2. 请谈谈滑雪运动对身体的好处。

    （提示：休闲滑雪是很好的有氧运动，能增强腿部、上肢力量。滑雪的运动量较大，相当于快速游泳。）

第四部分 规则与概念

1. 跳台滑雪的比赛场地由出发区、助滑坡、过渡区一、跳台、过渡区二、着陆坡和终点区组成。

2. 越野滑雪是运动员足蹬滑雪板、手持雪杖，运用登山、滑降、转弯、滑行等技术滑行于山丘雪原的运动项目，以完成比赛的时间排定比赛名次。

3. 高山滑雪是运动员从山顶按规定线路穿过用旗插成的门形向下滑行的竞速滑雪比赛项目。技术动作有直滑降、斜滑降、乙形滑降、起伏地滑降、犁式和半犁式滑降等，身体姿势分高、中、低三种。

4. 回转滑雪比赛线路长度为：男子600～700米，女子400～500米；坡度30度以上的段落占比赛全程的四分之一。标高差为：男子140～200米，女子120～180米。男子比赛线路上插55～75个门形，女子比赛线路上插45～60个门形。

5. 大回转滑雪是快速从山上向下沿线路连续转弯、穿越各种门形的比赛。比赛线路长度为：男子1500～2000米，女子1000米以上。

6. 单板滑雪场地长936米，平均坡度18.21度，坡高290米。高度差为120～200米。

7. 单板滑雪U型池赛共有两轮预选赛，首轮预选赛前6名选手直接晋级决赛；其余选手参加第二轮预选赛，前6名选手也获得决赛权。最后12名决赛选手进行两轮比赛，根据两轮决赛中的最好成绩排定最后的名次。

8. 跳台滑雪设有70米级台和90米级台两个项目。裁判员根据比赛选手两次（飞行）姿态判分，姿态得分与距离得分相加（距离分以飞行的米数来计算），最后按得分高低排定选手名次。

9. 北欧两项是跳台滑雪和越野滑雪两个项目的体育竞技比赛。

10. 第一天先进行跳台滑雪比赛，第二天进行越野滑雪比赛。比赛规定，运动员两个单项的成绩换算为得分再计总成绩和排列名次，得分高者名次列前。

第五部分 拓展阅读

"冰雪公主"李妮娜

李妮娜，1983 年出生，辽宁本溪人，中国著名女子空中技巧滑雪运动员，素有"冰雪公主"美称。自 2004 年年底以来，她在世界杯系列赛中以稳定的发挥六次夺得分站赛冠军，是中国第一个自由式滑雪世界杯总决赛冠军，第一个获得空中技巧世界排名第一的中国滑雪运动员，第一个世界锦标赛冠军。2014 年索契冬奥会，李妮娜参加了女子自由式滑雪空中技巧这一项目，作为谢幕演出，虽然只得了第四名，但仍露出了甜美的笑容。

第 **10** 课 **有舵雪橇、无舵雪橇和俯式冰橇**

第一部分 听和说

活动 1

🎧 听下面的对话，然后三人一组将其表演出来。

（滑雪障碍赛就要开始，一组队员正互相打气。）

A: 比赛马上就要开始了，我们要力争获得冠军！

B: 信心十足，夺取冠军。一定可以的，对吧？

C: 当然！比赛中要注意雪杆的位置，记住，一定要控制好雪橇。

A: 对，就按照训练的节奏进行比赛，我们能做好的。

C: 你们看到没？刚才一名选手因为没有控制好，发生了侧翻。

B: 我们可不能那样，一定要小心。

A: 我们那么努力的训练，肯定不会发生那样的情况。

C: 相信我们是最棒的！

A/B/C: 加油！加油！加油！

活动 2

👥 两人一组，根据以下所给情景设计对话。

> 情景 1：赛场观众对运动员的精彩表现发表着评论。
>
> 情景 2：比赛中，运动员没能控制动作，出现失误且摔出赛道。

第二部分 阅读

文章 1

阅读下面这篇关于有舵雪橇、无舵雪橇和俯式冰橇运动的文章，讨论文后的思考题。

有舵雪橇、无舵雪橇和俯式冰橇

　　雪橇运动起源于瑞士白雪覆盖的山区，后传到欧洲、北美和亚洲地区。雪橇运动有三种项目类型：有舵雪橇、无舵雪橇、俯式冰橇。1884 年英国首次举行雪橇比赛。1924 年有舵雪橇成为冬奥会比赛项目，无舵雪橇比赛于 1964 年成为奥运会项目，而俯式冰橇则在 2002 年进入奥运会。此前，俯式冰橇只出现在了 1928 年和 1948 年的圣莫里茨冬奥会上。

　　有舵雪橇，又称雪车，是一种二人或四人集体乘坐雪车在冰道上滑行的运动，也是速度最快的冬季运动之一。雪车用金属制成，形如小舟，车首覆有流线型罩。舵和方向盘控制方向。车底前部是一对舵板，车底后部为一对固定平行滑，车尾装有制动器。雪车是一项极其危险的运动，有翻车危险，胆小者不能参加。

　　无舵雪橇是一项冬季运动项目，单人或双人背部平躺在平底雪橇上，双脚向前，从冰道上滑下。雪橇由木头制成，底部为金属滑板。一对平行的滑板宽不超过 45 厘米。滑板前翅允许保持一定弹性，但不得装舵和制动器。冬奥会无舵雪橇比赛分男子单人、男子双人、女子单人、接力共四个小项。

　　俯式冰橇，又称钢架雪车。尽管其能达到的最高速度略小于无舵雪橇，但选手滑行时要头朝前俯卧在雪橇上，因此从某种程度上说，选手要具备更大的勇气挑战。俯式冰橇从传统雪车项目发展而来。第一次俯式冰橇比赛在瑞士举行，赛程从圣莫里茨到塞勒里那，获胜者得到一瓶香槟作为奖品。此项目曾是 1928 年圣莫里茨冬运会的比赛项目，20 年后，冬奥会再次在这里举行，俯式冰橇也再次被列为比赛项目。之后多年未曾在冬奥会出现，直到 2002 年盐湖城冬奥会重回赛场。从这次冬奥会开始，俯式冰橇又增设女子单人小项。

思考题：

　　1. 雪橇运动分为几种形式？

　　2. 无舵雪橇由什么制成？

　　3. 无舵雪橇与俯式冰橇运动的区别是什么？

文章 2

阅读下面这篇关于国际雪车联合会的文章，讨论文后的思考题。

国际雪车联合会

国际雪车联合会，原名称为国际有舵雪橇和平底雪橇联合会，最早起源于北欧，是国际有舵雪橇和俯式冰橇的管理机构，于 1923 年 11 月 23 日成立，2015 年 6 月正式使用此名称。正式工作语言为法语、英语、德语。总部位于瑞士洛桑。

1897 年，世界上第一个雪车俱乐部成立于瑞士圣莫里茨。1904 年，雪车运动已在自然雪道上展开。这项运动的兴起促成了 1923 年国际雪车联合会的成立，次年，国际雪车联合会成为国际奥委会一员，雪车项目也列入首届冬奥会比赛项目。俯式冰橇只在 1928 年和 1948 年的圣莫里茨冬季奥运会上被列为比赛项目，但直到 2002 年盐湖城冬季奥运会，这项比赛才又重新回归奥运赛场上。女性曾被允许参加早期的五人雪橇项目，但直到 1998 年，国际雪车联合会才正式批准女子雪橇运动为各大赛事的项目之一。2000 年，女子雪橇世界锦标赛首次举办；2002 年，女子雪橇成为冬奥会正式项目。

目前，国际雪车联合会管辖下列项目的比赛：奥运会有舵雪橇比赛、有舵雪橇世界杯赛、国际雪车联合会世界锦标赛、奥运会俯式冰橇比赛等。

思考题：

1. 国际雪车联合会何时成立？
2. 国际雪车联合会下辖的比赛有哪些？

第三部分 练习

请完成以下练习。

1. 简单介绍有舵雪橇、无舵雪橇和俯式冰橇在起源、发展、赛事规则等方面的区别。
2. 观看一场雪橇比赛，然后写一篇不少于 200 词的观赛感想。

第四部分 规则与概念

1. 雪车滑道全长 1500 米，平均坡度为 4° 30′，最大坡度为 8° 30′。弯道部分半径 20 米以上，滑道的护墙最少不得低于 50 厘米。

2. 有舵雪橇的滑道以混凝土或木材建成，宽度为 1.4 米，两侧均为护墙，护墙内侧高 1.4 米，外侧高 2 ~ 7 米。

3. 雪橇滑降比赛起点和终点间的标高差，男子为 700 ~ 1000 米，女子为 400 ~ 700 米。

4. 比赛线路中不得有石头、木板或树根等障碍物。如线路在树林中通过时，其宽度不得少于 20 米。线路应平坦，不得有突起物或上坡部分。

5. 大回转的起点和终点间的标高差，男子为 400 米，女子为 300 米。线路宽不得小于 20 米，旗门不得少于 31 组，旗门间隔最少 6 米。

6. 雪橇运动员服装包括比赛服、护肩、护肘、头盔和专用钉靴。

7. 靴钉为刷型并均匀分布于靴底。靴钉的长度不超过 14 毫米，间隔不超过 3 厘米。

8. 俯式冰橇比赛使用同有舵雪橇规格相同的滑道，但是运动员需俯身躺在钢架雪车上，头在前，脚在后。比赛使用的俯式冰橇重量，男子不超过 43 千克，女子不超过 35 千克；雪橇和运动员总重，男子不超过 115 千克，女子不超过 92 千克。

9. 选手不得加热雪板使其跑得更快。选手在比赛前将雪车送到起点放置一个小时，到比赛时雪板温度与送来时的温度差不能超过四度。

10. 无舵雪橇比赛中途允许选手掉落雪车。但是通过终点时，选手必须在雪车上，比赛成绩才算有效。

第五部分 拓展阅读

阿尔明·佐格勒

　　阿尔明·佐格勒，1974 年出生，意大利无舵雪橇运动员。由于他在准备比赛时冷静、理性且一丝不苟，他被其他运动员称为"冷血冠军"。从利勒哈默尔，到长野、盐湖城、都灵、温哥华，再到 2014 年的索契，每一届冬奥会的领奖台都给佐格勒留了一个位置。佐格勒连续六次参加冬奥运，共获得 6 枚冬奥会奖牌，其中金牌 2 枚。此外，他还获得了 16 枚世界无舵雪橇锦标赛奖牌。2014 年索契冬季奥运会，年满 40 岁的佐格勒是意大利代表团开幕式旗手、男子无舵雪橇单人铜牌获得者。凭借着这枚铜牌，他站在了和 20 年前相同的位置上，成为冬奥会历史上第一位在同一项目上连续六届获得奖牌的运动员。

第 **11** 课 现代冬季两项

第一部分 听和说

活动 1

🎧 听下面的对话，然后两人一组将其表演出来。

（参加现代冬季两项比赛之前，彼得发现做蹲起的时候大腿很疼，且无力。现在医生正在给他做检查。）

A: 你好，李医生！

B: 你好，彼得！怎么了？

A: 我感觉大腿拉伤了。

B: 我来看看。这儿疼吗？

A: 用力的时候稍微有些疼。

B: 做蹲起时，这里疼吗？

A: 疼，并且使不上劲儿。

B: 我知道了，你的大腿肌肉拉伤了，我给你一些喷雾，之后你要休息一两天。

A: 今天的比赛我还能参加吗？

B: 开玩笑，当然不能参加了。

A: 天啊！

活动 2

👥 两人一组，根据以下所给情景设计对话。

> ○ 情景 1：假设你是一个冬季两项比赛运动员，分享一下你开始练习冬季
> ○ 两项的故事。
> ○ 情景 2：最近你很疲惫，因此希望跟教练请假休息一下。

第二部分 阅读

文章 1

阅读下面这篇关于现代冬季两项运动的文章，讨论文后的思考题。

现代冬季两项

现代冬季两项是越野滑雪和射击相结合的运动。运动员身背步枪，每滑行一段距离进行一次射击，最先到达终点者即获胜。现代冬季两项运动起源于斯堪的纳维亚半岛，由远古时代的滑雪狩猎演变而来。在挪威曾发现大约 4000 年前两人足蹬雪板、手持棍棒追捕野兽的石雕。中世纪开始这项运动逐渐纳入军事训练科目。

1767 年，挪威边防军滑雪巡逻队举行了滑雪射击比赛，据记载，这是世界上最早的现代冬季两项比赛。1912 年，挪威军队在奥斯陆举行名为"为了战争"的滑雪射击比赛；这项比赛后逐渐在欧美国家开展，成为一种体育运动项目。1924 年被列为首届冬奥会表演项目；1958 年第一届世界现代冬季两项锦标赛举行；1960 年正式列入冬奥会比赛项目，并定名为"现代冬季两项"；1992 年冬奥会增设女子项目。

现代冬季两项比赛项目包括个人赛、短距离赛、追逐赛、接力赛，集体出发等。滑行路线设在丘陵起伏地区，运动员依一定的时间间隔单个出发，以滑冰方式按圈道竞速滑行；比赛有时间限制，每隔一定时间选手需射击一次。射击时，交替采用立射和卧射两种方式。脱靶会有惩罚：个人赛中，脱靶一次在选手最终成绩上加一分钟时间；其他比赛中，选手脱靶一次将被加罚滑行一个 150 米长的圈道。比赛项目不同，赛程和射击次数也不同。

思考题：

1. 请用你的语言阐述现代冬季两项运动的起源与发展。

2. 现代冬季两项是哪一年列入冬季奥运会正式比赛项目的？

3. 你能列举出现代冬季两项的比赛项目吗？

文章 2

阅读下面这篇关于国际冬季两项联盟的文章，讨论文后的思考题。

国际冬季两项联盟

国际冬季两项联盟为冬季两项运动的国际管理组织，总部位于奥地利萨尔斯堡，现任主席是挪威人维森伯格。

国际冬季两项联盟成立于 1993 年，是国际现代五项和冬季两项联盟（UIPMB）下辖的独立组织，与国际现代五项总会（UIPM）并行。1993 年 7 月 2 日，UIPMB 召开会议，将 1953 年就加入的冬季两项独立出来，成立国际冬季两项联盟，以期设立独立的联盟机构。会议同时选出了执行委员会，有 57 名联盟成员由 UIPMB 转至国际冬季两项联盟。同年 12 月 12 日，国际冬季两项联盟在奥地利萨尔斯堡成立。1998 年，国际冬季两项联盟正式与 UIPMB 分开；同年 8 月，国际单项体育联合会总会也认可其成为冬季奥运联盟成员之一。1999 年 6 月 1 日，国际冬季两项联盟正式在奥地利萨尔斯堡注册成立。

国际冬季两项联盟组织的赛事有：冬奥会冬季两项比赛、现代冬季两项世界锦标赛（男子 / 女子）、现代冬季两项世界杯、现代冬季两项欧洲杯、现代冬季两项青年世界锦标赛。

思考题：

1. 国际冬季两项联盟总部设在哪个城市？
2. 冬季两项联盟如何独立出来的？
3. 你能否列举出国际冬季两项联盟组织的赛事？

第三部分 练习

请完成以下练习。

1. 你认为现代冬季两项的运动员需要具备怎样的能力和素质？
2. 根据现代冬季两项的起源和发展谈谈你对这一运动的感受。

第四部分 规则与概念

1. 射击目标为黑色。射击后，目标前的白色闸门会关上，用来识别击中与否。

2. 在转播中也多以白色表示命中的目标，黑色表示未命中的目标。

3. 射击目标距离为 50 米远，目标分为内圈和外圈。

4. 卧射时目标直径为 45 毫米（内圈），立射时直径为 110 毫米（外圈）。

5. 开始区随不同赛事类型会调整成不同大小，但场地至少可容纳 30 人（集体出发赛的人数）。

6. 惩罚赛道为 150 米长的椭圆形水平赛道，没有上坡或下坡。

7. 运动员滑行时需全程背着步枪，枪口向上并不可装有子弹。只能在进入射击位置后才能装上子弹。

8. 比赛时，运动员要脚穿滑雪板，手持滑雪杖，携带枪支，沿标记的滑道，按正确的方向和顺序滑完预定的全程。

9. 个人赛采用单人出发，间隔时间为 30 秒或 60 秒。

10. 个人赛每次 5 发子弹，接力赛每人每次 8 发子弹。

第五部分 拓展阅读

冬季两项之王

奥利·埃纳尔·比约达伦，1974 年出生，挪威人，冬季两项运动员，人们称他为"冬季两项之王"。他是冬季两项世界锦标赛上最成功的运动员，共获得 40 枚奖牌，包括 19 枚金牌，是其他选手夺得奖牌数的两倍之多。在冬奥会历史上，他也是冬季两项项目获得奖牌最多的选手，共 13 枚，其中 8 金 4 银 1 铜。他本人也是冬季两项世界杯分站赛冠军的纪录保持者，一共赢得 95 场胜利，迄今为止无人能与之匹敌。

重竞技及其他项目

第 12 课 跆拳道

第一部分 听和说

活动 1

🎧 听下面的对话，然后两人一组将其表演出来。

（约翰想加入跆拳道社，但因为不是很清楚加入跆拳道社需要什么条件，所以有些犹豫。教练向他解释了跆拳道精神，说服他跆拳道社值得加入。）

A: 我想加入跆拳道社，但是不确定它是否像我想的那样。您能多跟我讲讲跆拳道吗？

B: 大部分人觉得跆拳道跟别的武术一样，就是用来打架的，事实上可不仅如此。

A: 我知道毅力和自制力是其中必须的，还有什么别的吗？

B: 真正的跆拳道精神是礼和诚。

A: 礼？这我可是第一次听说。

B: 是的，跆拳道教人知礼。其训练始于礼、终于礼，礼仪贯穿跆拳道练习的始终。

A: 听起来每个人都应该这么做啊。我决心要成为跆拳道社的一员。我能加入么？

B: 当然了！

活动 2

👥 两人一组，回答下列问题。

> 问题 1：在跆拳道比赛中，裁判员经常使用下列单词，你知道他们是
> 什么意思吗？"Chung"，"Hong"，"Cha-ryeot"，"Kyeong-rye"，
> "Joon-bi"，"Shi-jak"，"Keu-man"，"Kyong-go"，"Gam-jeom"，

"Shi-gan"，"Kye-sok"，"Kal-yeo"和"Ha-nal, Duhl, Seht, Neht, Da-seot, Yeo-seot, II-gop, Yeo-dul, A-hop, Yeol"。

［提示："Chung"（青）、"Hong"（红）、"Cha-ryeot"（立正）、"Kyeong-rye"（敬礼）、"Joon-bi"（准备）、"Shi-jak"（开始）、"Keu-man"（停）、"Kyong-go"（警告）、"Gam-jeom"（扣分）、"Shi-gan"（暂停／计时）、"Kye-sok"（继续）、"Kal-yeo"（分开）、"Ha-nal, Duhl, Seht, Neht, Da-seot, Yeo-seot, II-gop, Yeo-dul, A-hop, Yeol"（读秒 1～10）。］

问题 2： 跆拳道比赛中，如果运动员出现抓、推、背对对方，或假装受伤等行为时被判"警告"；如果出现扔对手或在格斗中在对手双脚离地时故意将其放倒，或故意攻击对手后背或脸部行为时被判"扣分"。这两种犯规行为分别判罚几分？

第二部分 阅读

文章 1

阅读下面这篇关于跆拳道运动的文章，讨论文后的思考题。

跆拳道

跆拳道是现代奥运会正式比赛项目之一，是一种主要使用手及脚进行格斗或对抗的运动。与大多数武术相比，跆拳道更注重腿踢和拳击。跆拳道起源于朝鲜半岛，早期是由朝鲜三国时代的跆跟、花郎道演化而来的，是韩国民间较普遍流行的一项技击术。"跆拳道"一词于 1955 年由韩国的崔泓熙先生创造，被韩国视为国技。

"跆"（TAE），意为以腿踢；"拳"（KWON），以拳头打击；"道"（DO），则是代表道行、礼仪修炼的艺术。跆拳道是受东亚文化影响下发展的一项韩国武术，以"始于礼、终于礼"的武道精神为基础。尽管跆拳道竞技者也会用手，但 70% 还是靠腿踢。跆拳道比赛主要有竞技、击破、品势、自卫。奥运会跆拳道比赛只采用竞技。跆拳道的套路共有 24 套，另外还有兵器、擒拿、摔锁、对拆自卫术及十余种基本功夫等。

跆拳道目前在全世界有两个体系：一个是在朝鲜和北美普及和发展的国际

跆拳道联盟（ITF），套路复杂多变；另一个是在韩国和世界其他地区普及和发展的世界跆拳道联盟（WTF），技术动作华丽，突出腿法的灵活运用，要求选手穿着相当完备的护具。奥运会采用的是 WTF 体系。

思考题：

1. 跆拳道的突出特点是什么？
2. "跆拳道"三个字分别代表什么含义？
3. 目前世界上的两大跆拳道流派是什么？

文章 2

阅读下面这篇关于世界跆拳道组织的文章，讨论文后的思考题。

世界跆拳道组织

国际跆拳道联盟（ITF），1966 年由韩国人崔泓熙先生在韩国首尔创立。朝鲜是目前世界上 ITF 跆拳道发展最好的国家。国际跆拳道联盟举办的重要赛事包括跆拳道世界锦标赛和世界杯，比赛项目有品势、竞技、特技、威力击破、预约团体竞技。此外，在全世界范围内举行的跆拳道其他赛事还有：青少年和中老年 ITF 世界跆拳道锦标赛、崔泓熙将军纪念杯赛、ITF 洲际锦标赛、ITF 公开赛等。

世界跆拳道联盟（WTF）于 1972 年在首尔成立，于 1980 年通过国际奥委会认证，如今已有 200 多个成员国。世界跆拳道联盟主办的重要赛事有：世界跆拳道锦标赛、世界青年跆拳道锦标赛、世界跆拳道品势锦标赛、世界跆拳道大奖赛等。世界跆拳道联盟认为，跆拳道是最系统、最科学的韩国传统武术之一，它传授的不仅仅是身体对抗技巧。通过身体和思想训练，跆拳道展示了它是如何强大人们精神和生活的。

思考题：

1. 国际跆拳道联盟的创立者是谁？
2. 世界跆拳道联盟主办了哪些赛事？
3. 世界跆拳道联盟认为练习跆拳道的益处有哪些？

第三部分 练习

请完成以下练习。

1. 一名跆拳道选手在比赛中输了，他一气之下把头盔摔在地上。世界跆拳道联盟对他处以终身禁赛的惩罚，将他永远逐出跆拳道界。请结合这个案例，以"武道精神"为题撰写一篇不少于250词的短文。

2. 请谈谈跆拳道礼仪与中国传统文化之间的关系。

第四部分 规则与概念

1. 比赛场区为水平、无障碍物、8米×8米的正方形场地。

2. 比赛台应高于地面0.6～1米，比赛台场地边界线外应有与地面夹角小于30度的斜坡。

3. 比赛时，运动员穿道服，系腰带，戴上头盔用以保护头部，并且穿上护甲、护腿等护具。

4. 护甲的颜色是红色或蓝色。护甲要穿在道服外面，头盔的颜色要与护甲的颜色一致。其他保护装备包括穿在道服里面的护裆、护臂和护腿。

5. 比赛允许运动员使用拳和腿的技术攻击对手的合法部位：一是头部，二是躯干。

6. 运动员只能攻击对手被护具包裹的锁骨以下、髋骨以上的躯干部位和锁骨以上的头部，禁止攻击对手后脑部位。

7. 击中躯干计1分；旋转踢技术击中躯干计2分；击中头部计3分（主裁判员读秒不追加分）；旋转踢技术击中头部计4分。

8. 一方运动员每被判两次"警告"或一次"扣分"，另一方运动员得1分。

9. 获胜方式包括以下几种：击倒胜；比分高胜；分差优势大胜；加时赛先得分胜；优势判定胜；对方弃权胜；对方失去资格获胜；主裁判员判罚犯规胜。

10. 特定比赛中，按照称重记录，体重轻者获胜。

第五部分　拓展阅读

跆拳道界的传奇人物——陈中

陈中，1982 年出生，中国女子跆拳道运动员，2000 年悉尼奥运会、2001 年世界杯、2004 年雅典奥运会和 2007 年北京世锦赛冠军，实现了奥运会、世锦赛和世界杯冠军的"大满贯"。2000 年 9 月 30 日，悉尼奥运会女子跆拳道 67 公斤以上级比赛，18 岁的陈中为中国赢得了第一枚也是世界跆拳道史上的第一枚奥运金牌。跆拳道于 1994 年被正式列为 2000 年奥运会比赛项目。中国在 1995 年组建跆拳道国家队，当时国外人士断言中国要获得这一项目的奥运金牌至少需要十年，陈中的夺冠把这个进程整整缩短了五年。陈中对自己充满信心，她说："我在这个级别可以说没有对手，对手只有我自己。"

第 13 课 举重

第一部分 听和说

活动 1

🎧 听下面的对话，然后两人一组将其表演出来。

（约翰大伤初愈，他想要尽快恢复到从前的身体水平。教练正说服他冷静下来，一步一步恢复。）

A: 教练，我热身做好了，可以开始练习了吧?

B: 可以。

A: 我感觉成绩恢复得太慢了。

B: 万事开头难，你的伤刚刚痊愈，恢复成绩需要一段时间，不要着急。

A: 我很担心能不能回到巅峰水平。以前抓举成绩很好的，但是受伤之后，我好像一点信心都没了。

B: 有压力才有动力，静下心来，集中精力做好训练，一步一个脚印重新开始。

A: 知道了，请教练放心，我会努力训练。

B: 你可以的，我相信你，加油!

活动 2

👥 两人一组，回答下列问题。

> 问题 1: "举重比赛"——打一成语。
>
> （提示:"斤斤计较"）
>
> 问题 2: 你知道奥运会举重比赛时杠铃片的重量和颜色吗？
>
> （提示: 25 千克—红色、20 千克—蓝色、15 千克—黄色、10 千克—绿色、5 千克—白色、2.5 千克—红色、2 千克—蓝色、1.5 千克—黄色、1 千克—绿色、0.5 千克—白色。）

第二部分　阅读

文章 1

阅读下面这篇关于举重运动的文章，讨论文后的思考题。

举重

举重是一项竞技奥林匹克运动，力量是其唯一的特点。举重比赛中，运动员以双手将杠铃举过头顶，举起的杠铃重量最大者即为胜。举重运动始于 18 世纪欧洲。最初杠铃两端是金属球，重量不能调整，比赛以举起某一重量的次数决胜负。后来，意大利人阿蒂拉将金属球掏空，通过往球内添加铁或铅块调整质量。1910 年，伯格将金属球改成重量不同、大小不一的金属片。1891 年在英国伦敦举行了首届世界举重锦标赛。奥运会举重比赛，男子项目始于 1896 年雅典奥运会，女子项目于 2000 年悉尼奥运会开始。

举重动作分抓举与挺举。抓举要求选手以一次连续动作将杠铃抓起并举过头顶。挺举较为宽松，选手需要先将杠铃置于双肩之上，依靠腿部力量使身体直立，然后再把杠铃举过头顶。

思考题：

　　1. 你能用自己的话简要描述举重运动的发展历程吗？

　　2. 举重动作分哪两种？

文章 2

阅读下面这篇关于国际举重联合会的文章，讨论文后的思考题。

国际举重联合会

国际举重联合会（简称国际举联），1905 年由法国倡议成立，现有协会会员 188 个，现任主席匈牙利人塔马斯·阿贾恩。国际举联的任务是组织和发展举重运动，制定举重规则，管理国际比赛，监督洲际和地区联合会的活动并协助国家和地区协会发展举重项目。国际举联设有技术、教练与研究、医务共三个专门委员会。国际举联的经费来自协会会员的会费、比赛电视转播费以及国际比赛组织者上缴的费用。该组织出版《国际举联公报》，每月一期，内容包括国际比赛、世界锦标赛、比赛规则和章程、会员地址的变更、代表大会和会议的报道等。

国际举联组织的赛事主要是世界锦标赛、世界青年锦标赛和奥运会举重比赛等。中国于 1936 年申请加入国际举联，1955 年得到国际举联的认可，1958 年退出，1974 年 9 月恢复在国际举联的会员资格。

思考题：

1. 国际举联成立于何年？现任主席是谁？
2. 国际举联组织的重要国际赛事有哪些？

第三部分 练习

请完成以下练习。

1. 观看一场举重比赛，谈谈抓举和挺举有什么不同？
2. 举重比赛亮白灯表示试举成功，亮红灯表示试举失败。当三名裁判员中的其中两位亮起白灯时，表示试举成功还是失败呢？

第四部分 规则与概念

1. 举重台为正方形，边长 4 米，由木头、塑料或质地坚实的材料制成，表面覆盖防滑材料。举重台不高于 15 厘米，周围 1 米内不得放置任何物品，包括杠铃。大台最小尺寸为 10 米 × 10 米。

2. 举重竞赛按运动员体重进行分级：青年和成年男子有 8 个级别：56 公斤级、62 公斤级、69 公斤级、77 公斤级、85 公斤级、94 公斤级、105 公斤级和 105 公斤以上级。

3. 青年和成年女子有 7 个级别：48 公斤级、53 公斤级、58 公斤级、63 公斤级、69 公斤级、75 公斤级、75 公斤以上级。

4. 赛前 2 小时运动员称量体重，时长为 1 小时。

5. 比赛先进行抓举，休息 10 分钟再进行挺举；抓举、挺举的试举次数均为 3 次，共计 6 次试举机会。

6. 上场顺序是根据运动员所要的杠铃重量、事先抽签顺序和试举过的次数来排定的。

7. 试举时所要重量轻的先举。如果第一次试举重量相同，抽签号小的先举。如果第二、三次试举重量相同，试举次数少的先举。如果试举次数也一样，则上次先举的仍先举。

8. 比赛场上的杠铃重量只能增加不能减少。每次试举成功后，必须增加 1 公斤的倍数。

9. 奥运会比赛是以抓举和挺举之和的总成绩来确定名次的。如总成绩相同，体重轻的名次列前。如体重又一样，那么先完成总成绩的名次列前。举重比赛不允许并列名次。

10. 运动员的每次试举时间规定为 1 分钟。从点到运动员名字到场上加重员加重结束，以两项分别结束的时间为准计时。如某个运动员连续试举，则时间限为 2 分钟，在此时间内杠铃没有提过膝部即判为失败。

第五部分 拓展阅读

占旭刚

　　占旭刚，1974 年出生，浙江省衢州市开化县人，中国著名男子举重运动员，中国奥运史上连续两次获得举重冠军的第一人。占旭刚生性直率又非常喜爱举重运动，10 岁开始练习举重，20 岁入选国家队，70 公斤级项目上达到世界超一流水平。1996 年亚特兰大奥运会上，夺得 3 项冠军，破 3 项世界纪录，达到运动生涯巅峰。2000 年悉尼奥运会，他在抓举 160 公斤排名第四的不利情况下，奇迹般地挺起了 207.5 公斤这个从来没有举起过的重量，以总成绩 367.5 公斤与希腊选手穆特鲁持平，最终凭借体重轻又一次蝉联这一项目的奥运冠军。

第 **14** 课 柔道

第一部分 听和说

活动 1

🎧 听下面的对话，然后两人一组将其表演出来。

（柔道比赛就要开始。彼得十分紧张，需要教练的指导。教练指导他如何平复心情。）

A: 教练，我有点紧张。

B: 别担心，放轻松，你已经进步很多了。

A: 我现在感觉脑子一片空白。

B: 放轻松，我相信你可以的，你也要相信自己。

A: 怎么做呢？

B: 听我说，深呼吸，闭上眼睛，告诉自己，我可以。

A: 好。我努力保持镇静。

B: 加油！你是最棒的！让我们看看你的本事！

A: 我觉得好多了。谢谢你，教练。

活动 2

👤 两人一组，回答下列问题。

> 问题 1： 你知道 2012 年伦敦奥运会上设置了哪几个级别的柔道比赛吗？
>
> 问题 2： 你知道柔道和空手道有哪些相同和不同之处吗？

213

第二部分 阅读

文章 1

阅读下面这篇关于柔道运动的文章，讨论文后的思考题。

柔道

柔道是一种以摔法和地面技为主的现代格斗术，它是一种对抗性很强的竞技运动，强调选手对技巧掌握的娴熟程度，而非力量的对比。比赛时要求选手对对手的四肢、脖子做出"锁臂""扼颈"等动作以使对手屈服；选手需将对手扔倒或压制在地直到对手认输，或清楚地将对手扔倒在地，方可取得胜利。柔道是奥运会比赛中唯一一个允许使用窒息或扭脱关节等手段制服对手的项目。

柔道运动由日本柔术演变发展而来。1882 年，嘉纳治五郎先生综合当时各派柔术的精华，创立了以投技、固技、当身技为主的现代柔道，同时创建了训练柔道运动员的讲道馆。"柔道"一词，即是由"日本讲道馆柔道"简化而来。柔道成形于 20 世纪初，20 世纪 50 年代成为世界性体育竞技项目。嘉纳治五郎于 1939 年逝世，讲道馆的后继者主动进行改革，如对体重分级、胜负方式重新判定等，使柔道成为世界范围内被广泛接受的运动竞赛项目。男、女柔道分别在 1964 年第十八届奥运会和 1992 年第二十五届奥运会上被列为正式比赛项目。

思考题:

1. 如何判定一场柔道比赛的胜负？
2. 你能阐述柔道运动的演变发展过程吗？
3. 男、女柔道分别在第几届奥运会被列为正式比赛项目的？

文章 2

阅读下面这篇关于国际柔道联合会的文章，讨论文后的思考题。

国际柔道联合会

国际柔道联合会，简称国际柔联，成立于 1951 年，总部位于日本，秘书处设在韩国，现任主席马瑞斯·委泽。现有会员 220 个，分属五个大洲联合会，分别是：非洲柔道联合会、泛美柔道联合会、亚洲柔道联合会、欧洲柔道联合会、大洋洲柔道联合会。每个柔道联合会下属若干个会员协会。俄罗斯总统普京是国际柔联的荣誉主席，于 2012 年 10 月 10 日被国际柔道联合会授予柔道八段，成为柔道运动的最佳形象大使。

国际柔联负责组织国际赛事，举办世界柔道锦标赛，管理奥运会柔道比赛项目。自 2009 年来，国际柔联每年组织的赛事有：世界柔道锦标赛、国际柔道大奖赛、国际柔道大满贯赛、国际柔道大师赛以及洲际公开赛。

思考题:

1. 你知道谁是国际柔联的荣誉主席和最佳形象大使吗？
2. 国际柔联主要组织哪些重要的国际赛事？

第三部分 练习

请完成以下练习。

1. 查阅资料，阐述柔道段位制的设立方法。
2. 观看青少年柔道训练，设计针对家长和孩子的采访问题。比如，可以问问他们对柔道运动的看法和感受。

第四部分 规则与概念

1. 比赛场地分比赛区和安全区，用榻榻米或类似榻榻米的合适材料铺设，通常为绿色。
2. 运动员穿蓝色或白色柔道服。上衣长度盖住大腿，上衣左襟压右襟。腰部系 4 ~ 5 厘米宽的腰带，腰带颜色代表运动员的段位。
3. 一场正式比赛时间为男子 5 分钟，女子 4 分钟。比赛设三名裁判员，主裁判在场上组织运动员进行比赛，评定技术，指示得分，宣布胜负。相对两角各有一名裁判，确保比赛在规定场地内进行。
4. 柔道比赛中，有三种方式得分：一本、技有、有效。
5. 一本：压制住对手，在满足"强有力""迅速""对手背部大部分面积触地"三个条件下以相当的力量和速度把对手扔出去的时候算一本。对手用手或脚拍打垫子或拍打对方身体两次或两次以上，或喊"我认输"算一本。用压技将对手压制 25 秒时也算是一本。

6. 技有：使用投技压制住对手，在判定一本的三个条件中有一项不足的时候算技有。或者使用压技压制对手 20 ～ 25 秒的情况也算是技有。两次技有相当于一次一本。

7. 有效：压制住对手，强有力且迅速地将对手扔出去，判定一本的三个条件中有两项不足的时候算有效。或者使用压技压制对手 15 ～ 20 秒的情况也算是有效。此外，当比赛一方受到第二个"指导"的处罚时，另一方获得一个"有效"得分。

8. 指导：使用标准以外的技巧，或者走出比赛场地等，情节较轻的犯规行为会受到"指导"的责罚。根据受到"指导"的次数，给对手加分。第四次"指导"直接导致选手犯规出局。

9. 犯规出局：把对手的脚从内侧拉伸（反关节动作）、抓住其头部撞击地面等存在严重危险性的犯规行为时所给予的惩罚，直接给予对手"一本"的分数。

10. 若比赛最后两名运动员得分相同，则进行加时赛，以黄金得分法则为准，先得分的运动员即获得胜利。

第五部分　拓展阅读

柔道女王——桂顺姬

　　桂顺姬，1979 年生于平壤，朝鲜著名柔道运动员。她作风顽强，技术高超，往往能在很短时间内以"一本"战胜对手，被誉为"柔道女王"。1996 年亚特兰大奥运会获得 48 公斤级金牌，是奥运会有史以来最年轻的柔道冠军；2000 年悉尼奥运会拿到 52 公斤级铜牌；2004 年雅典奥运会获得 57 公斤级的银牌；2001 年、2003 年、2005 年、2007 年世界柔道锦标赛冠军。她对柔道运动做出了巨大贡献，被授予"劳动英雄"的称号。

第 15 课 摔跤

第一部分　听和说

活动 1

🎧 听下面的对话，然后两人一组将其表演出来。

（彼得邀请约翰去看摔跤比赛。他们正在约定见面的时间和地点。）

A: 你看过摔跤比赛吗？我这里有两张票，要一起去看吗？

B: 好啊，只在电视上看过，很想去看。

A: 那正好啊！一起去看吧。比赛在首都体育学院体育馆举行。

B: 我不知道在哪里，要不先见面再一起去吧？

A: 好的，那坐 123 路公交车到蓟门桥西站吧。我在那里等你。

B: 几点到那儿呢？

A: 比赛七点开始，那我们六点半见面吧。

B: 知道了，那晚上见。

活动 2

👥 两人一组，回答下列问题。

问题 1：摔跤的比赛形式有哪些？

问题 2：你更喜欢看哪项比赛？跆拳道、柔道，还是摔跤？为什么？

第二部分　阅读

文章 1

阅读下面这篇关于摔跤运动的文章，讨论文后的思考题。

摔跤

　　摔跤是一项运用多种技能、技巧、方法将对手摔倒在地的竞技运动。摔跤是世界上最古老的武术之一，历史悠久。在希腊、埃及、中国和日本的文字记载中，摔跤运动在这些国家占据显著地位。现代摔跤运动起源于希腊，在古代奥林匹克运动会上，摔跤比赛野蛮凶残，是最受瞩目的运动。

　　目前国际摔跤比赛形式有古典式和自由式两种，比赛时按体重分级进行。古典式摔跤禁止抱握对手腰以下部位、做绊腿动作以及主动用腿。相反，自由式摔跤允许运动员借助自己或对手的腿进行攻击或防御。

　　古典式摔跤在 1896 年首届现代奥林匹克运动会上就被列为比赛项目。自 1908 年起，摔跤成为夏季奥运会的常设项目。自由式摔跤则是在 1904 年被正式列为奥运会比赛项目。2004 年的夏季奥运会增加了女子摔跤项目。摔跤选手不但出现在奥运会赛场，还征战在各类大型搏击比赛中，如终极格斗冠军赛(UFC)、战极、Strike Force 等比赛。

思考题：

　　1. 你能用自己的语言描述摔跤这一运动吗？
　　2. 古典式摔跤和自由式摔跤的区别是什么？

文章 2

阅读下面这篇关于国际摔跤联合会的文章，讨论文后的思考题。

国际摔跤联合会

　　国际摔跤联合会，简称国际摔联，是业余摔跤运动的国际主管机构。前身是国际摔跤项目联合会，1912 年成立于比利时安特卫普，2014 年 9 月更为现名。国际摔联的职责是制定比赛规则和章程，举办各种国际摔跤项目比赛：古典式摔跤、男子和女子自由式摔跤，以及其他形式的摔跤比赛。世界摔跤锦标赛是国际摔联主办的标志性赛事。

国际摔联负责监督奥运会摔跤项目。此外，还负责许多其他国际赛事，如：英联邦运动会、泛美运动会、洲际锦标赛、洲际杯赛等。摔跤比赛按体重分级：48 公斤级、52 公斤级、57 公斤级、62 公斤级、68 公斤、74 公斤级、82 公斤级、90 公斤级、100 公斤以上级。奥运会比赛也采用此分级标准。

中国于 1954 年加入国际摔联，1958 年退出，1979 年恢复会籍。

思考题：

1. 国际摔联的职责是什么？

2. 国际摔联举办的主要赛事有哪些？

第三部分 练习

请完成以下练习。

1. 简述中国式摔跤的运动特点。

2. 2013 年 2 月，国际奥委会投票取消即将举办的 2020 年夏季奥运会摔跤比赛。然而，同年 9 月 8 日，国际奥委会又宣布摔跤比赛重回 2020 年夏季奥运会赛场。了解这一事件的背景信息，对其原因加以分析，写一篇不少于 250 词的文章。

第四部分 规则与概念

1. 奥运会的摔跤比赛有两种不同的项目：古典式摔跤和自由式摔跤。

2. 在摔跤比赛中，"倒地"记作得分。

3. 古典式摔跤采用站立抓抱，选手不能用腿绊对手或抓握对手腰带以下的部位。

4. 自由式摔跤采用多种俯卧抓抱法，比古典式摔跤更自由，但也有一定的限制。

5. 自由式摔跤中，脚踢和掐脖子是犯规动作，而绊倒对方和抱腿摔是许可的。

6. 各级别比赛前一天，运动员称量体重，时间持续 30 分钟。离开磅称时，运动员抽签号，并依此为基础编排配对。

7. 如果有一名或数名运动员未参加称量体重或者体重超重，称量结束后，依据从小号到大号的原则重新排列运动员的序号。

8. 依据运动员所抽的签号进行分组配对。按抽签的顺序，如：1 对 2，3 对 4，5 对 6，依次进行配对。

9. 比赛按参赛的人数分两大组进行淘汰赛，直到各组产生最后一名获胜者，他们将进行冠亚军的决赛。

10. 在比赛中，除负于两名参加决赛的运动员参加争夺第三至第八名的复活赛外，其他比赛中的负方将被淘汰，其最终名次将根据比赛所获名次排列。

第五部分　拓展阅读

亚历山大·卡列林

亚历山大·卡列林，1967 年出生于苏联的西伯利亚，哲学博士，是公认的现代最伟大的古典式摔跤手，被称作"俄国熊"。他共参加了 887 场古典式摔跤比赛，仅输过两场，是现代奥运会历史上唯一一名连续三届奥运会男子 130 公斤古典式摔跤冠军获得者，在世锦赛和欧锦赛中分别夺得 9 枚和 12 枚金牌。2000 年奥运会结束后正式退役。2001 年，国际奥委会主席萨马兰奇为卡列林颁发了奥林匹克勋章。

第 16 课 自行车

第一部分 听和说

活动 1

🎧 听下面的对话，然后两人一组将其表演出来。

（小轮车赛已经开始检录，蒂姆的计时块出现了设置失误，裁判正在帮他修正。）

A: 请注意！请参加自行车越野拉力赛的运动员到检录处检录。

B: 裁判，我的计时块安装正确吗？

C: 不对。计时块必须按照比赛须知进行安装。

B: 裁判，是这样吗？

C: 正确。

B: 裁判，衣服两侧都需要贴上号码布吗？

C: 是的，必须按照要求着装并在胸前和后背佩戴号码布。

B: 好的，谢谢！

活动 2

👥 两人一组，回答下列问题。

问题 1: 比赛前运动员的自行车需要接受检查，如果不合格，如何处理？

问题 2: 比赛中运动员伤势比较严重，是否必须要退出比赛，接受治疗呢？

第二部分 阅读

文章 1

阅读下面这篇关于自行车运动的文章，讨论文后的思考题。

自行车运动

自行车，又称脚踏车或单车，通常是两轮的小型陆上车辆。自行车运动是指以自行车为工具而比赛骑行速度的体育运动。自行车比赛于 1896 年被列为奥运会比赛项目。目前自行车比赛主要包括场地自行车赛、公路自行车赛、山地自行车赛和小轮车赛。

场地自行车赛在赛车场进行。赛车场为封闭的椭圆跑道，跑道周长 250 米，跑道宽 5 ~ 9 米，弯道坡度 25 ~ 45 度。比赛采用的自行车为死飞轮，不得安装变速装置和刹车。除 1912 年外，场地自行车赛一直是现代奥运会的比赛项目。

公路自行车比赛始于 19 世纪的欧洲。最早的自行车赛于 1868 年 5 月 31 日在巴黎的圣克劳德公园举行，世界首次女子自行车赛于 1888 年在悉尼市郊的阿什菲尔德举行。公路自行车赛如今是最为流行的骑车运动。环法自行车赛是最负盛名的公路自行车赛。

山地自行车赛一般在地势崎岖地带举行，通常包括越野赛和速降赛两种类型。越野赛赛程一般为 30 ~ 50 公里，速降赛是运动员从下山的崎岖赛道上高速滑下的一种比赛。

小轮车比赛在人工自建的越野跑道上进行。尽管比赛用自行车对成人来说看似儿童玩具车大小，但它可以承受在崎岖陡峭的山路骑行，也耐得住运动员在平路上进行的各种特技表演。小轮车比赛于 2008 年北京奥运会正式成为比赛项目。

中国自行车运动于 1913 年前后由欧洲传入。环青海湖国际公路自行车赛、环海南岛国际公路自行车赛以及其他场地赛、山地赛促进了我国自行车运动的发展。

思考题:

1. 什么是自行车运动?
2. 你知道哪些自行车比赛项目?
3. 你能说出在中国举办的自行车赛事吗?

文章 2

阅读下面这篇关于国际自行车联盟的文章,讨论文后的思考题。

国际自行车联盟

国际自行车联盟,简称国际自联,是世界自行车运动和国际竞技自行车比赛的管理机构。1900 年成立于巴黎,总部在瑞士艾格尔。工作用语为英语和法语。中国于 1939 年加入国际自联,1958 年退出,1979 年恢复会籍。

国际自联的主要职责包括:给选手发比赛证,管理不同项目(如男子和女子、业余和专业的山地自行车赛、公路和场地自行车赛、自行车越野赛、预选赛、室内自行车赛等)的赛别和计分排名。国际自联举办的主要赛事包括自行车各类项目的世界锦标赛、世界杯等。

获得国际自联世界锦标赛的冠军会被授予白色的彩虹战衣,胸前有五种不同颜色的条纹:从下至上依次是绿色、黄色、黑色、红色、蓝色,和奥运五环的颜色相同。所有自行车项目的世界锦标赛都延承此传统。

思考题:

1. 国际自联是哪一年成立的?
2. 国际自联的职责有哪些?
3. 为什么国际自联世界锦标赛冠军要身着彩虹战衣?

第三部分 练习

请完成以下练习。

1. 观看一般奥运会场地自行车比赛录像,撰写 250 词左右的观后感。文章要突出参赛选手的情感和表现。
2. 你对中国自行车比赛未来的发展有何看法?跟同伴分享一下你的观点。

第四部分 规则与概念

1. 场地自行车赛：奥运会男子比赛项目包括计时赛、个人争先赛（3 圈）、4000 米个人追逐赛和团体追逐赛、记分赛；女子项目有争先赛、500 米个人计时赛、记分赛、3000 米个人追逐赛。

2. 个人追逐赛是场地自行车赛的比赛项目之一，两名选手分别位于跑道上两个相反方向的位置，枪响同时出发，在规定的距离内互相追逐（通常男子为 4 公里，女子为 3 公里）。如果运动员追上对手或与之并排，本场比赛即结束。如未被追上，则到达终点用时最短的运动员获胜。获胜者参加下一轮比赛。

3. 团体追逐赛，每队派 4 名选手参加比赛。基本规则与个人追逐赛相同，目标是最短时间到达终点或追赶上另一队选手。团体赛中，第三名车手位置至关重要，因时间是按照第三名选手自行车前轮通过终点线计算的。

4. 计时赛中，运动员在同一起点按规定时间间隔单独出发，出发顺序由抽签决定。以每名运动员到达终点成绩判定名次，优者列前，如成绩相等名次并列。

5. 记分赛比赛前以抽签排定运动员顺序。赛前指定一名领骑者，比赛时由领骑者领骑一圈，到达起点线时鸣枪，比赛开始。每 10 圈设冲刺圈，取前 4 名计分，得分按 5、3、2、1 计分；任何一名运动员超过主集团一圈，即获得 20 分。最终以运动员比赛中的总得分排列名次。

6. 公路自行车赛：选择环型往返路线，路面要有起伏和斜度，起终点尽可能设在同一地点。运动员赛前在集合处检录。

7. 公路大组赛的所有运动员从起点线集体出发，以运动员到达终点的顺序排列名次。

8. 公路大组赛中，运动员之间可以相互配合相互帮助，如交换食物、饮料和配件，但不可以相互推行。如果赛车发生故障，可以从团队的器材车上或收容车上获得帮助，也可以在赛段固定维修站获得帮助。

9. 山地自行车赛：根据规则要求，每一圈一般 4 ~ 5 公里，比赛骑行时间一般不超过 90 分钟。大会组委会选一名成绩较好的队员骑行一圈，根据骑行时间进行成绩预测，然后根据所预测的数据来确定比赛的圈数。

10. 如果一位顶级女子山地车赛选手骑完一圈要用 30 分钟，那么，比赛组委会将把比赛的赛程规定为 4 圈，这样，比赛的最佳总时间就有可能是正常的 2 小时。

第五部分 拓展阅读

自行车王子——黄金宝

黄金宝，1973 年出生，香港自行车运动员，被香港媒体封称为"自行车王子"，日本自行车界则封其为"亚洲之虎"。

黄金宝 17 岁加入香港自行车代表队，开始自行车运动生涯。他在多项大型自行车赛事中获得奖项，是香港首位获得世界冠军的自行车运动员，曾两次获得亚运会公路自行车项目金牌，成绩斐然。2007 年场地自行车世锦赛上，黄金宝夺得 15 公里追逐赛冠军，这也是中国选手首次夺得自行车男子世界冠军。2012 年伦敦奥运会男子公路自行车赛，黄金宝以 5 小时 46 分 37 秒获得第 37 名，结束了他的奥运生涯。他五次征战奥运会的经历使其成为香港体育的代名词，体现了自强不息的香港精神。

第 17 课 射击

第一部分 听和说

活动 1

🎧 听下面的对话，然后两人一组将其表演出来。

（射击比赛就要开始。教练正给李明加油打气。）

A: 李明，你做完赛前练习了吗？

B: 做完了，教练。

A: 你的枪接受检验了吗？

B: 是的，已经检验合格。

A: 下午的比赛有信心吗？

B: 信心十足，应该可以打到 585 环。

A: 相信自己，保持冷静，把比赛当作一场训练。

B: 谢谢教练，我记住了，我一定全力以赴。

活动 2

👥 两人一组，回答下列问题。

> 问题 1：比赛结束，裁判员要求运动员停止射击。子弹夹是否被要求退出？
>
> 问题 2：8 秒射击结束，如果子弹没有射出，运动员是否应该举手示意？

第二部分 阅读

文章1

阅读下面这篇关于射击运动的文章，讨论文后的思考题。

射击运动

射击运动是射击运动员用枪支对准目标打靶的竞技项目。射击项目对运动员在压力下保持平衡、注意力集中、手眼协调、心理稳定和时间感觉等各项素质具有很高的要求。

奥运会射击项目的基本类别包括步枪、手枪、移动靶和飞碟。每个大类依枪支、目标靶和射程的不同分各个小项。射击运动员的技术称为射击术。

最初枪支用于狩猎和军事目的。现在，射击被当作是一种娱乐活动。射击运动首次被列入现代奥运会是在1896年雅典奥运会上。1907年世界射击联盟成立。美国、中国、俄罗斯和德国在射击项目上处于世界领先地位。截至2012年，中国射击健儿在奥运会上共斩获21枚金牌。其中，在1984年第二十三届奥运会上，中国射击运动员许海峰获得冠军，为中国赢得奥运史上第一枚金牌。

思考题：

1. 谈一谈你对射击运动的认识？
2. 射击比赛基本类别有哪些？
3. 优秀射击运动员应具备哪些基本素质？

文章2

阅读下面这篇关于国际射击联合会的文章，讨论文后的思考题。

国际射击联合会

国际射击运动联合会，简称国际射联，是国际射击运动管理组织，管辖包括气枪、手枪和飞碟项目的奥运会射击比赛和其他各类国际射击比赛。国际射击联合会于1907年成立，原名为国际射击联盟；总部设在德国慕尼黑，现任主席墨西哥人莱加里奥·巴斯克斯·拉纳；现有协会会员154个，分属非洲、美洲、亚洲、欧洲和大洋洲五个大洲联合会。国际射击联盟的正式用语为德、英、法、俄、西班牙语，工作用语为英语。中国射击协会于1954年加入国际射联。

国际射联主要负责制定技术规则、颁发裁判执照、协助国际奥委会组织奥运会的射击比赛。此外，还负责技术监督，组织四年一度的世界射击锦标赛，促进和发展教学计划与方法，奖励对国际射联有突出贡献的个人等。

国际射联组织的主要射击赛事包括奥运会、残奥会、世界锦标赛、世界杯上的各类射击比赛。

思考题：

1. 国际射联成立于哪一年？

2. 国际射联的主要职责是什么？

3. 国际射联组织的国际赛事有哪些？

第三部分 练习

请完成以下练习。

1. 撰写一个采访奥运冠军蔡亚林的采访提纲。

2. 请观射击比赛，撰写 250 词左右的观后感。

第四部分 规则与概念

1. 射击项目分为步枪项目、手枪项目、移动靶和飞碟项目四大类，每个小项比赛都包括资格赛和决赛。资格赛成绩最好的前 8 名或前 6 名选手进入决赛，资格赛和决赛成绩相加最高者获得冠军。如果出现相同成绩，则成绩相同的选手通过单发加赛决出最终的胜负。

2. 手枪项目分为 10 米、25 米和 50 米小项，选手采用立姿单臂持枪，无依托射击。资格赛每发子弹的成绩分为 10 环、9 环、8 环……以此类推。决赛每环再细分为 10 个环值，最高成绩为 10.9 环。

3. 步枪项目分为 10 米和 50 米小项，选手采用卧姿、立姿或跪姿进行射击。成绩计算办法与手枪相同。

4. 飞碟射击也叫泥鸽射击。飞碟射击比赛采用双筒猎枪，早期射击目标为活鸽，现用沥青、石膏等材料混合压制而成。比赛时，抛靶机按固定方向抛靶，射手依次在不同位置射击，以击碎碟靶为命中，命中多者为胜。

5. 移动靶射击比赛以小口径步枪立姿向距离 50 米的移动靶射击。早期移动靶多为跑动的猪靶，故又称跑猪靶。1900 年起被列为奥运会比赛项目。在后来的移动靶射击中，原始跑猪靶逐渐改为和 10 米气步枪相像的靶纸。

6. 步枪和手枪的标准靶由 10 个靶环构成，排列是从 1 环到 10 环。最外面的靶环为 1 分，靶心为 10 分。奥运会手枪项目和步枪项目都采用国际射联认可的电子靶。

7. 在飞碟项目中，碟靶的直径为 110 毫米，厚度为 25 ~ 26 毫米，重量为 105 克，颜色为白、黄或橙色等鲜艳颜色。决赛中必须使用闪光靶。

8. 步枪项目要求射手必须遵照国际射联的规定着装，包括射击上衣、射击裤、射击鞋、射击手套和射击皮带等。比赛前需进行检查，确保着装符合规则要求。手枪项目射手们不需要特殊着装，允许穿专用射击鞋，这种鞋稳定性强，鞋底坚硬，面料为皮革制品或纤维制品。双向飞碟的射手必须在其射击服上佩带国际射联正式的标志带，标志带长 250 毫米，宽 30 毫米，黄色镶黑边，必须永久性地缝制在肘尖下水平位置的射击服上，以便裁判员可以随时观察到射手在发射的瞬间是否犯规。

9. 步枪分为气步枪、小口径步枪和猎枪三种。气步枪用于 10 米项目；小口径步枪用于 50 米项目；猎枪用于飞碟项目。

10. 手枪分为气手枪和小口径手枪。气手枪用于 10 米项目；小口径手枪用于 25 米和 50 米项目。10 米项目的手枪和步枪子弹为 4.5 毫米；25 米和 50 米项目为 5.6 毫米。对于飞碟项目，通常使用的是 12 号猎枪弹，弹丸的装填量不得超过 24.5 克。

第五部分 拓展阅读

奥运冠军许海峰

许海峰，1957 年出生，中国著名射击运动员，中国射击队的领军人物。1984 年第二十三届奥运会男子手枪 60 发慢射冠军，是中国奥运会历史上首位冠军得主。

许海峰对中国射击事业做出了重大贡献，在中国射击界有很高的威望和知名度。但他从未以此来炫耀过，而是在射击事业上默默耕耘。他对自己要求"要想打好枪，先要做好人"。他也经常告诫自己："在待遇和荣誉面前要满足，但对事业和工作上要永远不要满足。"

户外与休闲文体活动

第 18 课 户外运动

第一部分 听和说

活动 1

🎧 听下面的对话，然后两人一组将其表演出来。

（张和李是邻居。一天早上，他们碰到了，都觉得天气很不错。张建议两家一起带着孩子到郊外骑自行车。）

A: 今天阳光真好。

B: 是啊，我们不该一直在室内待着。室外有很多活动可以参加的。你有什么想法吗？

A: 我想到郊外玩玩，呼吸一下新鲜空气。

B: 一起去吧！骑单车怎么样？

A: 好主意，孩子们早都期盼着骑车郊游呢。

B: 带上风筝，到了郊外可以陪孩子们放风筝。

A: 太棒了！我回去准备一下，一小时后出发怎么样？

B: 好的，一会儿大门口见。

活动 2

👥 两人一组，根据以下所给情景设计对话。

> 情景1： 一位新加入的户外运动爱好者想买一双专业的户外登山鞋，作为一名资深的户外运动爱好者，请给他一些建议。

情景 2： 你和你的朋友们一起郊游露宿，此时有一位朋友不会支帐篷，
现在你要帮助他完成这项工作。

第二部分 阅读

文章 1

阅读下面这篇关于户外运动的文章，讨论文后的思考题。

户外运动

户外运动是在自然场地展开的一组集体项目群，包括登山、攀岩、悬崖速降、野外露营、野炊、定向运动、溪流探险等项目。户外运动要求参加者徒手或使用专门装备攀登各种不同地形的山峰或山岭，挑战自我，拥抱自然。多数户外运动具有探险性、挑战性和刺激性，属于极限运动。

户外运动最早可追溯到 18 世纪的欧洲。法国著名科学家德·索修尔为探索高山植物资源，于 1760 年 5 月在阿尔卑斯山脚下的夏木尼镇贴出一则告示："凡能登上或提供登上勃朗峰之巅线路者，将以重金奖赏。"然而，直到 26 年后的 1786 年 6 月，夏木尼镇一位名叫巴卡罗的医生才揭下了告示。他经过两个多月的准备，与当地山区水晶石采掘工人巴尔玛结伴，于 1786 年 8 月 6 日首次登上了海拔 4810 米的西欧第一高峰勃朗峰。1787 年，由德·索修尔率领、巴尔玛做向导的登山队再次登上该峰，由此揭开了现代登山运动的序幕。

思考题：

1. 结合自身实际，谈谈你对户外运动的认识。

2. 户外运动的特点有哪些？

3. 户外运动如何产生的？

文章 2

阅读下面这篇关于世界极限运动会的文章，讨论文后的思考题。

世界极限运动会

极限运动在 20 世纪 60 年代起源于欧美，目前已发展演变成为一个包含几十个竞赛项目的新兴运动形式。极限运动倡导"追求自我、挑战自我"，它所涵盖的文化已影响并成为年轻人的一种 "追求自由空间、探索未知世界、创造自我价值"的生活理念。

世界极限运动会是全球极限运动中水平最高、影响力最大的传统盛会，由美国有线体育电视网创立并组织举办，每年一次。

最早的世界极限运动会于 1995 年夏季在美国罗德岛州的纽波特市举行。参赛者相互竞争以赢得比赛的金牌、银牌、铜牌和奖金。比赛常有新的技巧项目：托尼·霍克的 900 米滑板运动技巧，特拉维斯·帕斯特拉那自由式摩托车越野赛后空翻两周技巧，希斯·弗理斯比迄今为止第一的机动雪橇最佳赛前空翻技巧，以及托尔施泰因·霍格莫单板滑雪竞赛的三转空翻技巧。比赛期间，还举行世界极限运动会音乐节，为大家提供现场音乐演奏、运动员亲笔签名活动和其他一些互动活动。

经过多年的发展，世界极限运动会已经成为世界上最受欢迎的多项目极限运动盛会之一。运动会的各个赛事都会有电视直播。

思考题：

1. 谈一谈你对"追求自我、挑战自我"这句话的认识。
2. 世界极限运动会的举办方是？
3. 世界极限运动会有哪些赛事？

第三部分 练习

请完成以下练习。

1. 制定一个以"生命在于运动"为主题的户外活动计划书。
2. 谈谈你最喜欢的户外运动项目。

第四部分 规则与概念

1. 攀岩分不借助支持器械、只靠人体自身力量的自由攀登和借助器械的器械攀登，是一项刺激且很有挑战性的体育活动。

2. 攀冰是一项借助于装备、器械而进行的在冰瀑或冰挂上攀登的运动。冰大体分为冰壁和冰挂两种。

3. 定点跳伞（BASE jumping）是从悬崖和其他建筑物上跳伞的极限运动。"BASE"一词由定点跳伞4个热门地点的首字母组成：摩天大楼（Building）、天线高塔（Antenna）、大桥水坝（Span）和悬崖溶洞（Earth）。

4. 溯溪是在峡谷溪流的上下游之间，克服地形上的各处障碍，穷水之源而登山之巅的一项探险运动。其特点与乐趣在于不断克服一个接一个的瀑布、漩涡，急流勇进，逆水前行。

5. 冲浪指利用冲浪板越过浪头的水上运动。冲浪者需配备冲浪板和系在脚上的安全绳。

6. 蹦极，是一种利用有弹性的绳索，一端系着身体或足踝，另一端系在高处平台（通常高数十至过百米），挑战者从高台一跃跳下的活动。

7. 露营是一种户外休闲活动。露营者通常携带帐篷，离开城市在野外扎营，度过一个或者多个夜晚。露营通常和其他活动联系，如徒步、钓鱼或者游泳等。

8. 滑雪是指利用滑雪板在雪地滑行的一种冬季体育运动。滑雪运动主要分为北欧滑雪、高山滑雪和特里马滑雪。

9. 漂流是指利用橡皮艇或者竹筏，在时而湍急时而平缓的水流中顺流而下的一种户外运动方式。

10. 徒步是指有目的在郊区、农村或者山野间进行长距离的走路锻炼。由于徒步活动比较简单，不需要太讲究技巧和装备，因此是户外运动中最为典型和最为普遍的一种休闲活动。

第五部分 拓展阅读

费利克斯·鲍姆加特纳

费利克斯·鲍姆加特纳，1969 年出生于奥地利萨尔斯堡市，奥地利著名跳伞运动员、极限运动员。他多次挑战高空跳伞纪录，打破多项高度和自由落体纪录，被粉丝们誉为"无所畏惧的费利克斯"。

孩提时代，鲍姆加特纳就梦想着在空中飞翔。1999 年，他在马来西亚吉隆坡国油双塔定点跳伞成功，刷新世界最高大楼定点跳伞记录。2003 年 7 月 20 日，他利用一具特殊设计的人造纤维翔翼，成为成功飞越英吉利海峡第一人。2007 年 12 月 12 日，他在台北市的台北 101 大楼 91 层观景露台跳伞成功，再度刷新世界最高大楼定点跳伞记录。

2012 年 10 月 14 日，鲍姆加特纳乘气球升至约 3.9 万米的高空后，携着降落伞自由落体跳下并成功着地，创造了人类搭乘气球抵达的最高高度（3.9 万米）和人类自由落体最高时速（每小时 1357 公里）两项世界纪录。

第 19 课 定向运动

第一部分 听和说

活动 1

🎧 听下面的对话，然后两人一组将其表演出来。

（定向运动比赛马上就要开始。教练要求队长在开始前检查好所有装备。）

A: 队长，告诉大家，出发前一定检查比赛物品是否带全。

B: 教练，我们都检查几遍了。

A: 还有，一定要仔细看地图，边跑边看，选择最近最安全的路线和奔跑方向。

B: 教练，我们能选择更危险但更近的路段吗？

A: 不行，切记安全第一。

B: 知道了，教练。

A: 还有，记得打完一个点，划去一个点，避免遗漏和重复，以免耽误时间。

B: 知道了，请放心。

活动 2

👥 两人一组，回答下列问题。

> 问题 1： 地图和指南针在定向越野比赛中的作用有哪些？
>
> （提示：使用地图与指南针进行标定地图、对照地形、判定地形、确定运动点、确定运动方向、确定运动路线等。）
>
> 问题 2： 你知道地图六大要素吗？
>
> （提示：包括地貌、水系、建筑物、道路、植被和境界。）

第二部分 阅读

文章 1

阅读下面这篇关于定向运动的文章，讨论文后的思考题。

定向运动

定向运动（或定向越野）是指利用地图和指南针到访地图上所指示的各个点标，以最短时间到达所有点标者为胜。比赛地点常常设在森林、郊外、城市公园或大学校园里。

定向运动起源于瑞典，最初只是一项军事体育活动。1895 年，瑞典斯德哥尔摩和挪威奥斯陆的军营区举行了定向越野比赛，标志着定向运动作为一种体育比赛项目的诞生。1932 年，世界定向运动比赛第一次召开。

如今，定向运动由初期单一的军事训练逐步演变为包括各种各样的比赛或娱乐项目在内的综合性群众体育活动。常见的定向运动形式主要有：徒步定向、接力定向、百米定向、滑雪定向、夜间定向、专线定向、五日定向、校园定向、特里拇定向等。

定向运动涉及的基本技术包括地图正置及拇指辅行法、利用指南针、扶手法、搜集途中所遇特征和攻击点、数步测距和目标偏测。定向运动也是国际军体理事会的正式比赛项目之一，每次举办的比赛都能吸引十余个国家的军队运动队参加。

思考题：

1. 可以进行定向运动的场所有哪些？
2. 你知道定向运动的比赛项目有哪些吗？
3. 你能列举定向运动的比赛技术吗？

文章 2

阅读下面这篇关于国际定向越野联合会的文章，讨论文后的思考题。

国际定向越野联合会

国际定向越野联合会，简称国际定联，是定向越野运动的国际管理机构。总部设在芬兰首都赫尔辛基，工作用语为英语。1992年，中国定向运动委员会加入国际定联。

国际定联负责定向越野四个项目的比赛，包括徒步定向越野、山地车定向越野、滑雪定向越野和轮椅定向越野。国际定联致力于推广定向越野运动，促进其进一步发展。

国际定联1961年5月21日在丹麦哥本哈根成立。截至1969年，国际定联拥有16个成员国，其中包括两个非欧洲成员国日本和加拿大。1977年国际定联得到国际奥林匹克委员会认可。截至2013年，国际定联拥有79个定向越野运动联合体。

国际定联由公共选举的委员会进行管理，其中包括1名主席、1名高级副主席、2名副主席和7名其他理事会委员。国际定联秘书长负责该组织的日常事务。国际定联的几个常任委员会负责定向运动的发展，这些常任委员会包括：徒步定向组、山地车定向组、滑雪定向组、轮椅定向组、环保专家组、信息技术组、地图专家组、医疗专家组和赛事规则专家组。

思考题：

1. 国际定联哪一年成立的，总部设在哪里？
2. 国际定联负责的项目有哪些？

第三部分 练习

请完成以下练习。

1. 从强健体魄、培养思维意识、提升独立解决问题能力的角度，撰写一篇鼓励大学生积极参与定向运动的倡议书。
2. 为什么说定向运动是一项男女老少皆宜的体育项目？

第四部分 规则与概念

1. 地图上的定向路线用粉色或红色标记,起点用三角表示,终点用双圆圈表示,一系列点标用单圆圈表示。

2. 在实际地形中,白色和橙色相间的点标旗标志着运动员应该找到的点标位置。

3. 完成全赛程所用时间最短的运动员即获胜。

4. 运动员漏找或找错点标,则运动员的成绩无效。

5. 有以下行为判以警告处罚:代表队成员擅自出入预备区,但未造成后果者;在出发区提前取图和抢先出发者;接受他人帮助者;为他人提供帮助者;为从对手的技术中获利,故意在比赛中与对手同跑或跟跑者;不按规定佩戴号码者。

6. 有以下行为判以成绩无效:冒名顶替参加竞赛者;竞赛中使用交通工具者;有证据表明在竞赛前勘察过路线者;未通过全部检查点者;终点宣布关闭前未返回终点者。

7. 有以下行为判以取消比赛资格:弄虚作假者;有意妨碍他人者;蓄意破坏点标、打卡器和其他竞赛设施者;通过技术和其他手段伪造成绩者;未佩戴大会颁发的号码布者;丢失指卡者。

8. 运动员途中因伤病不能继续完成竞赛时,以退赛论处,退赛后应尽快向就近裁判员报告。

9. 出发前运动员因故退赛,领队或教练员应向起点裁判说明情况。

10. 运动员在竞赛中损害公众利益,视情节给予处罚。

第五部分 拓展阅读

明娜·考皮

明娜·考皮，1982年11月25日出生于芬兰的阿西卡拉，芬兰著名女子定向越野运动员。明娜·考皮曾8次获得定向越野世界锦标赛冠军，其中包括5枚接力赛金牌。2010年，考皮当选为芬兰年度"最佳运动员"。她也是芬兰自1947年评选年度最佳运动员以来首位获得这一荣誉的定向越野运动员。

当明娜·考皮还很小时，她便和兄弟姐妹一起练习各种运动。8岁时，她开始对定向越野这项运动有了兴趣。除了练田径与越野滑雪之外，她也玩玩网球，练练体操。但是她很清楚，自己比较善于跑步和滑雪。

十五六岁的时候，因为定向越野的奥秘太难理解，加上她的脚程似乎比定向技术还要快，明娜·考皮基本下定决心要成为越野滑雪选手。但到了18岁，她觉得定向越野其实没有那么难。大哥大姐们都已被选为定向越野选手，作为家里的小妹妹，能跟随他们的脚步是比较容易的。

第一年，真正的定向越野训练展开了，她定下目标，要参加下一届的世界青少年定向越野锦标赛。隔年，她做到了，而且居然拿下了两枚铜牌。离开青少年赛场后，她顺利入选国家队。2005年，明娜·考皮获得NOC北欧定向锦标赛中距离个人金牌。自此之后，明娜·考皮获得一个又一个的世界冠军，并成为世界定向越野运动界的传奇人物。

第 20 课 拓展运动

第一部分 **听和说**

活动 1

🎧 听下面的对话，然后两人一组将其表演出来。

（一次拓展运动训练中，约翰在路上碰到一个大沟。他很紧张，觉得自己越不过去。教练鼓励他要勇敢战胜恐惧。）

A: 教官，我害怕，这沟太宽了，我跳不过去啊。

B: 不试试，你怎么就知道自己不行呢？

A: 太宽了。我不行的。

B: 成功与失败就一步，勇敢地跨出去，我相信你。

A: 教官，再给我几分钟，我稳定一下情绪。

B: 好吧。听我的，深呼吸，两臂自然平伸，保持身体平衡，后脚蹬，身体向前跃，大步跨出去。

A: 我过去了，我竟然过去了。

B: 好样的！真勇敢。

活动 2

👥 两人一组，回答下列问题。

> 问题 1: 你是否参加过拓展训练？和你的伙伴分享一下你的经历。
>
> 问题 2: 拓展训练具备哪些特点？
>
> （提示：比如具有活动综合性、挑战极限性、集体个性化、高峰体验性、自我教育和潜能激发性等。）

第二部分 阅读

文章 1

阅读下面这篇关于拓展运动的文章，讨论文后的思考题。

拓展运动

　　拓展运动是一个国际的、非营利的、独立的户外教育组织，在全球拥有近 40 所学校，每年有 20 万人参与此项活动。拓展训练的目标在于通过运用户外的挑战性探险来促进参与者的身心发展，培养其社会技能。

　　拓展运动，又称外展训练、生存训练，原意为一艘小船驶离平静的港湾，义无反顾地投向未知的旅程，去迎接一次次挑战。拓展训练起源于"二战"期间的英国，原为训练年轻海员在海上的生存能力和船触礁后的生存技巧，之后逐渐被推广开来。训练对象也由最初的海员扩大到军人、学生、工商业人员等各类群体，训练目标也由单纯的体能、生存训练扩展到心理训练、人格训练、管理训练等。

　　如今的拓展训练项目涵盖水上、野外和场地三大类，通常利用崇山峻岭、翰海大川等自然环境以及各种专门的训练场地与设施，通过精心设计的活动达到"磨炼意志、陶冶情操、完善人格、熔炼团队"的培训目的。

思考题:

　　1. 拓展运动的目的是什么?

　　2. 拓展运动的起源是什么?

　　3. 拓展运动的基本类别有哪些?

文章 2

阅读下面这篇关于外展训练组织的文章，讨论文后的思考题。

外展训练组织

　　外展训练的奠基人是德国著名教育家库尔特·哈恩，他在"二战"期间训练英国年轻海员海上生存能力时最早提出了这一概念。1946 年，外展训练信托基金会在英国成立，其目的是推广外展训练理念、筹集资金创办外展训练（OB）学校。1961 年，美国人乔什·曼纳将外展训练的理念带入美国，并创建了全美第一所 OB 学校。1964 年，外展训练法人组织，即外展训练国际组织在美国成立，它是当前全球规模最大、历史最悠久的从事户外体验式教育的非营利机构。目前，OB 训练中心和学校快速发展，遍布世界各地。

美国户外领队学校于 1965 年成立，创立者是世界著名登山运动员保罗·佩特佐。这是美国非营利的户外技能教育机构，致力于教授学员环境伦理、户外技能、野外医疗救助、风险管理与评估、领导力与团队合作等课程，累积培训学员 28 万余名。

香港外展训练学校于 1970 年成立，是中国第一个外展训练专业培训机构。20 世纪 60 年代，香港教育环境普遍缺失人格教育，香港外展训练学校应运而生，为刚离校的学生提供短期集中训练，以促进年轻人的人格发展。近来，香港外展训练学校在领导力、有效沟通、诚信、团队合作等方面提供一系列成功学课程，成为亚洲户外体验教学的先驱。

思考题：

1. 第一所外展训练学校是如何建立的？
2. 美国户外领队学校和香港外展训练学校的培养目标分别是什么？

第三部分 练习

请完成以下练习。

1. 制定一个以"增强协作沟通，提升凝聚力"为主题的户外体验训练计划。
2. 谈谈你对学校开设拓展训练课程的认识？

第四部分 规则与概念

1. 飞夺泸定桥：个人挑战项目。模拟当年红军"飞夺泸定桥"的情景，队员站在 10 米的高空处，凭借身体自我平衡，跨过一段相隔半米有一个木板的软"桥"。

2. 空中单杠：个人挑战项目。队员从独立杆爬上顶端，站在小圆盘上，纵身向前跃起，双手抓住上前方的三角杠。

3. 悬崖绝壁：单人或双人合作项目。队员靠气和技巧在一面无任何抓手的绝壁墙上从一边攀登到另一边。

4. 信任背摔：个人心理挑战与团队合作项目。队员依次站到 1.4 米高的小平台上，背向后倒在下面队员用胳膊交叉的网上。

5. 雷区取水：团队合作项目。在直径 5 米的深潭中间有一盆水，队员用一根绳子，在不接触水面的情况下取到全体队员的救命宝物。

6. 有轨电车：团队激励项目。将队员分组，每组组员双脚站在木板上，手拉木板上的提绳，共同前进。

7. 模拟电网：团队协作项目。在大家配合下，所有人员在规定时间内从网的一边通过到网的另一边，人体所有部位不得碰触网的任何部分，且一个网眼只能使用一次。

8. 天梯：双人合作项目。参训的两名队员在有安全保护的情况下，相互配合，从天梯低端一直上到最高处。

9. 合力桥：团队合作项目。一人或两人一组，登上 9 米高吊板（共 3 块）。每块板下方由 4 ~ 6 人控制绳索以保证吊板平衡。上方人员靠自己的努力和相互配合踩过每一块吊板，最终成功到达彼岸。

10. 空中相依：二人合作项目。两名队员面对面、手推手，在两条钢缆上横向前进到另一端。

第五部分 拓展阅读

船夫与哲学家

从前，有一位哲学家乘船过河，划船的船夫虽然年龄已经很大，却一直在使劲地划船，非常辛苦。于是哲学家就对船夫说："老先生，你学过哲学吗？"船夫答道："哎呀，抱歉，我没学过哲学。"哲学家摊开双手说："那太遗憾了，你失去了 50% 的生命呀。"过了一会儿，这位哲学家看到老先生如此辛苦，又说："你学过数学吗？"那位老船夫说："对不起先生，我没有学过数学。"哲学家接着说："哎呀！太遗憾了，那你将失去 80% 的生命呀。"就在这个时候，突然一个巨浪把船打翻了，两个人同时落入水中。船夫看着哲学家如此费劲地在挣扎，就说："先生，你学过游泳吗？"哲学家说："我没学过游泳。"老船夫无奈地说："哎呀，那真抱歉，你将失去 100% 的生命了。"

　　头脑中的知识是不能帮你战胜现实生活中的惊涛骇浪的。虽然大家都讲，"知识就是力量"，但纯粹的知识本身并不能产生力量，知识必须要转化成你的生产工具或是劳动技能才能发挥它的作用。

第21课 飞镖

第一部分 听和说

活动 1

🎧 听下面的对话，然后两人一组将其表演出来。

（彼得和约翰现在都很闲。彼得提议玩飞镖打发时间，约翰立刻同意了。）

A: 我们两个玩一次飞镖比赛如何？

B: 好呀！玩飞镖我可是高手。指哪儿打哪儿！

A: 是吗？比比看！

B: 用磁性飞镖还是针式飞镖？

A: 国际比赛都用针式飞镖，我们就用这个吧。

B: 离靶心最近的先投？

A: 好啊。你先投。

B: 没问题。

活动 2

👥 两人一组，回答下列问题。

> 问题 1： 你能列举一些飞镖比赛过程中的礼仪用语吗？
>
> （提示："好运气""好镖""我运气好""比赛很好"等）
>
> 问题 2： 你能说说当前非常流行的飞镖比赛种类吗？
>
> （提示：501飞镖比赛、301飞镖比赛、21点、打飞碟、高得分、杀手、设定
> 目标、顺序得分、追杀）

第二部分 阅读

文章 1

阅读下面这篇关于飞镖运动的文章，讨论文后的思考题。

飞镖运动

飞镖是一种前端用金属制成、后端具有尾翼的细长镖具，参与者需用手将其投掷至靶子。飞镖运动讲究投射精准，集竞技、健身、娱乐于一体。飞镖最早起源于英国。据记载，古罗马军团被罗马皇帝派到遥远的不列颠岛，多雨的英国气候不便于士兵在外活动，于是他们在板棚中把箭投向用橡树横切面制成的靶子，由此逐渐形成现代的飞镖运动。

1896 年，英国人布莱恩·甘林发明了现代镖盘的分区系统，极大地促进了飞镖运动在英国的普及开展。飞镖成为酒吧里一项受人欢迎的项目，并逐渐发展成为风靡全球的室内休闲娱乐运动。

飞镖运动于 20 世纪 80 年代在我国兴起，随着全民健身运动的深入开展，在 1999 年被正式列为体育竞技项目。从此以后，各地都掀起了飞镖热。1999 年、2000 年、2001 年连续举办了三届全国性飞镖大赛，涌现出了一大批优秀的职业飞镖选手。

思考题：

1. 你观看过飞镖比赛吗？谈一谈对飞镖运动的认识。
2. 现代飞镖运动是如何演变而来的？
3. 你是否同意青少年从事飞镖活动？为什么？

文章 2

阅读下面这篇关于世界飞镖联盟的文章，讨论文后的思考题。

世界飞镖联盟

世界飞镖联盟是飞镖运动的官方管理机构、世界飞镖巡回赛的组织者。创建于 1974 年，最初由 15 个国家代表组成。联盟接收各国为飞镖而成立的官方的国家组织作为成员。世界飞镖联盟作为世界性的飞镖组织实体，积极推动飞镖在这些联盟国家间的发展，致力于把飞镖运动推广为国际上认可的主要运动项目。

世界飞镖联盟主办的赛事主要是世界杯比赛，以及包括美洲杯、亚太杯、欧洲杯的其他洲际锦标赛。在全部的飞镖赛事所有项目（包括个人、双人、团队项目）中获得最好成绩的国家即成为世界冠军。世界杯赛上任何项目的获胜者为世界冠军，洲际锦标赛获胜者为区域冠军。

英国是世界飞镖运动的领先国家。英国飞镖组织是世界飞镖联盟成员之一，是英国飞镖运动的官方组织实体。每年一届的 PDC 世界职业飞镖锦标赛目前已成为世界飞镖联盟的最重要的赛事活动。

思考题：

1. 你能否用自己的语言简单阐述世界飞镖联盟是什么组织？
2. 世界飞镖联盟最重要的比赛是什么？

第三部分 练习

请完成以下练习。

1. 请为大学生飞镖队编写一段介绍词，不少于 150 词。
2. 如果让你担任飞镖比赛记分员，你事先应该熟悉掌握哪些知识？

第四部分 规则与概念

1. 飞镖的玩法多种多样，不同的玩法规则也有所不同，但基本的规则是一致的。
2. 每一轮掷三镖。
3. 从镖盘上崩出或脱落的飞镖不能计分，也不能重投。
4. 飞镖是两个选手或两队选手之间的比赛。双方的队员轮流投掷。
5. 开赛前的 9 次投掷通常作为个人赛前的热身；投掷的飞镖最接近靶心的一队首先开局。
6. 每个选手投掷一轮，共三镖，然后自己取回飞镖。
7. 如果选手脚越过投掷线或不小心绊倒而投了飞镖，该分不计，并且没有重投的机会。

8. 飞镖必须在镖盘上保持 5 秒钟以上。如果飞镖脱落或者插进了另一支飞镖，那么该分不计。

9. 选手可在任何时候走近镖盘去确认飞镖的位置，但在一轮投掷完成之前任何人都不能触摸飞镖。

10. 出于礼仪和安全的考虑，任何人都不能站在距离投镖选手 2 英尺以里的范围内。

第五部分 拓展阅读

菲尔·泰勒

菲尔·道格拉斯·泰勒，1960 年出生于英国的特伦特河畔斯托克，国际飞镖界的传奇人物。他在 200 余场职业飞镖巡回赛中夺冠，16 次获得世界冠军，绰号"力量"。1995 到 2002 年，连续八年获得世界冠军；1994 到 2007 年，连续 14 次打进总决赛。他创下的夺冠纪录无人能比。

泰勒在 26 岁之前是一个默默无闻的蓝领工人，后来他遇到了人生中最重要的一位伯乐——埃里克·布里斯托，20 世纪 80 年代最有名的飞镖选手之一。1990 年，泰勒首次获得了参加飞镖世锦赛的资格。1998 年他赢得第六个世界冠军，打破埃里克·布里斯托的 5 次世界冠军的成就，同时成为第一个连续四年赢得世界冠军的选手。菲尔说："我现在想赢得更多的冠军，将来没人能够超过我，就像彼得·希尔顿令人惊讶的 1000 场足球联赛上的纪录。"

第22课 钓鱼

第一部分 听和说

活动 1

🎧 听下面的对话，然后两人一组将其表演出来。

（约翰打算明天跟朋友一起去钓鱼。彼得也想一起去，但是又担心钓鱼有危险。）

A: 听说你们明天要去野外钓鱼？

B: 是呀。现在是钓鱼好季节，我等了一年，已经按捺不住了！

A: 钓鱼可是个休闲放松的好活动，我能跟你们一起去吗？

B: 可以，欢迎你加入我们的钓鱼团队。

A: 我听说野外钓鱼很危险，是这样吗？

B: 放心吧！这么多人在一起，不会有危险。

A: 草丛中会不会有蛇？我最怕蛇了。

B: 事先我们会做好防护措施，尽量避开草丛多的地方。

A: 我知道了。谢谢！我现在去准备钓具。

活动 2

👤 两人一组，回答下列问题。

> **问题 1：** 你认为鱼是不是变温动物？
>
> （提示：鱼的体温会随着水温的变化而变化，一般划分为暖水性鱼类、温水性鱼类和冷水性鱼类。）

问题 2： 钓鱼时所用的鱼饵都是一样的吗？

（提示：蚯蚓、米饭、菜叶、苍蝇、蛆等都可以做鱼饵，但钓不同的鱼需要用不同的鱼饵。）

第二部分　阅读

文章 1

阅读下面这篇关于钓鱼的文章，讨论文后的思考题。

钓鱼

钓鱼是在野外捕捉鱼类的一种活动，其寓意有引诱、欺骗行为的意思。根据钓鱼目的和性质的不同，钓鱼一般分为商业捕捞、休闲垂钓和竞技钓三种。商业捕捞以盈利为目的，休闲钓和竞技钓重在娱乐和比赛。

竞技钓鱼或休闲钓鱼对所钓鱼的种类有明确限定，禁止使用渔网捕捞，禁止鱼钩钩挂到除鱼嘴外鱼的其他部位。常用的钓鱼工具有钓竿、鱼线、鱼钩和鱼饵。用鱼钩把鱼钓起又称垂钓，垂钓者常有钓后即放的习惯。对于垂钓爱好者们来说，发现并成功钓起鱼的乐趣远大于鱼肉本身的食用和经济价值。

钓鱼的起源可追溯到古代先民的生产活动，现在逐渐演变成一种充满趣味、格调高雅、有益身心的文体活动。钓鱼不仅仅是茶余饭后的休闲活动；人们怀着对大自然的热爱，像小孩子一样静坐在水边池旁，享受这钓竿的颤动带来的欢乐。此时，即使是性情暴躁的小伙子，也会变得"静如处子"。

思考题：

1. 你参加过钓鱼活动吗？用你的语言谈谈对钓鱼的认识。

2. 钓鱼需要准备哪些工具？

3. 如何理解"静如处子"？

文章 2

阅读下面这篇关于国际钓鱼运动联合会的文章，讨论文后的思考题。

国际钓鱼运动联合会

国际钓鱼运动联合会是代表世界钓鱼运动组织的总联盟，1952 年在意大利罗马成立。国际钓鱼运动联合会通过举办国际钓鱼赛事，增进各国钓鱼爱好者之间的交流，提高参赛国家的声誉。目前，共有 69 个国家的 138 个钓鱼运动组织加入国际钓鱼运动联合会。

国际钓鱼运动联合会下设有国际（淡水）钓鱼运动组织、国际海钓运动组织、国际飞钓运动组织和国际抛竿钓运动组织等四个国际联盟。各联盟组织每年分别举办的各种钓鱼赛事达数十个，在全球垂钓行业中有绝对的权威性。由国际钓鱼运动联合会发起的国际垂钓锦标赛已经成为垂钓行业的奥运会。中国钓鱼代表队分别于 2003 年、2004 年参加了在斯洛伐克和比利时举行的第五十、五十一届世界淡水钓鱼锦标赛，自此中国垂钓正式走上了国际垂钓运动舞台。

思考题：

1. 国际钓鱼运动联合会成立于哪一年？总部设在哪个城市？
2. 国际钓鱼运动联合会下设哪些联盟，其名称是什么？

第三部分 练习

请完成以下练习。

1. 以"晚霞垂钓"为题，撰写一篇描述钓鱼场景的记叙文，不少于 250 词。
2. 当前许多人陶醉于钓鱼活动，请就这一现象谈谈你的看法与认识。

第四部分 规则与概念

1. 钓鱼比赛必须以溪流、江河、运河或湖泊作为赛场，所选赛场沿岸必须能完全利用上。水深至少 1.5 米，各赛区水深应尽量相同，赛区最小宽度为 25 米。每个钓位的两边应各有 1 米宽的中立区。
2. 比赛开始哨声未发出，所有选手的钩、漂一律不得入水。比赛结束哨声发出后，未入护的鱼不再计算成绩。

3. 比赛中上一尾鱼必须入护方能抛竿继续施钓。

4. 所有选手不得使用手抛饵或打窝器进行打窝；每次抛竿钩饵直径不得超过 2 厘米；比赛中不得串饵，违反本规定取消当事人本场比赛成绩。

5. 所有选手比赛中不得串通作弊、并护、恶意刮鱼，违反本规定取消当事人本场比赛成绩。

6. 所有选手比赛中的抛竿方向应该是本人竿架的正前方，不得以各种借口干扰相临两侧的选手，违反本规定取消当事人本场比赛成绩。

7. 边位选手禁止斜向抛竿，用钓边取巧的方法提高自己的成绩，违反本规定取消当事人本场比赛成绩。

8. 比赛选手可以飞鱼或使用抄网抄鱼入护；赛前钓具调试（调漂）不得在比赛池中进行，选手必须到裁判组指定地点调试。

9. 如果比赛中发现有串位、串号者，经证实后，取消当事人双方全场比赛成绩。

10. 按钓尾数或重量之和计算成绩，排定名次。

第五部分 拓展阅读

中国"钓鱼鼻祖"

我国最著名的钓鱼者是谁？应该首推商朝时期的姜子牙。他是中国古代的军事战略家，辅佐周文王、周武王推翻了商朝的统治。相传在结识周文王之前，姜子牙数年坚持钓鱼，但他的钓鱼方法尤为奇特，不曲钩、不设饵、不入水。事实上姜子牙并不是在钓鱼，而是在钓一位君王。后来，周文王封他为丞相，尊称他为"太公"。姜太公钓鱼的传说真实与否尚无从考证，但却衍生出了一句俗语"姜太公钓鱼——愿者上钩"，以比喻心甘情愿地落入别人的谋划。

第 23 课 棋牌

第一部分 听和说

活动 1

🎧 听下面的对话，然后两人一组将其表演出来。

（在去棋牌室的路上，小李碰到了朋友小赵，他们讨论起如何找棋友。）

A: 今天你又要去和王老师下象棋吗?

B: 没有，他只和张老师下，因为张老师比他下得好。

A: 这主意不错。和比自己强的人下棋才能发现自己的长处和不足。

B: 我知道了，不过下得最好的人找谁下棋呢?

A: 弈棋高手不愿意和低水平的人过招，也不容易找到合适的对手，他们喜欢自己和自己下。

B: 和自己下，这是为什么呢?

A: 因为可以把自己想象为对手，寻找下一步最为合理的招式。

B: 哦，我终于明白弈棋找高手的道理了! 我想我要去找一个比我强的人下棋了。

活动 2

👥 两人一组，回答下列问题。

> 问题 1: 请说出国际象棋、围棋与象棋分别在哪一年被列为亚运会比赛项目的?
>
> （提示: 国际象棋于 2006 年多哈亚运会列为比赛项目; 围棋和象棋是在 2010 年广州亚运会上列为比赛项目的。）

> 问题 2: 国际象棋是世界上最古老的搏斗游戏之一，与中国的象棋、围棋和日本的将棋同享盛名。请说出国际象棋的起源。

第二部分 阅读

文章 1

阅读下面这篇关于棋牌的文章，讨论文后的思考题。

棋牌

棋牌是棋类和牌类娱乐项目的总称。中国象棋、围棋和国际象棋已被列入体育运动竞赛项目，此外，还有蒙古象棋、五子棋、跳棋、国际跳棋、斗兽棋、飞行棋等诸多游戏棋类。另外，桥牌、扑克、麻将也是最为普及的大众休闲项目。

棋牌集竞技性、娱乐性、技巧性于一体，要求玩家高度专注、讲究策略、公平竞争，且受一定规则规矩的制约，因此是一项益智健脑的活动。赢得一局棋牌主要凭脑力，不靠运气。国际象棋已成为国际奥委会认可的一项活动。牌类游戏大多是民间游戏，游戏规则视不同的区域、文化、个人而有所不同。

思考题:

1. 你能列举一些棋类项目吗?
2. 棋牌运动的益处有哪些?

文章 2

阅读下面这篇关于世界国际象棋联合会的文章，讨论文后的思考题。

世界国际象棋联合会

世界国际象棋联合会，简称国际棋联，是联系世界各国国际象棋联合会的组织，全球国际象棋比赛的管理机构。1924 年成立于法国巴黎，总部现设在希腊雅典。1924 年，国际象棋被列为奥运会的比赛项目；1999 年，世界象棋联合会被国际奥委会认可为国际体育组织。

国际棋联负责计算选手的等级分，并以此积分为基础，将荣誉头衔授予激烈竞争的比赛中赢得胜利的选手，头衔包括：国际棋联大师、国际大师、国际特级大师和女子的国际象棋头衔。此外，国际棋联也将大师和特级大师的头衔授予解决棋谜和制作棋谜的优秀选手。

国际棋联主办或委托成员国协会举办的重大世界性比赛有：国际象棋世界冠军赛（包括公开组、女子组及青年组）和区域赛，以及世界国际象棋奥林匹克团体锦标赛等。

思考题：

1. 国际棋联成立于哪一年？总部设在哪个城市？
2. 国际棋联根据积分排名授予选手的头衔包括哪几类？
3. 国际棋联主办或委托成员国协会举办的世界性比赛有哪些？

第三部分　练习

请完成以下练习。

1. 弈棋是一种"斗智"艺术，是锻炼智力的一种娱乐活动。根据你的理解，以"弈棋"为题撰写一篇不少于 250 词的议论文。
2. 业余时间你喜欢玩什么棋牌游戏？谈谈你的理由。

第四部分　规则与概念

1. 国际象棋的棋盘是个正方形，由横纵各 8 格、颜色一深一浅交错排列的 64 个小方格组成。
2. 国际象棋的深色格称"黑格"，浅色格称"白格"，棋子就放在这些格子中移动。
3. 国际象棋的棋子共 32 个，分为黑白两组，各 16 个，由对弈双方各执一组。双方棋子的兵种是一样的，分为六种：国王（简称王）1 个，皇后（简称后）1 个，城堡、战车（简称车）2 个，主教、传教士（简称象）2 个，骑士（简称马）2 个，禁卫军（简称兵）8 个。

4. 国际象棋比赛时，白棋先走，黑棋后走，双方轮流走棋，一次走一步棋，直到把一方的"王"将死分出胜负或走成和局为止。

5. 围棋的棋盘长宽各有 19 条线，共有 361 个点；在棋盘上标有 9 个小圆点，称作"星"。正式比赛黑白棋子各 180 子。

6. 围棋比赛中，对局双方各执一色棋子，黑先白后，轮流下子。

7. 围棋比赛以己方的棋子在棋盘上的圈地多于对手为胜。

8. 象棋的棋盘由 9 条竖线和 10 条横线相交而成，棋子放在各条线的相交点上。双方棋手依次按规定位置走子。

9. 象棋棋子的颜色通常分为黑色和红色，双方各有 16 个棋子。

10. 只要一方的"将"或"帅"被吃掉，另一方即可得胜。

第五部分 拓展阅读

诸宸

诸宸，1976 年出生，浙江温州人，国际象棋女子特级大师和男子特级大师双料称号获得者，世界上第一位在青年、成年赛事上都获得世界冠军的棋手。1988 年获得国际象棋世界少年赛女子 12 岁组冠军。1994 年、1996 年两度获世界国际象棋女子青年冠军，并创造 13 局得 12 分的最高胜率记录。1998 年由诸宸和谢军、王蕾、王频组成的中国女队再次问鼎世界国际象棋奥林匹克团体赛，荣获女子团体冠军；中国女队首次突破"欧洲包围圈"，坐上冠军宝座。2001年诸宸获得女子世界冠军，是继谢军之后中国第二位国际象棋世界冠军。